P9-DNI-315

ESTHER &
DANIEL

Brazos Theological Commentary on the Bible

ESTHER & DANIEL

Samuel Wells
& George Sumner

BrazosPress

a division of Baker Publishing Group
Grand Rapids, Michigan

Published by Brazos Press
a division of Baker Publishing Group
P.O. Box 6287, Grand Rapids, MI 49516-6287
www.brazospress.com

Printed in the United States of America

Library of Congress Cataloging-in-Publication Data
Wells, Samuel, 1965–
    Esther & Daniel / Samuel Wells and George Sumner.
       pages cm. — (Brazos theological commentary on the Bible)
    Includes bibliographical references and index.
    ISBN 978-1-58743-331-3 (cloth)
    1. Bible. O.T. Esther—Commentaries. 2. Bible. O.T. Daniel—Commentaries. I. Title. II. Title:
Esther and Daniel.
    BS1375.53.W45 2013
    222'.907—dc23   2012044730

13   14   15   16   17   18   19   7   6   5   4   3   2   1

Esther

For Esther Jourdan
and Martin Wells, Jeremy Hare, Robert Glenny,
James Geoghegan, Francis Butler, Freya Shilson-Thomas,
Melita Gostelow, and Kezia Walter.

Daniel

This commentary is dedicated to Dr. Charles Forman,
the Kenneth Latourette Professor of Mission emeritus at
Yale Divinity School and my mentor, who taught me,
by his words and his life, what a faithful and
hopeful *missio ad gentes* might look like.

CONTENTS

SERIES PREFACE

Near the beginning of his treatise against Gnostic interpretations of the Bible, *Against Heresies*, Irenaeus observes that scripture is like a great mosaic depicting a handsome king. It is as if we were owners of a villa in Gaul who had ordered a mosaic from Rome. It arrives, and the beautifully colored tiles need to be taken out of their packaging and put into proper order according to the plan of the artist. The difficulty, of course, is that scripture provides us with the individual pieces, but the order and sequence of various elements are not obvious. The Bible does not come with instructions that would allow interpreters to simply place verses, episodes, images, and parables in order as a worker might follow a schematic drawing in assembling the pieces to depict the handsome king. The mosaic must be puzzled out. This is precisely the work of scriptural interpretation.

Origen has his own image to express the difficulty of working out the proper approach to reading the Bible. When preparing to offer a commentary on the Psalms he tells of a tradition handed down to him by his Hebrew teacher:

> The Hebrew said that the whole divinely inspired scripture may be likened, because of its obscurity, to many locked rooms in our house. By each room is placed a key, but not the one that corresponds to it, so that the keys are scattered about beside the rooms, none of them matching the room by which it is placed. It is a difficult task to find the keys and match them to the rooms that they can open. We therefore know the scriptures that are obscure only by taking the points of departure for understanding them from another place because they have their interpretive principle scattered among them.[1]

As is the case for Irenaeus, scriptural interpretation is not purely local. The key in Genesis may best fit the door of Isaiah, which in turn opens up the meaning of Matthew. The mosaic must be put together with an eye toward the overall plan.

---

1. Fragment from the preface to *Commentary on Psalms 1–25*, preserved in the *Philokalia*, trans. Joseph W. Trigg (London: Routledge, 1998), 70–71.

Series Preface   E S T H E R   &   D A N I E L

Irenaeus, Origen, and the great cloud of premodern biblical interpreters as-sumed that puzzling out the mosaic of scripture must be a communal project. The Bible is vast, heterogeneous, full of confusing passages and obscure words, and difficult to understand. Only a fool would imagine that he or she could work out solutions alone. The way forward must rely upon a tradition of reading that Irenaeus reports has been passed on as the rule or canon of truth that functions as a confession of faith. "Anyone," he says, "who keeps unchangeable in himself the rule of truth received through baptism will recognize the names and sayings and parables of the scriptures."[2] Modern scholars debate the content of the rule on which Irenaeus relies and commends, not the least because the terms and formulations Irenaeus himself uses shift and slide. Nonetheless, Irenaeus assumes that there is a body of apostolic doctrine sustained by a tradition of teaching in the church. This doctrine provides the clarifying principles that guide exegetical judgment toward a coherent overall reading of scripture as a unified witness. Doctrine, then, is the schematic drawing that will allow the reader to organize the vast heterogeneity of the words, images, and stories of the Bible into a read-able, coherent whole. It is the rule that guides us toward the proper matching of keys to doors.

If self-consciousness about the role of history in shaping human consciousness makes modern historical-critical study critical, then what makes modern study of the Bible modern is the consensus that classical Christian doctrine distorts interpre-tive understanding. Benjamin Jowett, the influential nineteenth-century English classical scholar, is representative. In his programmatic essay "On the Interpreta-tion of Scripture," he exhorts the biblical reader to disengage from doctrine and break its hold over the interpretive imagination. "The simple words of that book," writes Jowett of the modern reader, "he tries to preserve absolutely pure from the refinements or distinctions of later times." The modern interpreter wishes to "clear away the remains of dogmas, systems, controversies, which are encrusted upon" the words of scripture. The disciplines of close philological analysis "would enable us to separate the elements of doctrine and tradition with which the meaning of scripture is encumbered in our own day."[3] The lens of understanding must be wiped clear of the hazy and distorting film of doctrine.

Postmodernity, in turn, has encouraged us to criticize the critics. Jowett imag-ined that when he wiped away doctrine he would encounter the biblical text in its purity and uncover what he called "the original spirit and intention of the authors."[4] We are not now so sanguine, and the postmodern mind thinks interpre-tive frameworks inevitable. Nonetheless, we tend to remain modern in at least one sense. We read Athanasius and think him stage-managing the diversity of scripture to support his positions against the Arians. We read Bernard of Clairvaux and

2. *Against Heresies* 9.4.
3. Benjamin Jowett, "On the Interpretation of Scripture," in *Essays and Reviews* (London: Parker, 1860), 338–39.
4. Ibid., 340.

assume that his monastic ideals structure his reading of the Song of Songs. In the wake of the Reformation, we can see how the doctrinal divisions of the time shaped biblical interpretation. Luther famously described the Epistle of James as a "strawy letter," for, as he said, "it has nothing of the nature of the Gospel about it."[5] In these and many other instances, often written in the heat of ecclesiastical controversy or out of the passion of ascetic commitment, we tend to think Jowett correct: doctrine is a distorting film on the lens of understanding.

However, is what we commonly think actually the case? Are readers naturally perceptive? Do we have an unblemished, reliable aptitude for the divine? Have we no need for disciplines of vision? Do our attention and judgment need to be trained, especially as we seek to read scripture as the living word of God? According to Augustine, we all struggle to journey toward God, who is our rest and peace. Yet our vision is darkened and the fetters of worldly habit corrupt our judgment. We need training and instruction in order to cleanse our minds so that we might find our way toward God.[6] To this end, "the whole temporal dispensation was made by divine Providence for our salvation."[7] The covenant with Israel, the coming of Christ, the gathering of the nations into the church—all these things are gathered up into the rule of faith, and they guide the vision and form of the soul toward the end of fellowship with God. In Augustine's view, the reading of scripture both contributes to and benefits from this divine pedagogy. With countless variations in both exegetical conclusions and theological frameworks, the same pedagogy of a doctrinally ruled reading of scripture characterizes the broad sweep of the Christian tradition from Gregory the Great through Bernard and Bonaventure, continuing across Reformation differences in both John Calvin and Cornelius Lapide, Patrick Henry and Bishop Bossuet, and on to more recent figures such as Karl Barth and Hans Urs von Balthasar.

Is doctrine, then, not a moldering scrim of antique prejudice obscuring the Bible, but instead a clarifying agent, an enduring tradition of theological judgments that amplifies the living voice of scripture? And what of the scholarly dispassion advocated by Jowett? Is a noncommitted reading, an interpretation unprejudiced, the way toward objectivity, or does it simply invite the languid intellectual apathy that stands aside to make room for the false truism and easy answers of the age?

This series of biblical commentaries was born out of the conviction that dogma clarifies rather than obscures. The Brazos Theological Commentary on the Bible advances upon the assumption that the Nicene tradition, in all its diversity and controversy, provides the proper basis for the interpretation of the Bible as Christian scripture. God the Father Almighty, who sends his only begotten Son to die for us and for our salvation and who raises the crucified Son in the power of the Holy Spirit so that the baptized may be joined in one body—faith in *this*

5. *Luther's Works*, vol. 35, ed. E. Theodore Bachmann (Philadelphia: Fortress, 1959), 362.
6. *On Christian Doctrine* 1.10.
7. *On Christian Doctrine* 1.35.

God with *this* vocation of love for the world is the lens through which to view the heterogeneity and particularity of the biblical texts. Doctrine, then, is not a moldering scrim of antique prejudice obscuring the meaning of the Bible. It is a crucial aspect of the divine pedagogy, a clarifying agent for our minds fogged by self-deceptions, a challenge to our languid intellectual apathy that will too often rest in false truisms and the easy spiritual nostrums of the present age rather than search more deeply and widely for the dispersed keys to the many doors of scripture.

For this reason, the commentators in this series have not been chosen because of their historical or philological expertise. In the main, they are not biblical scholars in the conventional, modern sense of the term. Instead, the commentators were chosen because of their knowledge of and expertise in using the Christian doctrinal tradition. They are qualified by virtue of the doctrinal formation of their mental habits, for it is the conceit of this series of biblical commentaries that theological training in the Nicene tradition prepares one for biblical interpretation, and thus it is to theologians and not biblical scholars that we have turned. "War is too important," it has been said, "to leave to the generals."

We do hope, however, that readers do not draw the wrong impression. The Nicene tradition does not provide a set formula for the solution of exegetical problems. The great tradition of Christian doctrine was not transcribed, bound in folio, and issued in an official, critical edition. We have the Niceno-Constantinopolitan Creed, used for centuries in many traditions of Christian worship. We have ancient baptismal affirmations of faith. The Chalcedonian definition and the creeds and canons of other church councils have their places in official church documents. Yet the rule of faith cannot be limited to a specific set of words, sentences, and creeds. It is instead a pervasive habit of thought, the animating culture of the church in its intellectual aspect. As Augustine observed, commenting on Jer. 31:33, "The creed is learned by listening; it is written, not on stone tablets nor on any material, but on the heart."[8] This is why Irenaeus is able to appeal to the rule of faith more than a century before the first ecumenical council, and this is why we need not itemize the contents of the Nicene tradition in order to appeal to its potency and role in the work of interpretation.

Because doctrine is intrinsically fluid on the margins and most powerful as a habit of mind rather than a list of propositions, this commentary series cannot settle difficult questions of method and content at the outset. The editors of the series impose no particular method of doctrinal interpretation. We cannot say in advance how doctrine helps the Christian reader assemble the mosaic of scripture. We have no clear answer to the question of whether exegesis guided by doctrine is antithetical to or compatible with the now-old modern methods of historical-critical inquiry. Truth—historical, mathematical, or doctrinal—knows no contradiction. But method is a discipline of vision and judgment, and we cannot know in advance what aspects of historical-critical inquiry are functions

---

8. *Sermon* 212.2.

of modernism that shape the soul to be at odds with Christian discipline. Still further, the editors do not hold the commentators to any particular hermeneutical theory that specifies how to define the plain sense of scripture—or the role this plain sense should play in interpretation. Here the commentary series is tentative and exploratory.

Can we proceed in any other way? European and North American intellectual culture has been de-Christianized. The effect has not been a cessation of Christian activity. Theological work continues. Sermons are preached. Biblical scholars turn out monographs. Church leaders have meetings. But each dimension of a formerly unified Christian practice now tends to function independently. It is as if a weakened army had been fragmented, and various corps had retreated to isolated fortresses in order to survive. Theology has lost its competence in exegesis. Scripture scholars function with minimal theological training. Each decade finds new theories of preaching to cover the nakedness of seminary training that provides theology without exegesis and exegesis without theology.

Not the least of the causes of the fragmentation of Christian intellectual practice has been the divisions of the church. Since the Reformation, the role of the rule of faith in interpretation has been obscured by polemics and counterpolemics about *sola scriptura* and the necessity of a magisterial teaching authority. The Brazos Theological Commentary on the Bible series is deliberately ecumenical in scope, because the editors are convinced that early church fathers were correct: church doctrine does not compete with scripture in a limited economy of epistemic authority. We wish to encourage unashamedly dogmatic interpretation of scripture, confident that the concrete consequences of such a reading will cast far more light on the great divisive questions of the Reformation than either reengaging in old theological polemics or chasing the fantasy of a pure exegesis that will somehow adjudicate between competing theological positions. You shall know the truth of doctrine by its interpretive fruits, and therefore in hopes of contributing to the unity of the church, we have deliberately chosen a wide range of theologians whose commitment to doctrine will allow readers to see real interpretive consequences rather than the shadow boxing of theological concepts.

The Brazos Theological Commentary on the Bible has no dog in the current translation fights, and we endorse a textual ecumenism that parallels our diversity of ecclesial backgrounds. We do not impose the thankfully modest inclusive-language agenda of the New Revised Standard Version, nor do we insist upon the glories of the Authorized Version, nor do we require our commentators to create a new translation. In our communal worship, in our private devotions, in our theological scholarship, we use a range of scriptural translations. Precisely as scripture—a living, functioning text in the present life of faith—the Bible is not semantically fixed. Only a modernist, literalist hermeneutic could imagine that this modest fluidity is a liability. Philological precision and stability is a consequence of, not a basis for, exegesis. Judgments about the meaning of a text fix its literal sense, not the other way around. As a result, readers should expect an eclectic use of biblical translations, both across the different volumes of the series and within individual commentaries.

We cannot speak for contemporary biblical scholars, but as theologians we know that we have long been trained to defend our fortresses of theological concepts and formulations. And we have forgotten the skills of interpretation. Like stroke victims, we must rehabilitate our exegetical imaginations, and there are likely to be different strategies of recovery. Readers should expect this reconstructive—not reactionary—series to provide them with experiments in postcritical doctrinal interpretation, not commentaries written according to the settled principles of a well-functioning tradition. Some commentators will follow classical typological and allegorical readings from the premodern tradition; others will draw on contemporary historical study. Some will comment verse by verse; others will highlight passages, even single words that trigger theological analysis of scripture. No reading strategies are proscribed, no interpretive methods foresworn. The central premise in this commentary series is that doctrine provides structure and cogency to scriptural interpretation. We trust in this premise with the hope that the Nicene tradition can guide us, however imperfectly, diversely, and haltingly, toward a reading of scripture in which the right keys open the right doors.

R. R. Reno

ABBREVIATIONS

Biblical Books

Acts	Acts	Job	Job
Amos	Amos	Joel	Joel
1 Chr.	1 Chronicles	John	John
2 Chr.	2 Chronicles	1 John	1 John
Col.	Colossians	2 John	2 John
1 Cor.	1 Corinthians	3 John	3 John
2 Cor.	2 Corinthians	Jonah	Jonah
Dan.	Daniel	Josh.	Joshua
Deut.	Deuteronomy	Jude	Jude
Eccl.	Ecclesiastes	Judg.	Judges
Eph.	Ephesians	1 Kgs.	1 Kings
Esth.	Esther	2 Kgs.	2 Kings
Exod.	Exodus	Lam.	Lamentations
Ezek.	Ezekiel	Lev.	Leviticus
Ezra	Ezra	Luke	Luke
Gal.	Galatians	Mal.	Malachi
Gen.	Genesis	Mark	Mark
Hab.	Habakkuk	Matt.	Matthew
Hag.	Haggai	Mic.	Micah
Heb.	Hebrews	Nah.	Nahum
Hos.	Hosea	Neh.	Nehemiah
Isa.	Isaiah	Num.	Numbers
Jas.	James	Obad.	Obadiah
Jer.	Jeremiah	1 Pet.	1 Peter

2 Pet.	2 Peter		2 Sam.	2 Samuel
Phil.	Philippians		Song	Song of Songs
Phlm.	Philemon		1 Thess.	1 Thessalonians
Prov.	Proverbs		2 Thess.	2 Thessalonians
Ps.	Psalms		1 Tim.	1 Timothy
Rev.	Revelation		2 Tim.	2 Timothy
Rom.	Romans		Titus	Titus
Ruth	Ruth		Zech.	Zechariah
1 Sam.	1 Samuel		Zeph.	Zephaniah

✤ ESTHER ✤

by Samuel Wells

AUTHOR'S PREFACE

I am grateful to Michael Beckett, whose *Gospel in Esther* first brought to my attention the theological significance of the book of Esther. I am honored to be among those asked to write for this commentary series. It is a better book than it would otherwise have been because of friends and colleagues who read the manuscript and offered perceptive and constructive comments, including Walter Brueggemann, Rebekah Eklund, Michael Goldman, Stanley Hauerwas, Abby Kocher, Ephraim Radner, Rusty Reno, and Jo Bailey Wells. I am grateful to Chad Pecknold and Randi Rashkover for their invitation to contribute a chapter on Esther to *Liturgy, Time, and the Politics of Redemption*, which gave me an opportunity to explore some of these themes in a shorter format.

I have a goddaughter named Esther, and this book is dedicated to her, along with my other godchildren. To her and her parents I am grateful for friendship through sunshine and rain. Through my godson Martin and his parents I have learned truthfulness and courage. Through my godson Jeremy and his family I have discovered faith and faithfulness. With my godson Robert and his parents I have sought discernment and wisdom. For my godson James and his family I am grateful for everything that family can be. With my godson Francis and his parents I have enjoyed study and persistence. Through my goddaughter Freya and her parents I have been given mercy and love. Through my goddaughter Melita and her family I have been given tenderness and gentleness. Through my goddaughter Kezia and her parents I have been offered friendship and understanding.

Mordecai is like a godparent to Esther. But where would Mordecai have been without Esther? And where would I have been without my godchildren and their families? Thank God for them, and for the book of Esther, which teaches us to play, to adapt, and to remember.

INTRODUCTION TO ESTHER

This is not the commentary I expected it would be. I thought Esther was a book about exile: about ingenuity, a dramatic escape, a subtle yet disarming providence. But writing a commentary disciplines the scholar to look at the text beyond the piety of the devotional reader or the eclectic appetite of the preacher. And at some point in the meditative attention that is the preparation of a theological commentary, I realized that this was a book not about exile, but about Diaspora. It included ingenuity, but it was more about the formation of a political imagination. It included a dramatic escape, but there was no whiff of miracle. And if it was about providence, it was of a kind largely unknown to the rest of the canon.

My thoughts came to focus on the terrible date decided by lot for the extermination of the Jews. A date just a few weeks before Passover. But here is the bitter irony. If the Jews were to wait for Passover for their deliverance, it would be too late. The story of the God who had visited a people in slavery in Egypt and delivered them by his mighty hand and made a covenant with them and brought them into the promised land and given them the temple in which to be made holy for ever—this story was no longer enough. The book of Esther is a story of a people who found—were finding—that the Passover story, the story Christians tend to assume is *the* story of the Old Testament, was not enough. If they were to survive, the Jews had to make their own story.

Christians have also adapted the Passover story. Therein lies the poignancy in offering a theological commentary on Esther. In what ways does the Christian adaptation of the story resemble, and in what ways does it differ from, this Jewish one? In what sense is Purim *the* Jewish adaptation of Passover—a Passover the Jews make for themselves? Or is it simply one adaptation among many? And could Esther offer Christians a richer way of understanding the Jews, one beyond the stereotypes of rituals, laws, and Pharisees? These are among the emerging questions with which this commentary is concerned.

Two words are needed by way of introducing this commentary. First, form: a word on the distinctive judgments and specific choices I have made in going about this project. This I offer in the first subheading below. Second, content: an overview of the key theological themes that arise in addressing this vivacious book. This I offer in the remaining five subheadings.

Commenting on a Commentary

What I have tried to do is to offer a commentary whose form does justice to the content of the book of Esther. More precisely, I have worked to keep my prose poised between hilarity and horror. This poise is the unique characteristic of the story. The book of Esther is a narrative of the Jews' deliverance from the greatest peril they have ever faced; even Hitler did not have a plan for the complete extinction of the Jews quite as comprehensive as Haman's decree. Yet the combination of chance and resourcefulness that enables the Jews to escape this horrifying peril is narrated with a ready eye for farce, an appetite for slapstick, and a pervasive sense of the ridiculous. Such dimensions are invariably brought out in Jewish renditions of the story that mark the annual Feast of Purim. Thus the book resists solemn exegesis.

The mistake for the commentator is to concentrate so hard on one of these two themes—hilarity or horror—that the other one becomes obscured. On the contrary, the interplay and intersection of these two dimensions of the narrative constitute the book's most distinctive characteristic. A Christian commentator has three things to learn from this interplay of moods. First, faith is at once both deadly serious and hilariously funny. Second, the humor is not a relief from the seriousness, or a way to make the solemnity more digestible; it is at the heart of the serious character of faith. Third, while Christians may learn from Jews about the interplay of humor and horror and discover the importance of inhabiting both, and find resources to stay at such a point of intersection, Christians may appropriately and legitimately differ from Jews in their understanding of precisely what is so serious and what is so funny. The contribution of the book of Esther may lie as much in the way it keeps the reading community in the crossover between humor and horror as in the precise narrative details that embody that crossover. And the role of the commentator may be more to identify and stay with the crossover than to elucidate all the contributing circumstances.

So the style of this commentary is one that explicitly seeks to bring to the surface both the horror and the humor—and highlight the interplay between the two. Some readers may be less familiar with commentaries that pinpoint humor in the Bible. If so, this commentary may be a little different from some more conventional ones. The difference is designed not for self-indulgence or entertainment but to offer commentary that truly reflects the mood of the text.

Yet to read the story after the Nazi Holocaust is to read it differently from the way it might have been read before. There really was a Haman, an enemy of the

Jews. He really did exterminate one third of world Jewry. Not only did the kind of threat described in the book of Esther genuinely arise; it was to a significant degree carried out. This is no longer a figurative tale—and a challenge to the imagination. This is now an appeal to engage with contemporary realities—and a challenge to the memory. Is it still valid to speak of this story as lying on the intersection between hilarity and horror? Or is it more valid than ever, given that the horror is no fantasy? These questions have no clear answers, but remain at the forefront of post-Holocaust exegesis of this poignant book.

The book of Esther is a fast-paced and dynamic drama. This has dictated the way I have arranged the material for commentary. Because it is a drama I divided it into scenes and sought to allow the shape and pace of the action to dictate the interpretation. Thus I have not pursued a verse-by-verse exegesis, but interpreted each verse primarily within the context of its surrounding narrative.

Thus much for respecting the character of the story. Now, a brief word on my method of exegesis. Esther is a book of the Christian Bible. In *Introducing Christian Ethics*, Ben Quash and I outline three approaches to understanding the authority of scripture:[1]

1. To look *behind* the text means to assume the text is less important than the insights and events the text describes and records. The Holy Spirit was at work in those moments, and the text is an account of the work of the Holy Spirit.
   a. One view sees the true significance in the events the text describes and regards the Bible as an accurate account of those events.
   b. Another view sees the true significance in the patterns of life represented in the scriptural record.
2. To look *within* the text means to locate authority in the sacred words themselves.
   a. In one view the writing of the scriptures was done through the power of the Holy Spirit, and thus the text is genuinely holy and an incomparable source of truth. Thus the Bible is *perspicuous*—it has a single, plain meaning that is accessible to any reader in any context.
   b. Another view arises in reaction to weight of research and speculation about the original text and the events and words behind the text and, in contrast, regards the form of the text *as the church now has it* as the principal object of study. This is sometimes connected to a move away from identifying the author's original intention and accept that a text may have several legitimate meanings and that it may take on a life of its own long after the author composed it.
3. To look *beyond* the text, into the world the text creates, means to concentrate interpretation on living the text faithfully by following in its steps and

1. Samuel Wells and Ben Quash, *Introducing Christian Ethics* (Oxford: Wiley-Blackwell, 2010).

understands the Holy Spirit as acting primarily in the community reading the text. It means to pay more attention than the other approaches to where and why the text is being read.

This commentary does not give a lot of attention to the first approach. I include, for example, no discussion of the historicity of the story the book tells. The place of the story in the canon is not jeopardized by concerns about whether all (or some) of the events described actually happened, and happened in the precise way described in the story. Neither do misgivings about some elements of the story—for example, the degree of slaughter recorded in Esth. 9—mean the book should be regarded as of lesser status than other canonical books.

Instead my approach is a combination of 2b and 3. It does not regard the Bible as perspicuous. As already noted, the meaning of the book of Esther must be affected by reading it after the Holocaust. A person who reads the book today in ignorance of Nazi history would not be likely to read the story in the same way as a person who was familiar with this gruesome episode in European history. I take for granted that the text has no single, fixed meaning. But the journey from 2b to 3 is the move from saying there are many possible meanings to asserting that some meanings are more faithful than others—faithful, not necessarily to the text itself, since it is not entirely clear what that might mean, but faithful to the church that has sought to embody the text and faithful to the God whose Holy Spirit breathes through the text, and sensitive to the ways the text may mean different but overlapping things to Jews and Christians respectively.

Esther as Christian Scripture

Thus my attention focuses upon the form of the text as the church now has it, rather than as the principal object of study. The first question that then arises is, What *is* the form of the text as the church now has it? There is no simple answer to this question. The Hebrew text of Esther was the one translated by Jerome, and henceforth the six additional Greek "additions" found in the Septuagint not only became detached from the story, but their precise locations within the narrative were forgotten. Despite this they are considered integral to the Orthodox and Roman Catholic canon. In addition there are also the "A-Text," which refers to four Greek manuscripts that date from the tenth to the thirteenth centuries that seem more comfortable with Esther's Jewish identity and make more direct reference to Abraham and to God's intervention, and Josephus's account, included in his *Antiquities*, which in addition to telling the story offers reflections on its contemporary interpretation.

The six additions that take their place in the Apocrypha change the character of Jerome's text considerably, in ways that make Esther similar to Daniel, Ezra, and Nehemiah: God is very much a character in the story, Purim is obscured, and prayer and apocalyptic play a significant role. Reid offers a helpful summary of the roles these additions perform in the story.[2] They fill in gaps, such as the reason for Haman's antipathy to the Jews; they frame the story with a dream and its interpretation; they develop characterization; they attend to Hellenistic concerns, such as religious identity; and they add theatrical elements. The irony is that many of these features, whose absence from the Hebrew I highlight in the commentary and take to be vital to its interpretation, could well have been crucial for enabling Esther to be accepted as a canonical book.

Nonetheless I offer a commentary based on the NRSV as presented within the Protestant canon today. As this brief survey of the alternatives hints, to do otherwise would be to need to address a very different, and in some senses directly contradictory, set of theological issues. For example, any consideration of the Hebrew text as presented in the NRSV has to engage with the absence of God from the book's vocabulary. An examination of the Greek additions has no such engagement to make: on the contrary, it turns into a discussion of God's providential intervention in history. I take the additions and interpolations to be coming from a hand that regards the Hebrew text as theologically unacceptable or at best inadequate. Such a view has been shared by some in every century that has followed. Yet it is precisely those apparently unacceptable convictions that make the book so provocative for Christian interpretation today.

Of all the issues surrounding Esther's place in the canon, one stands out. The Hebrew text never explicitly refers to God. How significant is this omission? There are undoubtedly junctures at which God does not seem far away. Most notable are Mordecai's words to Esther: "For if you keep silence at such a time as this, relief and deliverance will rise for the Jews from another quarter, but you and your father's family will perish. Who knows? Perhaps you have come to royal dignity for just such a time as this" (4:14). These words not only suggest that God has providentially arranged for Esther to become queen, but further argue that even if this providential orchestration is not met with Esther's active participation, God will find another way. The other most telling moment lies in Zeresh's words to Haman: "If Mordecai, before whom your downfall has begun, is of the Jewish people, you will not prevail against him, but will surely fall before him" (6:13). Here Zeresh prophesies on God's behalf against her own husband; it is not explicit that God will act on behalf of the Jewish people—only that the Jewish people are indestructible and sure to win out within Haman's lifetime.

The silence in relation to God may be read in a number of ways. It could be subtlety and understatement—although this is not a book in general given to understatement. It could build a community among readers who can read between the lines. It could come from an era when dramatic interventions and revelations and appearances were not the conventional style of Jewish literature as they came

2. Debra Reid, *Esther*, Tyndale Old Testament Commentaries 13 (Downers Grove, IL: InterVarsity, 2008), 156–59.

to be in the intertestamental period. Or it could be saying, positively, that God's action is at most hidden and that the Jews had best rely on their own wits rather than wait hopefully or passively for the intervention of God.

This lack of mention of God has led many to regard the book of Esther in its Hebrew form as theologically unacceptable; what is it then doing in the Christian canon of scripture? Hostility to the book in Christian circles is commonplace, aptly summarized as follows: "It contains no promise to the Church, makes no mention of the gospel, has no type or prophecy of the Messiah, does not once introduce the name of God or recognize his providence, reveals none of 'those precious and fundamental doctrines' found elsewhere in the Old Testament, and is not quoted in the New Testament."[3] My question is not, however, Does Esther deserve a place in the Christian canon? That is not a question I see any value in addressing. It has been there for most of two millenniums, and Christian theology has taken shape assuming its presence there. I assume it is there through the gift and mercy of the Holy Spirit. Instead, my question is, rather, Given that Esther is a part of the canon, what does the church know that it would otherwise not know? Five answers stand out.

First, scripture may tell a story, but it is not a simple linear story where threads remain consistent throughout. Esther is written from a different perspective from those books that assume the promised land or exile. This is a Diaspora context, and not one that the book takes to be transitory: it is more or less permanent.[4] Thus the emphasis shifts away from the conventional forms of authority and identity—monarchy, law, land, temple. Purim, as we shall see, is a very different festival from Passover and, I argue, a parody of the whole Passover tradition. The Old Testament is not a seamless robe, any more than it is an unambiguous anticipation of Christ. The point is not that Esther's theology and understanding of providence need to be brought in line with the Old Testament—indeed the Bible—as a whole. It is more that any biblical theology has to ask itself whether it has taken seriously the searing questions posed by the book of Esther.

The most searing of those questions is that of how the Jews are to survive when God seems so reluctant to come to their defense. Thus, second, Esther asks the church what is its understanding of the Jews. The existence of the Jews is a sign of God's promise and faithfulness; their suffering and vulnerability seem to be a sign of the opposite. The Old Testament is predicated on the covenant in which God calls Israel to "be holy as I am holy." It is not clear in the book of Esther that either party is genuinely keeping its side of the bargain. In the absence of the activity of a transcendent God, Esther tells the story of how the Jews rely on their own devices and find resources they never knew they had. There are resemblances to the way Israel survived adverse circumstances in the days of Joshua and the judges; but

3. Jo Carruthers, *Esther through the Centuries* (Malden, MA/Oxford: Blackwell, 2008), 13.
4. Carruthers's definitions are helpful: "exile" signifies "a dispersed community in which identity is centered on a homeland" and "Diaspora" indicates "a coherent yet nonterritorial identity recognized by other characteristics such as religion or race" (ibid., 33).

the differences are as striking as the similarities. Esther is a meditation on what it means to be a Jew, opposed by the world and apparently abandoned by God, and yet with fathomless ingenuity and indomitable spirit. The question for the church in relation to the Jews has to be, Has anything really changed?

What has changed for the church is, of course, Christ. And this offers a third area of canonical reflection. The narrative presents significant resonances and dissonances with the story of Jesus. Esther risks a great deal by going into the place of danger, being at intimate quarters with the enemy, facing a loss of her identity, and in the end laying down her life for her people's salvation. Most interestingly, she sets this story in motion *before* the crisis arises that makes her actions so necessary. These are all christological resonances. She does so, however, without any sense of God's prior activity, without any specific regard to the Jewish law, and with an outcome—the impaling of Haman and the slaughter of the enemies of the Jews—that contrasts with the one who died for the ransom of the many. Esther is a study in how salvation can be rendered very differently from the way it is embodied in Jesus—and yet still be called salvation and inform an understanding of what salvation in Jesus means.

Fourth, the inscrutability of God is a theme at the heart of scriptural interpretation. It is hard to imagine the book of Esther without the background of faith in God. The book is, after all, in the Jewish and Christian canon and not accessible anywhere else. It is like a footnote in which an author acknowledges without contradiction a profound criticism of her argument in a source that would otherwise not have been available. The setting is the aftermath of Jerusalem's fall (in the foreground) and Saul's failure (in the background). These details assume a theological frame of reference. Ahasuerus is a savage parody of God: but even in him we can still discern an assumption that God rules the world and can do pretty much as God pleases. The trouble is, what God pleases. Esther is a story of how a people profoundly hurt by the absence of their hitherto faithful God may end up believing in themselves.

Fifth, and finally, there is plenty for the church to consider about itself. The closing chapters of Esther are full of explicit and tacit guidelines on how a community may retain its integrity and identity in troubled times. One would like there always to be an intimacy between God and the church, a settled trajectory for the church to perceive its role in God's story from the coming of the Spirit on the disciples to the coming down of the new Jerusalem dressed as a bride. But it isn't always like that. Esther says it never was always like that. But do not despair. Make provision. Develop habits. Improvise. Use your enemies' foolishness and malevolence against themselves. Fall back on your traditions. Keep united. And salvation will come.

Esther and Israel: A Story of Survival

The key question the book of Esther addresses is this: How to navigate the dangerous waters of exile, between the two extremes of spineless assimilation and fruitless resistance? This is the question at the heart of the book. It is as well by way of introduction to take account of the alternatives available.

The scriptural alternatives are largely as follows: Joseph, Moses, Daniel, and Ezra. Within the portrayal of Ezra comes the more ambiguous figure of Nehemiah. In the background is the apocryphal figure of Judith. In addition there are the contexts and perspectives of Lamentations and Isaiah. Each requires some analysis.

Joseph, like Esther, is a kind of orphan. His presence in the Egyptian court is likewise one of some secrecy. His time in prison is not entirely unlike Esther's time in the harem. Like Esther, Joseph gets one shot at impressing the ruler—in his case, as a diviner. Surprise and coincidence play a role in both stories. Both Joseph and Esther become trusted advisers with formal roles. Neither of them makes plans for their people to return home. Neither is particularly concerned with the details of ritual observance. Each of them decisively intervenes to save their people. Yet in each case, successful as their intervention may be, they cannot ensure permanent safety for the Jews.

There are significant differences. Joseph is a lone Jew in Egypt. He is there because he has been rejected by his people. He does not know in advance that his people's destiny lies in his hands. He is not serving an arbitrary and careless despot. With the exception of Potiphar's wife, he has no archenemy to combat among Pharaoh's advisers. While not highly visible in the narrative, God emerges decisively as the author of the whole story, in a way not found in Esther: "Even though you intended to do harm to me, God intended it for good, in order to preserve a numerous people, as he is doing today" (Gen. 50:20). And yet there is a shadow over Joseph's story—that of the way his policies opened the path for the Jews' subsequent enslavement. In general, however, the similarities far outweigh the differences. Joseph is undoubtedly a type of Esther. Both exhibit a confidence that the Jews can find a home away from home, provided they keep their wits, make the most of opportunities, and keep the ear of the ruler.

Moses is also a kind of orphan. Like Esther he finds a home at court that his people had lost elsewhere. Like Esther he comes to public visibility at a crucial time of danger for his people. Moses's ruler is much more of an arbitrary tyrant than Joseph's—if not quite so easily manipulated as Esther's. Moses is, even more explicitly than Esther, the deliverer of his people. Deliverance in each case involves large-scale casualties on the part of the enemy. In each case a festival commemorates the dramatic events.

But there are two overwhelming differences. For Moses, deliverance fundamentally means departure. There is a promised land to enter, and the dust of Egypt is good for no more than shaking off from the feet. Even more significantly, deliverance for Moses is God's doing. God's hand is on everything, from the plagues to the hardening of Pharaoh's heart—and the centerpiece of the story is an astonishing miracle, the parting of the sea. The climax of the narrative is the making and renewal of the covenant at Sinai: thus there is both the emphasis on specific ethical and ritual obedience and a divine promise of abiding security—two items notably absent from Esther. The story of Moses is a celebration of what God has done; the story of Esther is a celebration of what the Jews can do.

Daniel resembles Esther more in era than in ethos. Whereas Joseph and Moses tell the story of the exodus (including its prologue), Daniel embodies the exile. While the setting of Daniel and Esther may be only a hundred years apart, their context is very different. Daniel is set in Chaldean, and later Persian, Babylon during the exile. Esther is set in Persian Susa, one of four capitals of the Persian Empire and one of countless locations of the Diaspora. Both Daniel and Esther embody the conviction that the Jews have much to offer their Gentile rulers and mean them no harm: what is good for the Jews is what is truly good for the empire.

But where Daniel and Esther differ is on what to do when there is a parting of the ways between the empire and the Jews. Daniel focuses on individual confrontations over expressions of Jewish piety and the upholding of the Jewish law; in each case God does remarkable things that show who is really in control of events. The message is that eventually God will restore Israel to its home just as Daniel and friends were delivered from fire and lions. Esther includes individual confrontations, but is a much more elaborate and cohesive tale concerning the well-being of the Jews as a whole. While Mordecai's defiance of Haman has certain echoes of Daniel, and the comeuppance of Haman echoes the fate of Daniel's detractors, Esther allows for no description of God's explicit intervention. Stealth and sleight of hand, rather than bullish spirit and unbending loyalty, are the politics of the day for the Jews. Esther is not apocalyptic literature: the revelation of God is precisely what is missing.

The book of Judith is set 150 years before Esther, and yet its theme addresses the Hellenistic context, rather than the Persian one. Like Deborah, Jael, and Esther, Judith stands out as a woman of initiative and public prominence who turns the tide of history through taking on a level of authority typically, in her era, assigned to men and acting in a crisis for which no normal guidelines seem to apply. Like Esther she adopts the penitential attitude of sackcloth and ashes before taking on a daunting assignment (Judith 9:1). Unlike Esther, however, she sees God as all powerful and prays to God regularly. God is on her side, the side of the oppressed; and this is the same God who created the world. She credits God, rather than herself, in her moment of triumph. Unlike Esther she has no male accomplice. She lives in a community where Jewish law is central, as is the worship of God in the temple under the authority of the high priest. Unlike Esther she has ready access to a military solution to her nation's problems. She can hope not just to avert her enemies among the population, but to defeat her enemy's army itself. This is beyond the imagination of the book of Esther. More personally, Judith is a model of chastity, a virtue hard to associate with Esther. And yet, for all these differences, the resonances with Esther—gender, palace politics, a lustful and drunken leader, banquets, and the Jews' postexilic vulnerability—are strong.

Zerubbabel, Ezra, and Nehemiah collectively offer another counterpart to Esther. They too address the context of life under the Persians. They too see a natural and healthy partnership between the king and the Jews, with beneficial outcomes for each party. The books of Ezra and Nehemiah may even consider events ostensibly contemporaneous with the drama described in the book of Esther. But these figures and their books are largely taken up with the following concerns: return from exile, ritual and ethical adherence to the law, the restoration of the walls and temple of Jerusalem, and the maintenance of the Jews' racial and religious purity and integrity. What is most striking about these concerns is that they are almost entirely absent from the book of Esther. In the event of a massacre like that plotted by Haman, Nehemiah would have been no safer behind the walls of Jerusalem than Esther would have been in the citadel of Susa. But their strategies, perceptions, and goals are remarkably different for figures located in similar contexts. It is ironic that Ezra held out against the taking of foreign wives when the book of Esther tells a story of how the Jewish people were saved from annihilation only by a woman who took a foreign husband, albeit the king himself.

Perhaps the best way to assess Esther's politics is to highlight the ways in which she both echoes and differs from these distinguished forebears. For Esther, the goal is not return to the promised land. The method is not confrontation with the ruling authorities. The assumption is not that God has a plan for deliverance. The heart of Jewish identity is not in close observance of the law. For Esther, the Jews need access to power. They need the willingness to do what it takes to attain that access. They need to be resourceful and alert, with one eye behind their backs watching for unscrupulous enemies, and one eye on how to consolidate their seat at the right hand of the power. The key lesson, embodied in the life of Esther herself, is that it *is* possible to live in two worlds simultaneously. It *is* possible to be called Esther and Hadassah. It *is* possible to be the object of others' desires and an obedient agent in someone else's game, and yet to be biding one's time and waiting one's moment to bring about exactly the outcome one seeks. In short, it *is* possible to survive and thrive as a Jew, yet have no land, no king, no temple, and not even a carefully practiced law to call one's own. The book of Esther is not a fairy story. It is a profound challenge to the dominant reading of the politics of exile.

Moving from political and social strategy to theological ethos, points of comparison arise in relation to a number of figures and books. Ruth is another female character with a book named after her. Like Esther, Ruth is a story of redemption from a point of utter despair. The dynamic is somewhat different: Ruth's predicament is a personal one brought about by misfortune that seems, initially, to have no political dimensions. Esther's crisis is a political one that she had no hand in bringing about but holds the only possibility of averting. Both stories seem to be about redemption of a kind that depends on imagination and circumstance and excludes decisive intervention from God. But Ruth's story hints at a larger perspective in its concluding reference to the family from which came David. Both books are presented as historical but have a parabolic quality.

The most obvious character with whom to dialogue about the absence of God would seem to be Job. And yet Job and Esther differ in four significant regards. First, the book of Job is very much focused on the plight of one individual, rather than the jeopardy of the Jews as a whole. Second, the book is very much one of fable and poetry, rather than historylike narrative. Third, questions of theodicy, even if not conclusively answered, run through the book of Job; Esther is not concerned with justice as much as survival. Fourth, God is very much a character in the book of Job. Thus while both Job and Esther offer perspectives on the absence of God, that absence is very differently rendered in the two books.

Esther provides as strong a contrast to Lamentations as one can imagine. They are without doubt both set in the context of the destruction of Jerusalem and the exile—Lamentations being in the more immediate, Esther in the more remote aftermath. But there the similarity ends and the differences take over. Lamentations is a series of lyric poems focusing on the expression of grief, anger, despair, guilt, shame, and also hope and forgiveness, addressed in personal terms but without narrative shape. The book of Esther is entirely narrative, is almost without personal perspective—most speech is reported—and has little or no interest in a cosmic perspective that places the plight of the Jews in relation to the overall purposes of God. Esther is not concerned with theodicy, but with active steps to set things straight. It takes no time to linger over personal sins and shortcomings that invited punishment or repentance, but instead takes a pragmatic if sometimes playful view that even in dire straits, imaginative interventions can save the day. Most of all, Lamentations longs for God to restore what has been lost: it concludes with these words: "Restore us to yourself, O LORD, / that we may be restored; / renew our days as of old— / unless you have utterly rejected us, / and are angry with us beyond measure" (Lam. 5:21–22). Esther, by contrast, has no hint that destiny lies in returning to Jerusalem and rebuilding walls and temple and restoring law and kingly rule—and no hint that God has such things in store.

More subtle is the relationship between Esther herself and the Suffering Servant of Second Isaiah. In general the scope of Isa. 40–55 is way beyond that of the book of Esther: it places Israel's dereliction in the light of God's primordial, historical, and eschatological purpose. It has a much more nuanced and constructive view of foreign rulers: its Cyrus is capable of taking some of the dignity of a king of Israel—and is thus a very different figure to Esther's puffed-up and clumsy Ahasuerus. But more particular interest lies in the comparison between the way Esther allows herself to be put through hardship and virtual captivity in order to come into the king's chamber and later faces extreme danger in coming before the king to entreat for the Jews' protection. The initial experience in the harem can largely be ruled out, since Esther enters it before there is any genuine jeopardy for the Jews, and thus it seems an unlikely point of comparison to the notion of the Suffering Servant, whose vocation is specifically tied to a time of hardship and distress. But the connection between Esther's kenosis before Ahasuerus and the submission of the Suffering Servant is a genuine counterpoint. In both cases the subjection has a profoundly redemptive intention and effect. If one is going to consider Esther as a potential Christ figure, as I do in this commentary, then one may also reflect on the resonances with the Suffering Servant of Isaiah.

Esther and Jesus: A Story of Salvation

The correspondences between the narrative of the book of Esther and the economy of salvation are on the face of it so slim that many, perhaps most, theologians and preachers ignore or dismiss the book for the purposes of crafting an overview of God's purposes. But is this too hasty?

The christological dimensions of the story may be examined in three dimensions. First, Esther takes upon herself the plight of her people, faces ultimate danger on their behalf, places herself in the lion's jaw, as it were, and brings about not only her own restoration but the salvation of her people. This broad outline makes a formidable case for seeing the parallels between Jesus's story and Esther's. The conversation with Mordecai in Esth. 4 is crucial in this reading. Esther knowingly takes on all these responsibilities. She wavers at first, but her wavering only highlights the risk and the sacrifice involved. There is of course no question of Esther herself having anything like the associations that surround the second member of the Trinity; the point is not that Esther is like Jesus ontologically, but that the narrative shape of her story has strong resemblances with the story of salvation as seen in Jesus. This commentary seeks to take these resonances seriously and pursue their details in the text.

Why have these resonances not drawn further attention? It may be that only in recent times have resistances to seeing a woman as a Christ figure began in many places to be overcome. The nature of Esther's life in the harem and subsequently in marriage to a Gentile may be seen as expressing her suffering, but may in many quarters have seemed unsavory in a Christ figure. It may be that the salvation Esther procures is too this-worldly for many Christian appetites. And besides being this-worldly, it has a bloodthirsty character that is not generally associated with Christ's salvation—although the history of the Crusades and many imperial ventures might suggest otherwise.

What these resonances should do is draw further attention to the character of Esther as it develops through the book, from passive pawn of others' designs through ambivalence to active, imaginative, brilliant, and decisive actor on the world political stage. In the space of a few short chapters the story presents a compelling figure and invites as much scrutiny toward her humble beginnings as her vaunted conclusion.

Second, the sequence of chapters in the book of Esther discloses an interesting illumination of Christ's incarnation. The conventional pattern of theological analysis assumes a sequence that begins creation-fall-covenant-incarnation. But in the book of Esther the incarnation precedes the fall. I take the fall to be the

moment when Haman becomes first minister and Mordecai's refusal to acknowledge Haman triggers the momentous decree. One of the most fascinating aspects
of the book's plot is that by the time all this happens Esther is *already* queen. She
did not become queen as a strategy to offset catastrophe. She was already queen
by the time catastrophe dawned.

The christological illumination of this is to give weight to the conviction that
the incarnation is not simply God's response to humanity's fall, but is a part of
the overflowing and manifestation of God's very nature; in other words, there
would have been an incarnation had there been no fall. This is a venerable debate
in Christian theology, and perhaps the most illuminating one of them all—for it
defines the nature of God as much as if not more than any other question. We are
given no reason why Esther sought to become queen. Indeed Mordecai's words in
4:14, "Perhaps you have come to royal dignity for just such a time as this," indicate
that even Mordecai had no particular understanding of why Esther should enter
the king's circle. In entering the harem she embodies her people's condition of
exile, much as Jesus embodies Israel's sojourn in Egypt when he is taken there
after his birth in Bethlehem.

Third, a number of other typological inferences offer themselves and may be
given greater or lesser weight depending on one's judgment about the central
connection between Esther and Christ. I begin the commentary by noting Ahasuerus's portrayal as God, albeit a very different God from the God of Jesus Christ.
Perceiving Ahasuerus as a parody of the first person of the Trinity enhances the
resonance of Esther pleading at his right hand later in the story. Haman is as an
explicit an embodiment of evil as takes human form in the pages of the Bible.
While Satan appears in Job and in the Gospels, he is not flesh and blood in the way
Haman is. Mordecai is perhaps the most complex figure of all. He seems to be the
astute operator set to become the wise statesman, but it is his refusal to bow before
Haman that provokes the terrifying decree. He is perhaps as complex as Israel.

Esther and the Church: An Invitation to Faithful Witness

While my interest as a pastor, preacher, and theologian alerts me to the questions
of scripture, Israel, and Christ, my background as a scholar in Christian ethics and
a leader of a Christian community directs my attention particularly to the setting
and nature of the church and its perception of its relationship to the world. This
latter encounter has been portrayed in a host of different ways, ranging from the
hostile to the congenial.

My book *Improvisation: The Drama of Christian Ethics* offers an understanding of
the church's relationship to the world.[5] It endorses Hans Urs von Balthasar's notion
of a dramatic reading of the Christian story, synthesizing a lyric reading tied up with

5. Samuel Wells, *Improvisation: The Drama of Christian Ethics* (Grand Rapids: Brazos / London:
SPCK, 2004).

personal poignancy and feeling with an epic reading too detached from incarnational involvement to be truly embodied. It locates the church as the fourth act of a five-act drama, whose sequence is creation-Israel-Jesus-church-eschaton. Living in act 4 means recognizing that the decisive moment in God's story has already happened and therefore having the courage and patience to live knowing that God's eschatological consummation (act 5) will complete all that faithful witness leaves unresolved. The mistakes the church makes can in many respects be traced to misunderstanding which act it is in and assuming that no definitive sign of God's will has been seen (and thus living in act 2), or assuming that it must make the decisive intervention (living in act 3), or assuming that it must conclude the story correctly (act 5).

Improvisation is a helpful way of thinking about ethics because Christians cannot simply replicate the story they find in scripture. Improvisers in the theater are schooled in a tradition so thoroughly that they learn to act from habit in circumstances that spontaneously arise. This is what I take the practice of Christian ethics to be: forming habits that ensure responding to novelty, crisis, or challenge is not a dilemma requiring anxious effort but a stimulus to apply old wisdom and familiar practices in new settings. There are three key elements of the improvisatory imagination.

First is the understanding of status, a mode of interaction chosen rather than imposed, and referring not to social class or conventional aggregations of power but to the ways people maneuver interactions and conversations into forms that reaffirm the mode of relationship that suits them best. Status, in this sense, is not something you are or have; it is the way you choose to interact. High status and low status are not inherently good or bad ways of operating: they are simply ways that reflect a person's estimation of themselves and their facility in adopting styles that achieve their desired outcomes. If one has a gun pointed at one's head, a low-status response might be, "Please don't shoot! I have a family and I am no threat to you!" A high-status response might be, "Go on. Make my day." Expert status players can alter their status at will. When this is done well, and their interlocutors enjoy it, observers call it charm; when it is done less well, and their interlocutors dislike its outcomes, observers call it manipulation. The significance for ethics is that the church understands how status works and the status it may be called to play in differing circumstances.

In the book of Esther, Haman is the classic obsessive high-status player. His clash with Mordecai is all about demanding that Mordecai respond in low-status terms and then overreacting when Mordecai refuses to do so. It demonstrates how high-status players frequently get into conflict with one another and often lack facility in negotiating such conflict. Esther is a status expert, able to be subservient and ever pleasing in the harem, able to alter her status frequently as she leads Ahasuerus on, and then able to be utterly high status when her honor is impugned by Haman while Ahasuerus is momentarily absent.

Second is the practice of overaccepting. Anything an interlocutor says or does, whether friendly, hostile, or neutral, is considered an offer. The respondent has three options in return. The first is to accept; this means to work with the grain of the offer, even at great disadvantage to oneself. The second is to block the offer; this means to reject the premise of the offer. The third is to overaccept the offer; this means to accept the premise of the offer but fit the offer into a much larger narrative than had been in the imagination of the person making the offer. A friend was approached by a sex worker who said, "Would you like a good time?" To accept would be to say, "Yes, how much?" To block would be to say, "No, thank you." Instead my friend overaccepted and said, "I'd like to talk to you. I don't think what you're offering me right now is what I'd call a good time. If I can buy you a drink I'd like to talk to you about what I would call a *really* good time." Sometimes accepting all offers is a scary commitment. But blocking is not always an option. It sometimes requires violence and sometimes is futile. Overaccepting is especially significant for those who lack sufficient power simply to block threatening offers.

The key scene in the book of Esther comes in Esth. 4 where Esther, having accepted her role in the harem, initially blocks Mordecai's counsel to use her royal influence to save the Jews. However, after some deliberation, during which Mordecai persuades her that blocking will be futile and she will die with all her race, she overaccepts the offer and not only brings about salvation for the Jews but contrives to put Mordecai in a position of considerable power. This small story of overaccepting portrays the larger wisdom of the book—that the Jews must overaccept their Diaspora existence, rather than spinelessly accept or uselessly block.

Third is the practice of reincorporation. This is when discarded elements from earlier in the narrative begin to reappear, especially at moments when redeeming these discarded elements offers the resolution to what seemed insurmountable problems. Children are often highly attuned to reincorporation and refuse to believe they have reached the end of the story until elements and characters earlier set aside finally reappear. Charles Dickens's novels are notable for immense and rapid reincorporation in their closing chapters, where it sometimes seems almost every character in a sprawling narrative comes back into the story in a new way. One influential writer describes improvisation as like walking backward.[6] Instead of walking *forward* to face the daunting emptiness of an unknown future, the improviser walks *backward*, seeing discarded material, near or far, as a host of gifts enabling the continuance and resolution of troubling narratives.

Reincorporation is not quite so significant in the book of Esther as the previous two motifs, but like both of them it figures at 4:14. When Mordecai says, "Who knows? Perhaps you have come to royal dignity for just such a time as this," he is saying that a collection of events whose true meaning had remained for some time elusive were now coming back into the story in a crucial way. This is a dramatic reincorporating move.

The significance of introducing these themes from the practice of improvisation in the theater is not simply to amplify the dramatic qualities of the book

---

6. Keith Johnstone, *Impro: Improvisation in the Theatre* (London: Methuen, 1981), 116.

of Esther. It is to highlight the ways the text may inform and instruct debates in Christian ethics. Status is a perpetual feature of every human interaction and a constant theme in the relation of the church to the surrounding society. Faithfulness is not about settling on one kind of status as appropriate, but about becoming expert status players who can embody servant ministry at the same time as resurrected glory. Sometimes it means speaking truth to power, a high-status activity; sometimes it means being all things to all people, that by all means one may save some, a low-status approach.

Status may illuminate the debate between ecclesial ethicists, notably Stanley Hauerwas, and some of their antagonists, such as Jeffrey Stout.[7] When Hauerwas calls on the church to have a greater sense of its identity and to locate that identity in the narrative of Israel and Jesus and in practices such as baptism and Eucharist that seek to embody that narrative, he is making a high-status demand to the church to have a greater esteem for, and confidence in, its distinctive qualities and sources of truth. However, many beyond the church hear such a demand as a call for the church to flex its muscles and assert its authority all the louder, in the face of the apparently prevailing tide of secularism. Meanwhile when the call sounds like a plea for Christians to withdraw to a sectarian citadel—a high-status proclamation that Christians are better than the world and do not need their contemporaries of other faith persuasions or none—then antagonism quickly flares up, as invariably happens when extreme high-status positions are adopted. But the high-status claim *within the church*—that Christians have a distinctive understanding of truth and the possibilities of life and should base their philosophy and ethics on that understanding—does not automatically invoke a high-status claim addressed *by the church to the world*. Quite the contrary: Hauerwas's work constantly criticizes the assumption that it is the church's birthright or responsibility to run the world. The irony is that many of Hauerwas's critics regard his argument for the distinctiveness of the church as wrong precisely because it makes it *harder* for the church then to run the world, where he has the more modest proposal that Christians should allow themselves to be run by the Holy Spirit. This is where Hauerwas's critics often misunderstand him.

The book of Esther can bring clarity to this dispute about status. Withdrawal for the Jews is out of the question. There is simply no place to which the Jews could possibly withdraw. Sectarianism is taken out of the debate altogether. But in her moment of crisis, Esther calls upon the Jews to reassert their identity and practices by fasting for three days. Esther plays different status roles depending on her different contexts: she makes no virtue of stubborn inflexibility. Hers is a teleological ethic: she fits her whole form of life around what will bring salvation for the Jews. By contrast Mordecai's insistence on playing high status gets the Jews in trouble. His high-status behavior from Jew to Gentile triggers antagonism. Esther

---

7. Stanley Hauerwas and William H. Willimon, *Resident Aliens: Life in the Christian Colony* (Nashville: Abingdon, 1989); Jeffrey Stout, *Democracy and Tradition* (Princeton: Princeton University Press, 2003).

saves her high-status moments for the occasions when they flatter Ahasuerus and facilitate the right results. The obsession of Ahasuerus and especially Haman with status leaves them open to manipulation and downfall. Esther never falls into such a mistake. Unlike Haman, Esther never makes her desire for a particular status an end in itself: it is always something she employs to a greater end. To invoke the language of Augustine, Haman "enjoys" being high status—ridiculously so.[8] Haman thus enjoys what should only ever be used. Esther, by contrast, enjoys only the salvation of the Jews: everything else, most of all her status, she uses to that end. Hence Hauerwas's exasperation with his critics: status is simply something one uses for the sake of what alone should be enjoyed: bringing the church into faithful imitation of Christ through the Holy Spirit. To be overly concerned about how one social form best equips the church to influence the world—something that will inevitably vary over time—is to enjoy what should be used.

Another issue highlighted by status that is raised by Hauerwas's work is that of the language of exile. Hauerwas and others, notably Walter Brueggemann, often employ the language of exile to point out to Christians, particularly members of the Protestant churches in the United States, that their country is not their home. This has significant strengths. It distinguishes between the United States and the church, emphasizing that the United States is not the church, however much many American Christians have treated it as if it were. It sharpens the sense Christians have that they are and should expect to be in tension with key assumptions of their social and political culture. But the book of Esther again clarifies what is lacking in this portrayal. The book of Esther is not about exile. It is about life in the Diaspora. There is no question of going home in this book. One can only hope to find peaceful coexistence in foreign territory. Once one invokes the language of exile one has to be explicit about where precisely home is. And while home has to be heaven, in eschatological terms, there remains a sneaking suspicion that there was a time when American Christians really did get Christianity right—be it the 1950s, or the 1930s, or the 1820s—and that becomes an unspoken template for all thoughts of return. (Hauerwas, Brueggemann, and others do not endorse these suspicions, but neither do they provide a detailed alternative to them, so the force of them remains.) The language of Diaspora has no such thoughts of return. It does not risk the nostalgic overtones of the term "exile" to quite the same degree. It is provisional, but more or less permanent. And it requires constant adaptive tactics for survival, rather than shrewd strategies for eventual dominance. The book of Esther illuminates why the language of Diaspora would suit the rhetoric of such figures as Hauerwas and Brueggemann rather better than the language of exile.

The practice of overaccepting has similar resonances with Esther and with the contemporary church. People's first reaction to the notion of overaccepting is frequently, But surely there are some things one *must* block? In these cases the

---

8. Augustine, *On Christian Doctrine*, trans. J. F. Shaw (Edinburgh: T&T Clark, 1892), 9.

significance of overaccepting sinks in only when it is made explicit that there are many circumstances where one simply cannot block. The situation of the Jews in Esth. 4, after Haman's decree, is a perfect example of such a circumstance. The poignancy of Esth. 4 is that one might assume—most people at most times do—that the only options are passive acquiescence (acceptance) or futile defiance (blocking). But Esther finds a way to overaccept. That is the heart of her story. And that is the heart of Christian social ethics. Ethics are often conceived as a contest between principles—which invariably require blocking—or outcomes—which invariably assume a level of accepting. But the ability to make a block effective assumes the employment of, or complicity with, a level of force or coercion that ought to invite further scrutiny. (For example, one might say abortion is wrong; but if that therefore implies that abortions must be stopped, then it means working through legislation and encouraging coercive enforcement of legislation. Thus a principled stand ends up having a consequential approach to law enforcement.) By contrast Esther has no power to block. She has to find a way to renarrate Ahasuerus's story in such a way that Haman emerges as his enemy, not his friend. She has to find a way to persuade him not to erase Haman's decree—Persian law does not allow legislation to be blocked—but to overaccept Haman's decree with a subsequent decree. Thus while status puts its finger on some of the more controversial debates in contemporary Christian ethics, overaccepting offers the key to how the church may, while remaining faithful to its tradition, witness in challenging circumstances without assuming that its role is to seize control.

Reincorporation is central to the church's understanding of the reign of God. Reincorporation describes how people discarded earlier in the story reappear as gifts. This is how the church sees the least of these as the key to unlocking the door of God's future. Act 5 of the divine drama is made up of the reincorporated discarded material of the previous acts. Thus living eschatologically in act 4 means spending time with those discarded from the drama—the downtrodden, oppressed, and of no account—who will inevitably be present in act 5. Reincorporation identifies why the conclusion of the book of Esther is troubling to Christians. The issue is not primarily whether the slaughter is excusable because of the extreme circumstances or whether it is exaggerated in keeping with much other hyperbole in the narrative. The issue is that, if God works by drawing the discarded events and people back into the drama at the end in new and reviving ways, this does not look like the way God works. Of course the book never says that this is how God works. Which might lead Christians to the wry conclusion that, while the church has a great deal to learn from the book of Esther about status and overaccepting, the language of reincorporation may clarify a decisive parting of the ways between the Jews' resourceful dependence on their own devices and the true reincorporating politics made possible by the God of Jesus Christ. Not that, of course, the church has often been such a shining example of such a politics.

The Challenge of Esther

The foregoing reflections have yielded the following conclusions. The intersection of existential threat and hyperbolic humor is not incidental to Esther but inseparable from its meaning. The book of Esther has significant precedents and parallels in Old Testament literature both in terms of its political ethics and its spiritual disposition. The book of Esther has illumination to shed on Christ's incarnation and passion, death and resurrection. The book of Esther has important things to say about the church's political and social ethic, and these may be highlighted using the categories of theatrical improvisation.

The most specific challenge of Esther lies in the way it offers a story of salvation, but one different in marked respects from the way salvation is depicted in the Old and New Testament texts more central to the tradition. There is no directly identified action of God that brings salvation about. There is no dialogue with God in which God's people wrestle with God's purposes and their appropriate role in bringing those purposes about. There is no sense of a promised land, in Canaan or in heaven, that lies in the near, middle, or far distance as the home of God and/or the destiny of those involved in the struggle to realize God's purposes. There is no sense of a temple, constructed or embodied, to focus God's reconciling word to God's people or the people's imprecatory word to God.

More than that, there seems to be a degree of criticism of such convictions. These convictions—that Israel's heritage and destiny lie in God's holiness, manifested in liberating action, coded in covenant, represented by land, maintained by king, restored in temple—are what we might think of as the spine of the scriptures. It is not that the scriptures exclude countertestimony, searching inquiry, profound lament. But such countertestimony presupposes the core testimony. And Esther's countertestimony challenges that core testimony in a unique way, by presenting an ethic more or less shorn of God. If the Jews wait for Passover to come it will be too late: that is how the lot falls. There is a hint of piety in Mordecai's sackcloth and ashes and in Esther's fast—but besides these glimpses, the Jews are left very much to their own devices. Meanwhile there is an element of parody in the portrayal of Ahasuerus, the unpredictable ruler with cumbersome and sometimes ridiculous but nonetheless irrevocable laws. If one were in any degree given to lament God's absence or silence, such a portrayal gives exaggerated vigor to such protest. In this commentary I use the term "Passover" to indicate the spine of the scriptures and the word "Purim" to indicate the alternative vision offered by the book of Esther.

Thus fundamentally the book of Esther is a challenge to Israel to discern when to take its destiny into its own hands; a challenge to the church to learn how to balance refusal with compliance and find a faithful way between the two; and a challenge to God to show a face, different from that of Ahasuerus, that the Jews desperately need in their constant search for salvation.

SETTING

ESTHER 1–2

Ahasuerus and His World (1:1–8)

Ahasuerus is God. That is how the book of Esther begins.

There is much speculation over the presence or absence of God in the book of Esther. But the book begins with the one who is in charge of all the events and circumstances and arrangements and threats that affect the Jews. He holds the whole world in his hands. All 127 provinces, to be precise. There may be life beyond the lands that Ahasuerus rules over, but it hardly matters. Ahasuerus rules the whole of the world as far as the Jews are concerned. All the world that counts. The book of Esther is about coming to understand, survive, and eventually thrive in Ahasuerus's world.

Esther begins in a time and a place that is at once the hazy land of fairy tale and the epicenter of the known world. The story it tells is a timeless tale of how people of dignity, courage, and guile can survive in even the most perilous situation, and it is a precise account of how quick thinking and amazing coincidence saved the Jews from being wiped off the face of the earth. Thus it combines the preposterously far-fetched with the existentially urgent.

To read Esther means to keep this tension in mind throughout. If one forgets the existentially urgent, one can make the mistake of seeing this simply as a burlesque, a comic tale of disguise and reversal, of goodness vindicated and evil trounced. In fact, this is a story as significant as the exodus, because it concerns how Israel was saved from obliteration, a fate it came perilously close to experiencing. Yet if one forgets the preposterously far-fetched, one makes a mistake of equal magnitude. This is not a story to be read in a pious way, and its huge numbers and incredible coincidences are not to be dwelt upon in meticulous devotion. It is a farce and should be enjoyed as a farce. That is its charm, its appeal, and a crucial dimension of its meaning.

In the opening verses we meet the whole world, or at least its executive representatives, gathered at the table of the almighty. The guest list cascades upon us. The **officials and ministers** are there, and the **nobles and governors of the provinces**. What is more, it seems the whole **army** has turned up. This is quite some banquet. And it goes on for six months. There are many exaggerations and absurdities in the book of Esther, but this one is the greatest by some distance. Can this really be any fun for anybody? It may be a picture of heaven—a great banquet with everyone who is anyone present. But almost every picture of heaven becomes a hell once the momentary and spontaneous becomes the eternal and obligatory. Ahasuerus either has no understanding of this or has patience for only one thing—broadcasting his pomp and circumstance.

From the very start we have a vivid picture of this empire. It covers all the world that counts; its ruler is wealthy and lavish in his tastes; it is wasteful and prodigal; and it sees power and authority as existing for the benefit of those who hold them, not for those who are subject to them. We are given plenty of words to stress that this is a royal occasion—**royal throne**, **reign**, **kingdom**, **majesty**, **palace**. This is clearly the summit of royal aspiration. Here we have the dream of heaven and the realities of earth portrayed in one and the same moment. This is everything we need to know about how things are and how they will always be. Eventually **these days were completed**. In other words, perfection has been reached. The peoples of the earth have feasted and the king of the earth is on his throne. Just as the animals gathered around Adam (Gen. 2:19–20) and just as the nations will stream to the mountain of the Lord's house (Isa. 2:2–3), so this is a picture, albeit a parody, of created order and eschatological fulfillment.

The paradox of this portrayal lies in the way it engages with a constant debate in the Old Testament. That debate concerns whether kingship highlights or obscures the way God is fundamentally king. The ideal king points to the kingship of God; the less-than-ideal king points away from God to himself. The ambivalence about the description of Ahasuerus lies in whether this is a parody of a king of Israel or a parody of God. The latter is the stronger resonance, but the question of the former context sharpens the irony.

The whole world is at the feet of Ahasuerus. The story begins with him, and not with its Jewish protagonists. The irony is that he never ceases to think the story is about him. From beginning to end, he remains happy in his ignorance. The very idea that a story about him would be included among the Jewish and Christian scriptures, and yet not named after him, is absurdly beyond his imagination. This irony is at the heart of the theology of Esther.

And what does Ahasuerus do at this perfect moment? What he does best! He holds a second banquet. Later Esther will hold two banquets where it seems that one would have done: here Ahasuerus shows that gilding the lily is a royal habit in Persia. What the first banquet had in duration, the second banquet has in quality. The fittings are breathtaking: **couches of gold and silver** for the reclining guests, **a mosaic pavement of porphyry, marble, mother-of-pearl, and colored stones** would you believe, and a full selection of **golden goblets** from which to sip (or slurp) the **royal wine**. These people know how to have a good time.

This second banquet took place **in the court of the garden of the king's palace**. In Mesopotamia, then as now, gardens are uncommon. They are very special. The climate is dry, the ground is dusty, rain can be rare. While not the language of the book or the civilization portrayed in it, Arabic gives us an insight into the setting of this second banquet. In Arabic the word "garden" has a particular resonance. The Arabic word for "garden" is "paradise." Paradise means flowing water in a desert, green shoots in dry ground, lush beauty in the middle of arid wastelands. After all, Eden is depicted as being in this same part of the world. And this second banquet takes place over **seven days**—skimpy, really, by the standards of the previous one, but a number with resonances of completion and fulfillment, a number with a hint of perfected creation. Here, perhaps, is the Sabbath at the end of the long period of onerous partying.

The court of the garden of the king's palace is a parody of the Jerusalem temple. The temple is the only other building in scripture that gets this kind of attention to exotic detail and exquisite texture. Here we discover **white cotton curtains and blue hangings tied with cords of fine linen and purple to silver rings and marble pillars**. The fixtures are built to last, and the fittings are dressed to impress. This is a place of worship for the god of the whole world—Ahasuerus. There is even a hint of a connection with the Jerusalem temple in the reference to **golden goblets**, which could perhaps have been brought by Nebuchadnezzar from Jerusalem, as one Targum suggests. If the Targum's insight is pursued, one may see an analogy between the goblets and Esther herself—objects of Jewish beauty dragooned into servicing the king's pleasure. This is an early hint of the character of Jewish assimilation and the parody of Israel's glory at work in the Persian Empire.

But one very significant difference is that **all the people present in the citadel of Susa, both great and small**, were at the second banquet. That means there were a lot of people, and Ahasuerus would have needed a lot of **golden goblets**. But what it really means is that the *Jews were there*—right at the holy of holies. This was the heart of the palace at the heart of the citadel at the heart of the city at the heart of the empire at the center of the world. And the Jews were there. They must have been, because **all the people** were. From the very beginning of the story one of its key themes is vividly portrayed—the permeability and impenetrability of the circle of royal power. Just as the Jerusalem temple had been open to all yet closed and secret, so access to the god at the center of the Persian universe was unthinkable and yet possible. Ahasuerus is a dizzying figure beyond the reach of ordinary mortals—and yet there are chinks in the surrounding walls, and they are ripe for exploitation by serious and systematic Jews, as Mordecai and Esther will later demonstrate. We are being prepared for a lesson in how to weave a path through this Byzantine labyrinth.

Just as one day all the nations will stream to Jerusalem to worship the God of Israel, so at this moment the Jews in Susa are flocking to **the court of the garden of the king's palace**, to pay homage to the ruler of the earthly universe. All the peoples of the earth are streaming to the mountain of the lord Ahasuerus, and the Jews are there—but there seems to be nothing distinctive about them. These are the realities of life in the Diaspora. This is what you need to know. Not to admire, not to be appalled by, not to scorn, not necessarily to imitate—just to know.

This is what we have discovered so far. There is a ruler of the world, and he is impossibly wealthy and absurdly lavish in his tastes. Yet in this empire there is a place for Jews. It is not the place they had in Jerusalem, and it is not clear what compromises they have been driven to in order to find such a place. But this place is not just about tolerance and forbearance: when everyone celebrates, the Jews celebrate too. Like everyone else, they get an invitation to the heart of the empire when occasion arises. There is nothing fundamentally unsustainable about their place in this world, parody of the true state of things as it may be.

The opening scene tells us one more thing about the Persian world. It is governed by laws—or at least decrees. **The king had given orders to all the officials of his palace**: this was a place of due process and regulated authority. That should be good news for a minority community, perpetually glancing behind its back for enemies among the rulers or the people. The rule of law reigns here. However, that is good news only if the laws are good laws. And already we have strong reason to doubt that, for the first decree we come across from the ruler of the known world is for all the officials **to do as each one desired**. It is open season for anyone close to the throne to set about using their power as they see fit. The context is permission for drinking with abandon. But the implication is that pretty much anything can be done with abandon in this court. The serpent has been busy and persuasive in the garden: there really is no tree from which one may not eat. This is power not for a purpose but for the exhilaration of its possession and exercise: power for its own sake. The irony here is that we are about to discover that Ahasuerus cannot do as he desires if he wants to make the queen the subject of those desires.

Already we have in place the twin paradoxes that form the foundation of the political ethic of the book of Esther. The empire is about unimaginable wealth and power; yet there is a place in it for Jews. And the empire is governed by the firm hand of law; yet its laws are ridiculous. It seems the only way to be safe is to have a close eye on the lawmaking process. And in an empire like this, that can only mean being close to the king. Which sounds like not just the safest, but also the most dangerous place to be—as the book goes on to show.

It is not hard to detect a subversive tone in this opening scene, directed not just in mockery at the Persian Empire, but more significantly in lament of exasperation at the God of Israel. Like Persia, God's world is one of untold wonders and splendors; and yet there is a place, sometimes a dangerous place, in it for Jews.

Meanwhile God's world is one of laws, and the ways of God are ones that one may know with some confidence; and yet sometimes God's ways are beyond belief and beyond comprehension. It is in finding a way to live in both the Jewish world and the Persian world, it seems, that the political ethic of the book of Esther lies. And the early signs are that, while Ahasuerus's hand, particularly after a glass or eighty of wine, is none too steady, the hand of God is not to be taken for granted either. It will therefore take shrewdness, cunning, and a sharp sense of timing to survive in this world.

Cost of Defiance (1:9–22)

It out turns that someone very close to the king gets to exercise some of the king's privileges and enjoy some of the king's wealth and power. Now we may get to see what it is like to be close to the king—a position that already seems so necessary and yet so vulnerable. **Queen Vashti** holds a **banquet**. We hear very little about her banquet, aside from knowing it is **in the palace** (and thus not the garden) **of King Ahasuerus** and it is **for the women**. Which women, precisely, and how long the banquet lasted—let alone the quality of the soft furnishings and the size of the drinking goblets—we are not told. We are simply to assume that the luster of Queen Vashti's banquet added to the luster of the king's world record-breaker—if not in duration or quantity, then at least in looks, charm, and personality.

The climax of creation and salvation is upon us. We may step back for a moment and see this parody not just in its Old Testament context but also across the whole of the Christian Bible. In the New Testament Jesus's resurrection is the culmination of creation and the inauguration of the eschaton. It takes place at the very moment of the end of the seventh day of the week in an idyllic garden scene. It is the ultimate Sabbath at the end of the Sabbath. It is the new dawn. Here now, early in the book of Esther, once again in parody, is the drumroll finale to the 180 days of patrician banqueting and one week of plebeian feasting. The book's first decree has been carried out in full, and **the king was merry with wine**. Again we have an absurd and embarrassing paradox: the empire has engineered a grand stage, but, when the vital moment comes, the king is drunk.

Being drunk is no serious obstacle to Ahasuerus. It is, perhaps, normal for him. The whole empire, the whole world, quivers at the mercy of his drunken whim. That is a permanent state of affairs. But what happens next is, like the opening scene, both general and very precise. It is general, because it shows that the empire is both dangerous and stupid; being ridiculous certainly does not make it harmless. It is precise, because it opens a window of possibility for the Jews and a warning lesson in how not to conduct themselves around a king with a distended belly, a short fuse, and a wafer-thin attention span.

Queen Vashti refused to come at the king's command. We are not told why. There are many things in the book of Esther that we might like to know but are not told. We never know why Mordecai enters Esther into the royal beauty pageant. Or why everyone loves Esther. Or why Mordecai refuses to bow to Haman. Or why Esther delays telling Ahasuerus her request. Or why Ahasuerus has difficulty sleeping. Or why Zeresh is so certain the Jews will prevail. We may speculate about these and other things, but they are simply stated as part of the plot of the story. And this development in the plot is as significant as any in the book, because on it rests much of what follows.

Vashti's refusal, whatever its motivation, shows the king cannot have whatever he wants. It exposes the farce of the Persian court. It shows how offending the pride of a powerful man in this empire can have widespread ramifications. It demonstrates the rapid communication system of Persian bureaucracy. It discloses the important detail that Persian laws, once passed, are irrevocable. And it creates a vacancy beside the king on the throne of the empire. In all these ways it fore-shadows the story that is to come. We will look at these in turn.

The king is attended by **seven** named **eunuchs**. On first reading this is yet an-other cascade of abundance—each name falling over the previous one, the king's every word obeyed by a superfluity of eager attendants. But on closer reading the role of the eunuchs here adds to the poignancy of the scene. Why would the king be surrounded by eunuchs? Presumably because he also desires to be frequently in the company of alluring women, and he wants to be sure his closest aides have no mixed motives for consorting between him and his companions. But surely . . . is he not all powerful? There could be no question of anyone for a moment imagining that their own desires could inhibit or divert the king's. That would make him less than the manly colossus one assumes such a powerful man must be. It would make him more like a eunuch.

If the portrayal of Ahasuerus is a playful but edgy parody of God, then the portrayal of the eunuchs is a playful but edgy parody of Ahasuerus. Only a man who fears his ultimate impotence needs to be surrounded by impotent men who remind him of his potency. We have already discovered that the judgment of the man that holds the scepter may be unsteady. We are now getting a hint that he may also be unsure of his own power. All the principal male characters in the book of Esther are inclined to overplay their hand—Mordecai somewhat, but disastrously, Ahasuerus publicly and arrogantly, and Haman compulsively and aggressively.

If there is a hint of a fall narrative here it lies in the transgression of the com-mand of the godlike figure and the inability of the man to maintain his authority over the woman. Both this moment and Mordecai's later refusal to bow before Haman play a role in the story akin to the fall of Adam: before these events, all is well; afterward, order is in peril. And yet in both cases the threat of chaos is portrayed in terms that make the one making the command look absurd. Law and its rule are upheld, and lawlessness averted, but at enormous cost. The dynamics of the relationship between man and woman become the central concern of this chapter. Is harmony between male and female a key symbol and determinant of harmony in creation as a whole? Genesis 2–3 and Rom. 1 would suggest so. Or is male-female disharmony a sign of the Persians' fundamental disorder, a disorder in which Esther and Mordecai, by dint of their harmonious partnership, will have the opportunity to outmaneuver their antagonists?

The king consulted the sages who knew the laws. Immediately we discover a despot who is not really in control. He needs sages to tell him his own rules. All the king's horses and all the king's men are needed to put the king's marriage together again. This is part of the farce of the story. Ahasuerus is a prisoner of his advisers. The cacophony of sages may know the rules—but they are not good advisers on how to play the game. Whereas everything Ahasuerus says is in reported speech, his adviser **Memucan** makes a direct speech that stretches to five verses. Who is really in control of the empire remains an open question throughout the book.

Ahasuerus is a man who has his personal and his public roles confused. He appears to be in the habit of using his public power for personal glorification; and he thus sees no reason not to use his personal relationship for public acclaim. Vashti, it seems, is his crowning possession. After 187 days of enjoying marble columns and golden goblets and porphyry mosaics, the guests get to see the queen herself. A person in a public role who cannot separate personal benefit from public responsibility is bound to lurch from one crisis to the next. One might anticipate that the public would complain first; but here it is the king's wife who refuses to play. As the book will show, it is never clear whether the role of queen in this empire is primarily a public or a personal one.

To those who have a hammer in their pocket, everything looks like a nail. To a sage who has the ear of the king of the whole world, legislation looks like the answer to every problem. This is part of the humor of the story, but it is not simply a fairy-tale detail. It is an abiding parody. It is notoriously difficult to legislate that people should be good. If they will not be good, of course, let them be obedient. But it is even harder to legislate that people be obedient. A law that is widely flouted and cannot be enforced brings the whole legal system into disrepute. This really is a threat to the empire—that its laws become subject to ridicule and its law enforcers become figures of fun. One of the key messages of the book is thus foreshadowed: the true threat to the empire does not come from loyal Jewish subjects dispersed across its provinces, but from sinister laws and machinations originating from the king's inner circle. It is not as if there is no threat whatsoever to the king: we are soon to find that two eunuchs have plotted against the king's very life. But this shows only how wide of the mark the sages have been—because the threat does not come from women, does not threaten the provincial domestic hierarchy, and remains invisible to the wise men of the land.[1]

It is not entirely clear why the king is obliged to keep his own laws. It is hardly as if he has a supreme court keeping constant vigilance and a concatenation of congressional hearings pending should he breach the constitution. Once again the portrayal of Ahasuerus hints at a critique of the God of Israel. Why can the

1. As Jon D. Levenson, *Esther: A Commentary* (Louisville: Westminster John Knox, 1997), 51, notes.

one who can do anything, who arrays the world lavishly and displays beauty extravagantly, not assist the Jews when they need help? Is God constrained by rules—is God tangled up, like a cat in a ball of wool, in an absurd system of laws? Or is God hiding behind precedent and pleading due process while the Jews are left to make their own arrangements? The immediate and burning **anger** of the king also hints at a bitter portrayal of God who is unfathomable at normal times, makes unreasonable demands at others, and then is brimming with fury and punishment when those demands are not met. There is a lot of anger in the book of Esther, and it epitomizes the cocktail of impotence and impatience at the heart of the empire.

The response to Vashti's refusal foreshadows later events in a number of further ways. It confuses a slight to the king's pride with a profound threat to the empire. It thus raises the question of whether anyone can tell the difference between honor and status, on the one hand, and social stability and popular well-being, on the other. Certainly no one has learned their lesson by the time the events of Esth. 3 unfold. Which way round is it? Does Ahasuerus have honor and renown so that he may better be king, or is he king so that he may better have honor and renown? The latter is undoubtedly the case. And that is the political problem at the heart of the empire from which all the subsequent problems are derived.

Out of the confusion between honor and stability comes absurd overreaction. Part of this is the burlesque style of the book. Part of it is the consistent ridiculing of the Persian court, a ridicule that never underestimates the system it is subverting. And part of it anticipates the absurd overreaction of Haman's law against the Jews in Esth. 3. This is the world of the bumper sticker that says, "You toucha my car, I smasha your face." Mindless machismo is mixed with empty threat. Once again the awesome and historic are juxtaposed with the absurd and laughable. The whole dynamic machinery of the Persian pony express swings into action— the king sends **letters to all the royal provinces, to every province in its own script and to every people in its own language**. All 127 provinces get their own translations, every scribe under the sun is put to work to pass on the vital news, the whole diversity of the empire listens with one ear to a matter requiring its urgent attention. But it turns out that the breathtaking decree is this: **every man should be master in his own house**.

And the decree turns out to be counterproductive. It is worse than just ineffective. It produces the opposite effect of that intended. The slight was to the king's honor. Now everyone in the empire, in every province, in the script of their own language, knows of the slight to the king's honor. Vashti's name is proclaimed abroad. Anyone who had never previously thought of the rewards of defying authority will quickly see it as the way to imperial fame. And the king's name is attached to an absurd decree that shows his ignorance of life outside the court— the world where events are not fundamentally shaped by decrees. What could be more dishonorable? And this foreshadows the counterproductive efforts of

Haman to assert his own honor and destroy the people of Mordecai the Jew—the result of which is his own impalement, the public execution of his ten sons, and the consolidation of Jewish power in the empire.

The counterproductive outcome of the decree is exacerbated by its irrevocability. We already know that Persian laws are ridiculous—the first law we encounter is the law that one must drink as much as one desires. The second law is even more ridiculous than the first, since it cannot be enforced, embarrasses those it is supposed to support, and is bound to be counterproductive. But this time we discover that Persian laws **may not be altered**. That is bad enough when they are foolish—but catastrophic when they are genuinely menacing. What emerges first as farce is set to be repeated as tragedy.

While the details of the decree and its proclamation all illuminate the nature of Persian politics, the most significant features of this episode concern the queen. **Vashti is never again to come before King Ahasuerus**. This again has a humorous dimension, since the punishment for refusing to come before the king turns out to be a ban on coming before the king. The king is the political, sexual, and social hub of the empire, however, and the decree ensures that Vashti is excluded from everything that matters in Persia. She also, more precisely, ceases to be queen. And, more pertinent to the plot, there is a vacancy: **let the king give her royal position to another who is better than she**. This is the cue for the entry of Esther into the story.

The key question about Vashti is not whether she should be regarded as a feminist icon. Some may choose to see her as boldly standing up for her dignity and independence in the face of systematic patriarchal degradation and consumption. These are worthy purposes. But the text offers no explanation about the motives for her refusal. There is no direct or reported speech to assist our imaginations. All we are told is that **Vashti refused**. The surrounding words **Queen Vashti refused to come at the king's command conveyed by the eunuchs** hint that this could be a question of status. She is a queen, she is being asked something that might be required of a concubine, and the request is conveyed not by the king but by eunuchs. But this is no more than a hint.

Instead, the question is whether one can ever simply refuse. The book of Esther is a story of two queens, one who refused and one who complied. And yet the one who apparently complied retained her integrity, her influence, and her legacy in a way the one who refused did not. Meanwhile the book of Esther is also a story of two Jews, one whose refusal created a crisis, and one whose compliance defused that crisis. Vashti and Mordecai are in different ways complements to Esther. The clumsiness and failure of Vashti's refusal to appear before the king throw the subtlety and success of Esther's compliance into sharp relief. The apparently selfish and headstrong nature of Mordecai's refusal to bow before Haman contrasts with the selflessness and nuance of Esther's compliance with the Persian court. When Daniel refused to bow, the question was one of idolatry. Here, no theological dimension is introduced.

Elsewhere I explore the nature and assumptions of a refusal like Vashti's.[2] I draw on the language of improvisation in the theater to describe a flat "no" as a block (see introduction). Such a block denies the premise of the proposal or invitation made by the other party. The art of improvisation is learning how to say "yes" even when the offer (the technical term for proposal) seems impossible, improper, or dangerous. The technical term for saying "yes" is to accept. The book of Esther can be read as a study in improvisation,[3] because it concerns a people faced with the gravest danger, a danger that they had no power simply to block. Thus they had to find another way to avert the danger, and that other way is what the book is really about. Vashti's story is a warning to the Jews: if they imitate her approach, they are going to be out of the story and into oblivion by the end of Esth. 1.

It is common for those new to the notions and nomenclature of improvisation to assume that faithfulness requires blocking, particularly in the face of danger and evil. But the example of Vashti demonstrates much of why this is a misunderstanding. Vashti is summoned to the king. His motives may or may not be demeaning: but either way, it is an invitation she determines to resist. But what does resistance mean?

Resistance means *assuming one has the power to prevent the feared outcome*. There is no sign that Vashti has that power. But if she did, it could be only by allying herself with forces that might be as unsteady and unworthy as the force she is opposing. This is how blocking assumes violence: for all its apparent faithfulness, blocking fundamentally configures conflict as the clash of opposing forces and assigns victory to the greater force. Those who say "this regime must be crushed" or "these evils must be stamped out," tacitly assume that they are on the side that has the superior physical force.

But having the superior physical force may blind one to more appropriate methods of engaging that which one finds disagreeable, dangerous, or domineering. The availability of superior physical force is more often an inhibitor of the moral imagination than a catalyst to it. One may win a physical battle. But having done so, one is no better prepared than one would otherwise have been for the battle that arises where one's force is inferior. That eventuality requires more imagination than force, and it is in the moral imagination, rather than in physical force, that the most significant elements of retaining identity, maintaining faithfulness, and overcoming evil truly lie.

Resistance also means *taking it upon oneself to close the story*. In theatrical improvisation a story is like a river: trying to block it is useless. One's fundamental role is always to keep the story going. The book of Esther is not interested in grand, tragic gestures that close the Jews' story, with their honor and dignity intact but their presence eradicated from the face of the earth. The whole point is to keep

---

2. Wells, *Improvisation*.

3. Samuel Wells, "For Such a Time as This: Esther and the Practices of Improvisation," in *Liturgy, Time, and the Politics of Redemption*, ed. Chad Pecknold and Randi Rashkover (Grand Rapids: Eerdmans, 2006), 167–87.

the story going. The Jews have no more power to prevent Ahasuerus's will taking effect than Vashti does.

One way of construing these issues is to consider the abiding disagreement between an ethic based on unwavering principle and an ethic resting on calculated outcome. Vashti may appear to be a noble woman of principle—but only if she is seen in isolation. Would her refusal be justified if it jeopardized the survival of her whole people? One shortcoming of principled ethics is its tendency to see questions in narrowly individualist terms and obscure the community of which the individual in question is a member. Esther and Mordecai do not have the luxury of seeking a pure motive entirely based on their own principles. Their responsibility is to keep their people's story going. It turns out that Vashti is indeed a member of a "people." Whether she realizes it beforehand or not, her actions affect every woman in the empire. The ability of women in Persia to negotiate the limitations of their social roles is inhibited by the results of Vashti's actions. Just as the punishment for Mordecai's pride will be the humbling of the Jews, so the price of Vashti's insubordination is the even greater subordination of women.

Meanwhile an ethic that concentrates on so acting that one may bring about a desirable outcome quickly resolves, like so much contemporary debate, into a battle of power and interest. Power—because of the assumption that one has the wherewithal to bring about one's desired result. And interest—because of the question "desirable for whom?" At first glance the book's presentation of Esther's methods in preference to Vashti's may appear to be an assertion of opportunism over principle. But on closer examination the book bears out some familiar criticisms of an ethic based on evaluating outcomes. Most notably, that the ostensible context for the story is the origin of the Festival of Purim places events in a far longer time span than ethics based on results tend to do. Esther is not just concerned about her own survival but about the flourishing of her entire people—and not just in the Susa of the time but in all times and places.

Moreover there is the complex question of the role of providence in the story. The ethic of likely consequences assumes no one is going to set things straight unless one does so oneself. In some ways this may seem to be a lesson this story teaches. But there are traces that make a counterclaim, that the Jews' story is not their own. In 4:14 Mordecai says, "For if you keep silence at such a time as this, relief and deliverance will rise for the Jews from another quarter." And in 6:13 Zeresh says, "If Mordecai, before whom your downfall has begun, is of the Jewish people, you will not prevail against him, but will surely fall before him." This language seems to assume some kind of providence, albeit one that excludes the name of God. So the book of Esther steers a path that seems to rule out straightforward principled approaches. But meanwhile it takes an approach based on assessing consequences to be inadequate descriptively (because they exclude providence) and prescriptively (because they envisage too short a time span). The precise nature of the path it genuinely proposes is the subject of the book.

Vashti lingers in the mind of the Jews as a stark portrayal of one approach to exile. As a pawn in Ahasuerus's empty game she is a vivid analogy for the vulnerability of the Jews in the Persian Empire. In the book of Daniel the Jews appear to block: they assert their own customs and traditions in the face of an inhospitable culture and a hostile ruling elite. They rely on divine intervention to rescue them when blocking jeopardizes their survival—although the survival of the whole people is never in jeopardy. In Esther there is little confidence in such an approach. The opening of the book explains why. Vashti's fate discloses that blocking is not an option. How then to survive and even thrive without losing their identity? It is time to find out.

Opportunity (2:1–7)

It takes a long time for the dust to settle after a six-month-long banquet, a citywide drinking week, and a spectacular slap in the face for the king. Ahasuerus spends an undefined period prowling around like a wounded lion, licking the wound of his **anger**. We discover three things straightaway, which summarize the lessons of the first chapter. Ahasuerus is a prisoner of his anger, he is a prisoner of his feelings for women, and he is a prisoner of his advisers. **He remembered Vashti and what she had done and what had been decreed against her**. The passive voice suggests that Ahasuerus had little awareness of his agency in relation to Vashti and the decree. Things happen *to* Ahasuerus—he has no understanding that he can shape or determine events. This creates the possibility for the Jews' jeopardy and the opportunity for their deliverance.

A theme more subtly introduced to the narrative at this juncture is that of memory. The king **remembered Vashti**. Not *Queen* Vashti, a dignified consort to his majesty: but simply Vashti. If one assumes Ahasuerus had been busy with a new woman each night and this was thus "one thousand women later,"[4] then either the king had been very, very angry or his desire for Vashti had been very, very great. This is not a king, as we shall soon discover, who has much of a memory. And yet this is a story that turns on the presence and absence of memory. And it is a story that is recorded faithfully and rehearsed annually precisely to foster a community of memory. The king's faulty memory opened him up to manipulation. All he can remember are his visceral feelings and the wrongs done to him. Everything else is in the vague haze of a hangover. The Jews have no intention of being caught out the same way.

There not being much to be done about the festering anger and aching pride, the servants set about addressing the lingering desire. We are by now used to those in the king's circle setting the agenda. Like last time, the plan is already fully fledged; but this time the attendants do not even take the trouble to phrase it in polite

4. Michael V. Fox, *Character and Ideology in the Book of Esther*, 2nd ed. (Grand Rapids: Eerdmans, 2001), 39.

formulas.[5] The bureaucracy of the empire swings into action once more: last time it was called upon to prevent the king being insulted, this time it is required to ensure the new queen, besides being youthful and alluring, is romantically inexperienced yet sexually adept. One wonders whether the royal **commissioners** would really be up to such a delicate task. Some things cannot seriously be delegated. Nonetheless there is no requirement that the young women be of a particular race or nationality. And that opens a door to the Jews. The gathering of all the women of beauty in the empire at the start of Esth. 2 mirrors the gathering of all the men of influence in the empire at the start of Esth. 1. While the king does not wish women to have too high a place in his world, it is equally clear he cannot be for a moment without them. But before one assumes such a search is simply a Gentile preoccupation, one may recall that David's desire for a new partner is described in 1 Kgs. 1:2 in similar terms. What really matters, as Esther is quick to discover and repeatedly able to use to her advantage, is the ability to **please the king**—a phrase that appears twice in the same verse.

This is the moment when the central characters make their first appearance. In three verses we discover some very significant things about them. They live in the **citadel of Susa**, and thus they are in close proximity to the king. Perhaps Mordecai has some role at the court. They have Persian names. It may well be the case that **Mordecai** and **Esther** relate to the Babylonian deities Marduk and Ishtar. Their names certainly have a similar ring to those two divine names. More certainly, Mordecai's and Esther's names indicate they are a regular part of Persian culture. Esther has two names, a Persian one and a Jewish one. This hints at her ability to assume more than one identity and play more than one role. Her name has more than one meaning, since in Hebrew it carries a sense of hiding. Already we have a sense that this is going to be a very different story from Daniel. Esther's skills are about covert concealment, not public confrontation.

Mordecai's heritage highlights key themes of the story to come. Coming from the house of **Benjamin** indicates the first of a great many connections to the Joseph story, wherein Joseph's brother Benjamin is a pawn in a complex game of Jewish and Gentile power. **Kish** is the name of King Saul's father, and **Shimei** is a renegade member of Saul's house. Saul is to become a character the shadow of whose failures lurks at the back of the narrative. Our heroes can trace their lineage back to the ruling class of Judah, who were the first to be removed by **Nebuchadnezzar**: this, then, is not to be a story of the common people. But the key term in the introduction of Mordecai and Esther is repeated three times in one verse: **carried away**. This is centrally to be a story about exile or, more precisely, life in the Jewish Diaspora, about how to navigate one's way in a culture and society where being a Jew is to be, not chosen, destined, and cherished, but ignored, despised, or exterminated. **Carried away** means, in its repeated emphasis, vulnerable, with

5. Carol M. Bechtel, *Esther*, Interpretation (Louisville: John Knox, 2002), 29.

one's destiny in the hands of others and in a land where the rules of engagement may turn out to be significantly different.

Immediately Esther epitomizes the pathos of the Jewish people: she has **neither father nor mother**. She has, in short, no home. She has to rely on others for her well-being. Israel knew it was being faithful to God if it cared for the widow, the orphan, and the stranger. Now Israel itself is an orphan and a stranger—and Esther is undoubtedly so. Thus Esther's identity is the identity of the Jewish people. And Esther's fate will be the fate of the Jewish people. It turns out she is **fair and beautiful**, and we shall later discover she "was admired by all who saw her" (2:15). This we already know is a minimum qualification for a woman intending to have influence in the Persian court.

Accession (2:8–18)

The narrative begins in earnest with the word **so**. Everything is in place for Esther to make her move. Yet the events are described in a way that minimizes Esther's agency. **The king's order and his edict were proclaimed**, and **many young women were gathered in the citadel of Susa in custody of Hegai**. Now is the moment: **Esther also was taken into the king's palace and put in custody of Hegai**. There is a studied ambiguity about whose doing this is. Did Mordecai put her forward? Did she stand out so dazzlingly that the king's commissioners spotted her from afar? The one thing that the grammar seems to rule out, with its sequence of passives, is that she asserted herself, either in favor of or against this development.

There would be good reason to shy away from this step. Esther is about to lose her identity. **Mordecai . . . charged her not to tell** who she was. She is about to break Jewish dietary laws, since **Hegai . . . provided her with . . . her portion of food**. And she is about to lose her virginity, with no serious prospect of marriage—just a life of seclusion in the harem. The best outcome imaginable is intermarriage—which itself runs counter to the Jewish law. This information is delivered in what is by now characteristic style—at once absurdly overblown and deadly serious.

And the place where the overblown and serious intersect is, once again, the law. Just as the Jewish law expresses the essence of what it means to practice the presence of God, so the Persian law is the quintessence of deadly absurdity. **The regulations for the women** decree that it takes a year to be ready for a night with Ahasuerus. We have had a law about drinking, a law about not answering your husband back, and a law about corralling beautiful women. Now we have a law about how and when to have sex. If Ahasuerus is a merciless parody of the God of the Jews, these random, ribald, and ridiculous decrees are a flat parody of the Jewish law. At the very least one may infer a playful satire on the preparations for encountering God in the tabernacle. Esther has **six months with oil of myrrh and six months with perfumes and cosmetics**; she has **seven chosen maids from the king's palace**.

Like the endless banquet in Esth. 1 and the countless advisers around the throne, there is now an interminable time of preparation to sleep with the king and a myriad of underlings eagerly supporting this industry. We know by now that the way to succeed in Persia is to get on the right side of the king's advisers. So Hegai becomes the protector who shelters Esther between the home of Mordecai and the home of Ahasuerus.

Esther's early prospects are favorable: she **pleased** Hegai **and won his favor**; she **was admired by all who saw her**; she had the wisdom to follow Hegai's instructions to the letter and thus **asked for nothing** (unlike Vashti, who demanded way too much), **except what Hegai the king's eunuch, who had charge of the women, advised**. But the consequences of failure are social obliteration. The metaphor here is not hard to perceive. These are the circumstances of the Jews even prior to their perilous state after Haman's decree. They are subject to disappear into the morass of Persian extravagance, indulgence, whim, and waste, and their lives are ones of virtual imprisonment with the cost of losing identity. This is a life of constant compromise, uncertain length, complete subservience, and dubious integrity. The harem is the epitome of exile.

Esther's approach, as we have seen, is very different from Vashti's. The contrast is highlighted by the reappearance of **Vashti**'s name as Esther receives her crown. Vashti blocks, Esther accepts. She allows herself the passive voice in relation to Mordecai, Hegai, and Ahasuerus. She puts up with the cosmetic treatments, the lengthy preparation, the role of the maids, the portion of food, the detail of Hegai's advice, and the prospect of a life of concubinage. There is no protest. Blocking is useless. As Fox points out, the harem is a fact of life; the narrator "perceives how women can be used as toys in the sexual games of the powerful, but he does not condemn the harem setup so harshly. He takes it for granted as he does all the peculiarities of the gentile state. Both are fields of obstacle and danger—but also opportunity—for the Jews who find themselves thrust into them."[6] As we shall see, accepting is not the last word. But it has to be the first word if the Jews are going to survive.

If the Jews have no access to conventional kinds of power, they have to develop the arts of alternative resistance—what Yoder calls "revolutionary subordination."[7] The most prominent one in this section of the narrative is secrecy. **Esther did not reveal her people or kindred**. We are not in the book of Daniel here. The narrative makes a number of different allusions to an underground form of power. It is best to keep one's counsel. It is good to be on close terms with the eunuchs. It is as well to **walk around in front of the court of the harem** every day, as Mordecai does, to find out what is going on. It is not a bad idea to become sexually satisfying in the highest degree: there seems to be plenty of advice to hand on this score, for

6. Fox, *Character and Ideology*, 36.
7. John Howard Yoder, *The Politics of Jesus: Behold the Man! Our Victorious Lamb*, 2nd ed. (Grand Rapids: Eerdmans, 1999), 162–92.

obvious reasons. Later there are various channels of communication between the different circles of the court. This is a story where conventional power is wholly outflanked by informal methods and networks.[8] These are the kinds of networks that become available only to those who realize they have no choice but to accept. It is somewhat galling for Esther to be handed around between the men named in this chapter—Abihail, Mordecai, Hegai, Shaashgaz, and Ahasuerus. But because she uses the arts of subordination, she attains the astonishing prize: her offspring is likely to be the next king of Persia. A Jew is poised to rule the world.

The combination of natural endowments, cosmetic refinements, honed techniques, and royal pleasures proves a winning one, and Esther proceeds from commissioner's corral to eunuch's parlor to king's bed and never descends to concubinal oblivion: instead, **the king loved Esther**. It is **the seventh year of his reign** and the time is ripe. And immediately, it seems, there was a wedding banquet. For the first and only time Ahasuerus knows his own mind. It is, granted, a mind shared with **all who saw** Esther; but it is the king's mind, nonetheless. Time for another **banquet**, to round out the business begun with the previous one. It is as if the king has been hungry for four years between Vashti's banquet and Esther's, like a prowling lion seeking whom to devour. Now his hunger is satisfied. It would be ingenuous to hope that this love would transform Ahasuerus and that, in loving Esther, he would find a true desire for all things good, becoming a Cyrus-like figure in the history of the Jews. The story gives us no encouragement for such a positive view. Love is a fleeting thing for Ahasuerus, as is pretty much everything else.

Two key themes of the book of Esther are highlighted at this celebratory moment. The political point is that what is good for the Jews is good for everybody. There is a large party for the **officials and ministers**. There is a great amount of general **gift**-giving. And there is a public **holiday** (perhaps an amnesty or a tax break—it is unclear). The empire is a much rosier place now that the Jews have a key role in it—although that role remains a secret for now.

The cultural point is that what takes place at Esther's coronation is a miniature Purim. If Purim means a great meal, a holiday, and a feast of **gift**-giving, then all these elements are already present as soon as Esther becomes queen. There is every sort of speculation about the relation of the Festival of Purim to the book of Esther, but the narrative here seems to be suggesting at the very least that celebrating Esther means sharing food, sharing gifts, and sharing freedom.

Decisive Intervention (2:19–23)

Once Esther becomes queen, remarkably little changes. Mordecai is still **sitting at the king's gate**. No change there. **Esther had not revealed her kindred or her people**. No change there either. There seems to be no difficulty in communicating

8. James C. Scott, *Domination and the Arts of Resistance: Hidden Transcripts* (New Haven: Yale University Press, 1990).

between palace and gate: when information reached Mordecai, he **told it to Queen Esther, and Esther told the king in the name of Mordecai**. There seems no difficulty preserving her identity; even when Esther passes Mordecai's information to the king, no eyebrow is raised about her connection to Mordecai. **Esther obeyed Mordecai just as when she was brought up by him**. Esther may have broken the Jewish law by marrying a Gentile, but her secrecy and her obedience are the ways she maintains her identity and integrity. Later in Esth. 4:11 we shall discover even more surprisingly that Esther has "not been called to come in to the king for thirty days." Only a moment ago she had his love, favor, and devotion. This does not seem to be a king preoccupied with the need to conceive a legitimate heir. The early signs are that Esther, in being folded into the heart of Persian power, has not given up as much as one might suppose. She and Mordecai make a fine team.

The larger narrative plot is about the salvation of the Jews, but this cameo is about the salvation of Ahasuerus. It directs immediate attention to where his best interests lie—not in the labyrinthine relationships and machinations and power games of courtiers and servants, but in paying attention to the Jews. We are told very little about the conspiracy **to assassinate King Ahasuerus**. It arose from anger. This perhaps goes without saying, since anger flows in the royal court as freely as wine. Handling a volatile temper under stress is something only the Jews appear able to do. It is part of their art of revolutionary subordination. Anyone would think that a wise king would hire reliable Jews, rather than perfidious eunuchs and headstrong courtiers, as his closest advisers and confidantes. But already we get a sense that deadly plans are part of Persian politics. The advisers and servants around the king are an unscrupulous lot. Those who get it wrong will be shipped to the gallows without delay.

In all these ways we are given another introduction to the events that follow. Esther 1 gave us banquets and law and anger and sexual power and honor and bureaucracy and eunuchs and the Persian world. Esther 2 has given us another banquet, more laws, more bureaucracy, an elaborate sequence of summonses, and more pregnant details: the deadly intent of figures within the court, and the contrast between the public show of royal Persian power and the private network of Jewish familial and ethnic allegiances. But the most important element is left till last. The assassination attempt and Mordecai's role in foiling it were **recorded in the book of the annals in the presence of the king**. The laws of the land may be as reckless as they are permanent. But the annals make up in thoroughness for the foolishness of the events they describe. Mordecai leaves Esth. 2 with no reward for his service; he might have expected his action to be celebrated in ways that might rival Esther's exaltation. But the king, as by now we know, is neither conscientious nor predictable. Mordecai, like Esther, keeps his counsel. Protest and self-promotion are not the tactics of this time and place.

CRISIS

ESTHER 3–4

Conflict to the Death (3:1–6)

It turns out there is more than one vacancy at the heart of the Persian court. Ahasuerus appears to have a role available for a first minister. Unlike last time, when the post of queen fell vacant, on this occasion the whole empire is not scoured for a suitable person to take up the position. Last time there were elaborate procedures and clandestine evaluations to identify the chosen figure. But not this time. We know of only one person who has so far proven able to give the king genuinely useful information and advice: Mordecai. But the king seems to have an eye patch in that direction. The job goes to another. We are not told why. Esther's progress was significantly aided by a member of the king's circle who went out of his way for her. Mordecai is not so lucky.

Two verses into the story proper, and already we are in the middle of a feud. **Mordecai did not bow down or do obeisance** to **Haman son of Hammedatha the Agagite**. Like many other things we might be curious to know in the narrative, we are not told why. But in this case one detail invites us to infer. Israel is in exile because of the mistakes made under its kings. They had not put their trust in God and followed God's ways. Their kingship had not magnified the Lord. This was not simply about worship and keeping the commandments; there were particular transgressions that continued to rankle in the memory. Israel's first king, a Benjaminite like Mordecai, was Saul. Saul lost God's favor, in a process that anticipates the way God lost patience with Israel centuries later. The error of Saul's ways can be traced back to 1 Sam. 15:2–3, where God tells Samuel, "I will punish the Amalekites for what they did in opposing the Israelites when they came up out of Egypt. Now go and attack Amalek, and utterly destroy all that they have; do not spare them, but kill both man and woman, child and infant, ox and sheep, camel and donkey." It turns out in 15:7–9 that "Saul defeated the Amalekites, from Havilah as far as Shur, which is east of Egypt. He took King Agag of the Amalekites alive, but utterly destroyed all the people with the edge of the sword. Saul and the people spared Agag, and the best of the sheep and of the cattle and of the fatlings, and the lambs, and all that was valuable, and would not utterly destroy them; all that was despised and worthless they utterly destroyed." And this was the decisive moment. For the Lord says in 15:11, "I regret that I made Saul king, for he has turned back from following me, and has not carried out my commands."

So for a Jew to encounter a descendant of King Agag of the Amalekites is to meet a living reminder of what is wrong and how it began to go wrong. For an Amalekite to be in a position of power over a Jew is to exert an ironic twist of the knife, that the people who were supposed to have been utterly extirpated have yet, half a millennium later, yielded a leader of the known world. To bow down to such a man is to consent in having one's whole sense of destiny discredited. Without this background it is hard to make any sense of the offense that triggers the annihilating decree and the slaughter that follows its eventual reversal.

This is the most charitable reading of Mordecai's actions. Some might call Mordecai's action prophetic. A prophetic action is one that (1) anticipates and displays the reign of God embodied in (2) a more faithful and just alignment of social relationships and (3) runs counter to prevailing wisdom in such a way that (4) renders the agent vulnerable to personal attack. Of these four dimensions of a prophetic action, Mordecai's refusal to bow undoubtedly fits the third and fourth. But it is hard to see how it meets the first two criteria. The story from 1 Sam. 15 presents a very particular perspective on the reign of God, suggesting that the will of God may be explicitly known and must be precisely followed, regardless of whether it seems vindictive, wasteful, or in contradiction of previous articulations. It also has a very particular perspective on a faithful and just alignment of social relationships, implying that God wishes total obedience for Israel and has little or no vision for the rest of creation. Only if these perspectives are endorsed can Mordecai's action be described as prophetic.

The narrative does not pause to evaluate what is being described: we are left to make our own judgments. Of two negative estimations of Mordecai's refusal, we may consider a modest one and a grand one.

The modest negative evaluation is that Mordecai has learned nothing from Vashti and nothing from Esther. Like Vashti, Mordecai blocks. The block is not so bald as Vashti's refusal, because we are given some narrative context to understand the significance of the block, which was not the case in Esth. 1, where we were told nothing about Vashti except that she was the queen and was holding a banquet. But it is a block nonetheless. In the language of theatrical improvisation, a "no" of this kind is legitimate only if it may be construed as part of a larger "yes." Mordecai's "no" may be narrated this way. One may see his encouragement of Esther to join the harem as saying "yes" to the customs of the Medes and Persians. This is not a blanket rejection of the authority of a power beyond the God and kings of Israel. Supporting this reading is Esth. 2 coming before Esth. 3: Esther's becoming queen is *not* a response to the crisis but a *worthwhile project in its own right*. But Haman is not a Mede or a Persian. He is an Agagite. Thus one could take Mordecai's refusal to bow to Haman as a statement that there could be no way that an Agagite could be a suitable first minister for the empire. This assumes that what is good for the Jews amounts to what is truly good for Persia, an assumption that runs throughout the narrative.

However, even if Mordecai's block is a little different from Vashti's, it still runs counter to the manner in which Esther finds ways to accept. Esther is wholly missing from Esth. 3, and so is the spirit in which she attains influence in the empire. Gone are the subtlety, self-effacement, patience, teamwork, humility, and carefully honed technique. Gone are the strategic partnerships with sympathetic elements in the king's entourage: not only will Mordecai not bow before Haman, but when **the king's servants who were at the king's gate said to Mordecai, "Why do you disobey the king's command?"** even **when they spoke to him day after day**, Mordecai **would not listen to them**. Who can blame them if they lose patience with him? This is not the philosophy of navigating Diaspora existence. It is the single-mindedness of a vendetta—albeit one with scriptural precedent and, perhaps, warrant.

The grand negative evaluation is that this moment, in which Mordecai's action swaps the tranquility of well-connected life for the crisis of imminent extinction, is a narrative of the fall. Like the fall of Adam and Eve, it is not the first event in the drama. The first event is the creation of the universe and the setting of the man and woman within it. The book of Esther, like the book of Genesis, spends its first two chapters portraying the universe and locating a man and a woman within it, dwelling on the splendors of the world and the best ways to enjoy what it has to offer. And then in the third chapter in each case there is a catastrophe, and the rest of the story is about how to recover from and transform that catastrophe.

The book is a salvation history in itself, albeit with greater and lesser elements of parody and irony. Part 1 is creation and incarnation: the whole world is displayed and then one particular Jew emerges at the center of that world, while remaining in some degree invisible. Part of that invisibility involves undergoing humiliations and deprivations. Part 2 is fall: from one momentous interaction, and the response to it, comes the prospect of eternal death for the Jews.[1] Here the incarnation is fully realized in its salvific dimension. Before moving to part 3, the significance of the sequence of Esth. 2–3 should again be noted. From a Jewish perspective this sequence says that the Diaspora, though dangerous, is not an inherently unsustainable condition for the Jews. There is a place for Jews in Persia. From a

---

1. Michael Beckett, *Gospel in Esther* (Cumbria, UK/Waynesboro, GA: Paternoster, 2002), 25, notes the connection between Mordecai and Adam.

Christian perspective this sequence means the incarnation is not dependent on the fall. Christ would have come whether or not Adam and Eve had fallen. The fall undoubtedly oriented Christ's coming toward the outcome of salvation, but the need for salvation does not determine the nature and timing of the incarnation. Esther's calling in Esth. 4 illuminates Christ's passion by demonstrating the cost of salvation.[2] Part 3 is rescue: captivity is led captive and, through transformatory meals, death is defeated and hope restored. Esther is a kind of Jesus, at the right hand of God (in the form of Ahasuerus), laying down her life for the salvation of the Jews. Part 4 is joy: victory, feasting, and reigning with God.

This is the context in which it makes sense to read Mordecai's refusal to bow as a kind of fall—albeit a fall that creates jeopardy, rather than one with the sense of having betrayed God. As in the Christian story of salvation, one person brings about the crisis: but it takes another person to clear it up. Esther is subject to both crises—both falls, that of Vashti and that of Mordecai—that come about when characters block and when counterparts and adversaries (Ahasuerus and Haman) overreact to those blocks with wide-ranging and vindictive laws. As a woman, Esther suffers from the consequences of Vashti's refusal to come before Ahasuerus. And as a Jew, Esther suffers from the consequences of Mordecai's refusal to bow before Haman. Her exile is one of gender and ethnicity. And yet she turns that exile into a blessing for all Jews, as we shall see. (Whether she redeems the women of the empire is another matter.)

Haman is the original cartoon villain. Esther and Mordecai are generally shrewd figures whose emotions are seldom disclosed. But we always know what Haman is thinking. Haman appears for the first time as an agent in the narrative only in Esth. 3:5—but by the end of 3:6 we know plenty about him. He is too head-in-the-air to have noticed Mordecai's snub until the royal servants point it out to him; once he notices, he is immediately full of anger, as befits a member of Ahasuerus's circle. **But he thought it beneath him to lay hands on Mordecai alone**. This is a man of some pride, new as he is to high office. And finally **Haman plotted to destroy all the Jews . . . throughout the whole kingdom of Ahasuerus**. Haman will stop at nothing to wreak maximum destruction and achieve permanent transformation on account of one stain on his honor—a stain he had not noticed before it was brought to his attention. (It is a feature of the narration that the main characters consistently fail to know things they might be expected to know: Haman that he has been slighted, Ahasuerus that Esther is a Jew, Esther that her life is in serious danger, Haman that the man Ahasuerus wishes to honor is Mordecai.)

Haman portrays what power means without God. There is no larger narrative that guides Haman how to direct and channel his power; it serves only one purpose—to inflate his honor. Honor without service is a monstrous idol. Haman's appetite to increase and protect his honor knows no bounds. Everything turns into fuel to puff up his honor. Like Ahasuerus's, Haman's honor craves display if

---

2. Beckett, ibid., 7, 17, helpfully highlights the christological character of Esther.

it is to be assured of its own existence. He is a quick learner, and if he has studied the behavior of Ahasuerus to this point, he will know that exercising power
means passing laws, making flamboyant gestures, drinking a lot of wine, winning
battles of honor, exhibiting rage, and using one's office to promote one's personal
image and agendas. Thus **Haman plotted to destroy all the Jews, the people of
Mordecai, throughout the whole kingdom of Ahasuerus**. This is a plan that
meets all the royal criteria. Not content to be first minister, Haman gradually as-
sembles all that he will need to become king. Again the political ethic is clear: by
unseating Haman, the Jews will be acting in the empire's best interests, since it is
only a matter of time before the one whose vitriol, violence, and vindictiveness
has first been turned on the Jews will finally turn on the king.

Terrible Revenge (3:7–15)

The portrayal of Ahasuerus reaches its lowest ebb. The king has appointed a first
minister; we have been given no reason for the appointment, and we already know
the man to be hasty, haughty, and full of hatred. It turns out that Ahasuerus is also
open to bribery. The sum involved is yet another astronomical exaggeration—the
kind that makes the cartoon character's eyes spiral like a yoyo. Ahasuerus is prepared to turn over his signet ring, the executive symbol of his legislative authority, and authorize genocide when he has not even inquired about the identity
of the people to be exterminated. It is still early in Esth. 3, and we have already
witnessed a lot of legislation. Drinking, domestic hierarchy, the assemblage of
beauties, cosmetic treatments, and bowing before the first minister—these form
the formidable raft of policies promulgated by the king. Now, more than ever
before, the ridiculous becomes the catastrophic. Between a thoughtless yawn and
a distracted sigh, Ahasuerus allows Haman to consign the Jews to obliteration.

Again one can detect here a criticism of the majority interpretation of the Old
Testament narrative. The **lot** for the date for the killing of the Jews **fell on the
thirteenth day of the twelfth month, which is the month of Adar**. Thus it fell on
the eve of the Passover. It is as if a gauntlet has been laid at the feet of the God of
Israel and the Passover tradition in which the action of God has been definitively
discerned. What use Passover, the narrative seems to say, when the Jews are all set
to be wiped out before they next celebrate it? The Jews need rapidly to invent a
new form of redemption, because if they wait for God's redemption, as disclosed
through the Passover, to take effect, it will in all likelihood be too late. The key
moment—the date of the Jews' destruction—is decided not by providential intervention, not by hostile action, but by lot—the epitome of chance, even fate. Once
again this seems a bitter demonstration of what it means to be a Jew in Diaspora
Persia. One's destiny is a matter of chance and whim.

The arteries and capillaries of Persian bureaucracy have flexed and stretched
through prior instructions concerning each man's mastery and every woman's

opportunity. Now they have something really to sink their teeth into. Five verses are given over to the details of implementing Haman's decree. The impression is of breathless speed, geographical extent, meticulous detail, and an empire galvanized by an astonishing decree. The process involves **the king's secretaries**, **the king's satraps**, **the governors over all the provinces**, and **the officials of all the peoples**. This activates the whole governmental system. It reaches **every province in its own script and every people in its own language**. Not a single person in the empire—the world—will be unaware. The decree is **in the name of King Ahasuerus** and is **sealed with the king's ring**. There can be no more impressive authority: it has come from on high. The instructions are unambiguous—**to destroy, to kill, and to annihilate**. No doubts there. And their target is to scorch the earth—to destroy **all Jews, young and old, women and children, . . . and to plunder their goods**. The comprehensiveness of the decree leaves the listener or reader speechless. The practice of *herem*, which Saul failed to impose on the Amalekites, is now being turned around and inflicted on the Jews. When Memucan presented a fully developed plan for cleaning up the national household in Esth. 1 it was absurd—but now that Haman has brought forward a ready-made plan for cleaning up the empire it is terrifying. All the color drains from the face. The news is delivered in portentous terms. We are reminded that Haman is an **Agagite**, and, lest there be any misunderstanding, it is underlined that this man is **the enemy of the Jews**.

Haman never names the people he has determined to eradicate. Ahasuerus never asks. They remain **a certain people**. The argument is that they are **scattered and separated among the peoples in all the provinces**, that **their laws are different from those of every other people**, and that **they do not keep the king's laws**. There are several levels to these arguments. After a chapter in which Esther has broken a good number of the precepts of the Torah, such as intermarriage and dietary prohibitions, it is a significant indication that the Jews were notable for their adherence to the law of Moses. Having seen Persian law brought into disrepute, one can hardly see the refusal to keep such absurd laws as a reason for reproach. Likewise it is hard to see why being **scattered and separated among the peoples** is such a dangerous thing, when the alternative would be concentrated and secluded. These words, **their laws are different from those of every other people, and they do not keep the king's laws**, name precisely the political question before the Jewish people. How can they keep their own law and identity and become neither a threat to their political masters nor a vulnerable group without protection in the face of hostile powers? This is precisely the question the book of Esther addresses.[3] Haman forces the question upon them and has his own, negative answer: but even without Haman, the question would be urgent and demanding.

A year after the September 11 attacks, which he experienced at close proximity, Rowan Williams noted the necessity of withholding from oneself and others the

3. Bernhard W. Anderson, "The Place of the Book of Esther in the Christian Bible," in *Studies in the Book of Esther*, ed. Carey A. Moore (New York: Ktav, 1982), 130–41 at 133.

identity of the person one is about to attack: "The terrorist, the suicide bomber, is someone who's got to the point where they can only see from a distance: the sort of distance from which you can't see a face, meet the eyes of someone, hear who they are, imagine who and what they love. All violence works with that sort of distance; it depends on not seeing certain things."[4] Haman sees Mordecai very close up indeed; but the rest of the Jewish people he sees, as Williams puts it, "at a distance." They are, after all, **scattered and separated among the peoples in all the provinces**.

The concluding note to the chapter underlines two consistent themes throughout the narrative. The first is that meals are the defining moment when status is affirmed and displayed, relationships are codified, and the Persian court takes stock of who and what it is. **The king and Haman sat down to drink**. Haman has everything he wants: the signet ring, the decree, and the jovial company of the king. He has become the lawmaker and the person who pleases the king. It is his finest hour. The celebration echoes the meal enjoyed by Joseph's brothers (Gen. 37:25) after they had thrown him into the pit—an event that later, like the decree against the Jews, includes the exchange of money (37:28). In both cases the destiny of Israel is in the hands of callous men who have their price. It is a reversal of Ps. 23:5: "You prepare a table before me / in the presence of my enemies" has become "my enemies set a table before you in my presence." Significant differences, however, bear out the contrast between Genesis and the book of Esther: Joseph's brothers do not, in the long run, control his destiny, since the Midianites intervene. And when Joseph's brothers awaken to Joseph's power over them later in the story, it is to their benefit, not death—the opposite of how things turn out for Haman. Joseph's brothers may be callous men, but they are of the same family and people as Joseph and thus subject to redemption.

The second consistent theme is that the Jews belong in the Persian Empire and there is a legitimate and happy home for them there. **The city of Susa was thrown into confusion** because catastrophe for the Jews apparently meant disaster for Susa. It also meant their king was not just a fool but a criminally negligent fool and that, if he could be manipulated to this end, there really was no limit to the malevolence that could emerge from his court. Whether such dismay was repeated throughout the empire is not recorded. Susa is here, as elsewhere, taken as a symbol for the king's whole domain.

The Only Way Out (4:1–17)

The fourth and pivotal chapter of the book of Esther is arranged in a dance. It begins with Mordecai and the Jews; there follows a sequence of three interchanges in which Esther initiates dialogue with Mordecai and in the process realizes what it

4. Rowan Williams, *Thought for the Day*, BBC Radio 4, September 11, 2002.

means for her to be a Jew; and it concludes with Esther and the Jews, during which Mordecai takes his place as one of the Jews. At the start of the chapter Mordecai is the representative Jew, wearing **sackcloth and ashes** and going **through the city, wailing with a loud and bitter cry**. By the end of the chapter the representative Jew is Esther, commanding the Jews in Susa, preparing to stand before the king, and commanding Mordecai.

This chapter is a study in another motif of theatrical improvisation, the role of status. Status is vital to the whole character of the book of Esther both because it is the source of much of the comedy (think of the highly ranked Haman in the lowly role of leading Mordecai around town in Esth. 6) and because it is at the heart of how a downtrodden person or people may still find a mechanism for social and interpersonal leverage.

Status draws attention to the element of power and role in every single interaction between two or more people. The crucial element in understanding status is to grasp the difference between the status a person *has* and the status that person *plays*. The building in which I currently work has a housekeeper who acts in almost every way as if he were the most senior person in the organization. The status he *has* is low, but the status he *plays* is high. The fascination lies in the difference between the two.

Johnstone, in the most articulate expression of the nature and flexibility of status, explains the dynamics of status interactions:

> You may be low in social status, but play high, and vice versa. For example:
>   TRAMP: 'Ere! Where are you going?
>   DUCHESS: I'm sorry, I didn't catch . . .
>   TRAMP: Are you deaf as well as blind?[5]

Johnstone goes on to describe his experiences of trying to introduce his theater-studies students to the ways status works:

> Those who hold eye contact report that they feel powerful—and actually look powerful. Those who break eye contact and glance back "feel" feeble, and look it. . . .
>   I change my behaviour and become authoritative. I ask them what I've done to create this change in my relation with them, and whatever they guess to be the reason—"You're holding eye contact," "You're sitting straighter"—I stop doing, yet the effect continues. Finally I explain that I'm keeping my head still whenever I speak, and that this produces great changes in the way I perceive myself and am perceived by others. . . . Officers are trained not to move the head while issuing commands.
>   People have a preferred status; they like to be low, or high, and they try to manoeuvre themselves into the preferred positions. A person who plays high status is saying, "Don't come near me, I bite." Someone who plays low status is saying, "Don't bite me, I'm not worth the trouble." In either case the status played is a defence,

5. Johnstone, *Impro*, 36.

and it'll usually work. It's very likely that you will increasingly be conditioned into playing the status that you've found an effective defence.[6]

In other words everyone works hard on their status interactions, even if they are unaware of doing so.

If a classroom teacher speaks slowly, keeps her head still, never touches her face, makes a long "errrrm" sound between comments, and is comfortable with silence, she is playing high status and will usually evoke respect but perhaps not love. If, by contrast, her movements are jerky, her hands frequently touch her face, the "erm" is brief and apologies are many, she is playing low status and may struggle to control her class. An expert status player swaps status at will to achieve the desired results and is invariably popular and effective.

Status, in this sense, is not so much bestowed as chosen. Life is not simply a battle to obtain high status—although Haman might see it that way. In the book of Esther status, at least for the Jews, is much more subtle than that. Adopting an apparently low status becomes at times a very effective means of retaining the initiative. Conventional relationships such as master-servant consistently illustrate the endless possibilities of manipulation in apparently fixed status roles. Such reflections are instructive as Christians come to appreciate the subtleties of their relationship to power and role and deepen their understanding of politics. The scriptures are full of status interactions and present an array of examples of the status complexities of Israel, Jesus, and the church.

Status is the key to understanding the political ethics of the book of Esther. The story begins with the status reversal of Ahasuerus and Vashti. He is the all powerful, the magnificent—but she is able to humiliate him. This is a lesson in one of the downsides of high-status behavior: it quickly attracts antagonism. Part of the absurdity in Memucan's decree later in Esth. 1 arises also from a status issue. In such a culture it is understood that a man commands respect in his household by his own authority. It is thus humiliating that he requires a law to gain such respect. Such a law recognizes that women in Persia are more than capable of playing high status even though they technically occupy low-status roles. It is embarrassing to recognize this reality so publicly.

In Esth. 2 we get a more complex lesson in the Jewish use of status. It seems that Mordecai is the brains and Esther is the beauty. He maneuvers and anticipates; she complies and obeys. The irony in Esth. 2 is that Esther achieves a role of great honor—that of Queen of Persia—by pursuing nothing but low-status methods—recommended treatments, eunuch's advice, and sexual submission.

In Esth. 3 Mordecai seems to have learned nothing from Vashti's determination (in Esth. 1) to play high status. Mordecai refuses to bow, thus preserving his status. But his inflexibility produces antagonism just as Vashti's did. Haman is an obsessive, but unsuccessful, high-status player. It seems that nothing motivates him other

6. Ibid., 42–43.

than to attain the trappings of majesty, the tokens of the highest status. What it must be to know that when one has a petty malevolence all the king's horses and all the king's men may be summoned to settle one's discomfort as brutally as one might wish. Haman, however, never approximates Ahasuerus's indifference: to be sufficiently distracted that one can dispense with a significant percentage of one's own population—and not even feel the need to know which—is high status in the extreme. Haman, by contrast, is constantly looking over his shoulder and anxious to maintain his honor. If Haman were truly operating in high-status mode, Mordecai would be so far beneath him as not to be worth the trouble of a decree.

In Esth. 4 we discover what this study in status has taught the Jews thus far. Mordecai plays low status for the first time. He is devastated and is content for the whole world to know it. He is not taking this on the chin. And he is in solidarity with the Jews, who likewise are **fasting and weeping and lamenting . . . in sackcloth and ashes**. This is a public ritual of lament and defeat. It is the only place in the book of Esther where Mordecai seems to embrace a conventional Jewish practice shaped around God's mercy and perhaps God's intervention in history. If one holds to a view of the book as maintaining a view of God closer to that of the Old Testament as a whole, this would be the place to focus one's attention. (One irony is that having been accused of being a people that "do not keep the king's laws" [3:8], the first thing we encounter after the passing of the decree is a Jew obediently *keeping* a law—yet another one, this time that **no one might enter the king's gate clothed with sackcloth**.) Esther's attempt to be high status misfires. She attempts to solve the problem with a new set of clothes. But it becomes clear that she does not know about the decree—which is somewhat embarrassing since the whole of Susa does—and her response of sending clothes thus seems painfully superficial and acutely ironic. (It might be noted in passing that Mordecai's block in response to Esther's gesture—**she sent garments to clothe Mordecai, so that he might take off his sackcloth; but he would not accept them**—is an example of the kind of block that does in fact keep the story going, since it is blocking a false premise, that there is nothing seriously the matter. Such a block is the only legitimate kind of block in theatrical improvisation.) This is the first status interaction between Esther and Mordecai. Mordecai makes a tentative—but still highly demonstrative—attempt to be low status, and Esther makes a bungled attempt to be high status.

The second status interaction immediately follows. Esther knows there is something she does not know. Once again the eunuchs symbolize powerlessness. There is no point pursuing a high-status approach. She needs to know what the matter is. Mordecai reverts to high-status mode. He tells **Hathach . . . all that had happened to him**, which seems narcissistic, since it had really happened to all the Jews. (The passive voice identifies Mordecai for a moment with Ahasuerus, who has a regular habit of forgetting his own agency.) Mordecai meanwhile seems to have access to **a copy of the written decree issued in Susa** (this was not a photocopy—to have one's own copy is a sign of eminence), and, even more extraordinarily, he seems to be aware of **the exact sum of money that Haman had promised to pay into the king's treasuries for the destruction of the Jews**. Full of his own importance and impatient with his minions, he dishes out instructions to Esther **to go to the king to make supplication to him and entreat him for her people**. The second interaction shows that scratch the surface and nothing has seriously changed in the relations of low-status Esther and high-status Mordecai.

The third interaction then follows. Esther plays ultralow status. Forgetting or ignoring her high-status role of queen, she pleads sympathy for the delicacy of her situation. Like the Jews as a race, she is hemmed in by the law (yet another law!)—**that if any man or woman goes to the king inside the inner court without being called . . . all alike are to be put to death**—and by the whim of the king—**I myself have not been called to come in to the king for thirty days**. She throws up her hands and says the task is beyond her. There is distinguished precedent for reluctance to hear the call of God. Moses, Gideon, Saul, and Jeremiah were all quicker to recognize their own inadequacy than they were to acknowledge God's sufficiency. But Esther's reluctance is based on her perception of danger rather than on personal unworthiness. That she is overstating the weakness of her position is hinted in the reference to the king dangling out his **golden scepter to someone**—an allusion so bawdy it would fit comfortably in one of the farces of Plautus on the Roman stage. But this is not a lewd line simply to poke more fun at the drunken, distracted, horny Persian king. The point is, he is a man who needs sex, and he adores the sex Esther gives him. No one compares to her. We already know that. So she has a lot more resources to call upon than she makes out.

And this introduces Mordecai's decisive response, which bears close analysis in status terms. It has three dimensions. (1) He affirms her low status—she is no safer in the king's palace than any of her fellow Jews elsewhere. Mordecai strips Esther of her royal safety buffer. (2) He pushes her even further down, suggesting that if she keeps silence, she may suffer while the rest of the Jews find another deliverer. The logic is not entirely clear—it would be curious if a deliverance that saved the Jews did not save Esther as well—but Mordecai is playing on Esther's isolation and guilt. There is an element of bullying and bravado in this speech, since Mordecai cannot know that there will be deliverance for the Jews or that Esther would be excluded from it. But it creates a poignant picture. She is alone at the bottom of the pit at this moment. (3) Suddenly the tables are turned and she becomes, like Joseph, in **royal dignity**, not for her own benefit but precisely to serve her people at **just such a time as this**. The rhetoric is masterful and rests on status. Esther is low because she is a Jew like any other. She is uniquely low because she is alone among even the lonely Jews. Yet suddenly she is stratospherically high, because she alone has royal status, and this is the defining moment in her and her people's existence, and only she can take the decisive step. Mordecai reinforces his high, and Esther's low, status before suddenly turning the tables and putting himself and his people at her mercy.

Finally there is a fourth interaction between Esther and Mordecai. Will she accept her newfound status, not to deny the crisis as she did in the first interaction, but to seize the moment as only an expert status player can? The transformation is immediate and dramatic. Esther barks out the instructions, and Mordecai meekly does **everything as Esther had ordered him**. She asserts her Jewishness, by calling for a fast. This is the only point in the narrative where Esther does something close to the traditions of her people—something designed to show her and their dependence on God. In contrast to Vashti, who rivaled Ahasuerus by holding a banquet, she subverts the Persian court by summoning a power it cannot comprehend: she holds a three-day fast. She behaves like a queen, by setting an example and commanding the obedience of her people in a common cause under her leadership. And she faces up to her own power and what only she can do: attract the attention of the roving scepter.

Esther turns a terrifying situation into an opportunity to take her place in salvation history. In an echo of Exod. 7:1–2, where Moses goes before Pharaoh, Esther is to go before the king and plead for the deliverance of her people. In an echo of Gen. 43:14, where Jacob says to his sons as they take Benjamin (Mordecai and Esther's ancestor) to Egypt, "As for me, if I am bereaved of my children, I am bereaved," Esther announces, **I will go to the king, though it is against the law; and if I perish, I perish.**

This elaborate dance of status between Esther and Mordecai is significant both within the narrative and beyond. Within the narrative it prepares the reader for the kinds of interactions Esther will need to bring about in order to rescue the Jews. It shows she will be well prepared for them. At the start of Esth. 4 there is no indication that Esther is a person of this level of interpersonal sophistication. But by the end she has become a woman of huge interpersonal and political skill. One lesson of the narrative is that Jews need to have this combination of interpersonal and political savoir faire if they are to survive their Diaspora existence. Mordecai and Esther are both aware of and ready to employ habits of piety associated with devotion to the God of Israel—practices of lament and fasting. That they adopt these without any hint of the prayer that would normally accompany them can be read in two contrasting ways. It could be as close as the story gets to identifying God; or it could be the adoption of conventional forms of piety for the strengthening and solidarity of the Jewish people in the absence of God. Esther is certainly portrayed as a woman with the qualities needed to interact with the powerful and the weak, the Jew and the Gentile—and perhaps God as well.

Beyond the narrative the purpose of this status analysis is to demonstrate that the relationship of faithful believers to their surrounding governing and cultural pressures is never static and is not simply about who holds the coercive power. There is no correct relationship of the church to the state, because the state is not a static theological category. When, for example, Jesus says, "Give therefore to the emperor the things that are the emperor's, and to God the things that are God's" (Matt. 22:21), how one hears such instruction depends on what kind of a state one is in. Is it, for example, a minority community under an oppressive regime, like in the book of Esther; a minority community in a failed state or in circumstances where conventional law and order is in abeyance or has broken down, such as Somalia or Afghanistan today; a minority community under a regime that is not oppressing the community but that the community believes to be oppressing other social groups or nations, as many activists see the United States in the era of Guantánamo and the School of the Americas; a nominally majority community with access to a regime that sees itself as having a divine mandate, a more conventional view of the contemporary United States; or a minority presence in an ordered state, where the state has limited notions of its ability to carry out a noble mission, perhaps a more European configuration?

The point is not to imagine the church has, must have, or must seek the power to determine which kind of regime it lives with. The point is, each of these kinds of regimes present Christians with significant challenges and opportunities, and the book of Esther is a dynamic account of how the Jews coped with one of the more extreme kinds of such alternatives. The book of Esther makes absolutely clear that holding the coercive power is no advantage in itself if it is not used wisely, and not holding coercive power, even when that power is in the hands of those bent on malice, is not a disaster so long as skills are developed to handle such a predicament. Being able to negotiate and animate the dance of status is, in the book of Esther, chief among those skills. This is because the expert status player is able to retain the initiative and outmaneuver even the most powerful person without such a person realizing what is going on or even, necessarily, becoming resentful about the way things come out.

To move to another improvisatory trope, that of overaccepting, what Esther discovers is that the choice is not simply between accepting and blocking. In the language of improvisation, one must dismantle the oppressive force of the apparent givens. Forces such as death, sin, and time appear to be givens. Givens are unchangeable realities that must simply be accepted.

Three kinds of givens mount up together against the Jews. One is the given of the opening political context. The Jews are a small minority in the Persian Empire and are potentially vulnerable. A second given is the arbitrariness of Persian laws in general and Haman's decree in particular. Such a law cannot be revoked. And with Haman at the helm, there is no doubt that it will be executed thoroughly. The looming date of the thirteenth day of Adar is the most significant given in the story. A third given is the social code of the period. The palace has a particular rule of conduct. A constant series of royal laws suggests how hidebound life in the palace is. In addition the wider social code assumes a number of static relationships such as the low status of women.

These givens seem overwhelming. That is the force of the story. However well one knows the story, one shares the Jews' dismay at their plight: **Mordecai tore his clothes and put on sackcloth and ashes. . . . There was great mourning among the Jews, with fasting and weeping and lamenting.** And yet, brick by brick, this mountainous wall teetering ready to collapse over the Jews is somehow dismantled. The process of dismantling establishes which factors really are givens and which, finally, prove not to be.

The scriptural narrative constantly rejoices in the subverting and overcoming of such givens, and the book of Esther shares that delight. The new given proclaimed by the book of Esther is that deliverance will come to the Jews: in Christian vocabulary, the gospel of salvation. If there is only one given, only one unvarying determinant, everything else in all creation is set free to become a gift. That is, nothing is profane.

It is not just that all *may* be incorporated into the story of salvation, but that all can *enhance* that story by their incorporation. In fact the story of salvation is precisely about creatively incorporating as gifts all things that might otherwise have been destructive givens. Thus actors—and the church—do not simply accept the givens of society and the world and stoically try to fit their discipleship around such givens; instead they *over*accept these apparent givens by fitting them into a much larger story—the story of the ongoing relationship between God and the people of God. Thus they transform the fate of accepting givens into the destiny of *overaccepting gifts*.

Mordecai shows Esther that blocking is not an available option. If you tacitly accept, he says to her, **you and your father's family will perish**. (Commentators are bewildered about whom Mordecai could be implying by the words **your father's house** in relation to the orphan Esther, but it seems quite clearly a euphemism for himself.) Therefore, says Mordecai, overaccept. Take your femininity, your long training in the harem, your vulnerability, your membership of the Jewish people—givens that may seem challenging or unjust—and treat them as gifts by incorporating them into the larger story of saving your people. Each of these apparent givens does indeed become a gift in the course of Esther's sequence of banquets for and petitions to the king.

Esther, in a decisive moment, overaccepts not only her situation but also Mordecai's appeal. **Go**, she says, **gather all the Jews to be found in Susa**. She overaccepts her Jewishness, by asking for the joint action of the Jews in Susa in solidarity with her. She overaccepts her position as queen, by recognizing that it is not an end in itself but a means to a much higher end. She overaccepts her cousin's petition, by going further than he had dared ask. She overaccepts her whole story, by perceiving that she has been placed on earth for exactly this moment. And she overaccepts even her own death, by realizing that her fundamental choice is between a redemption and futile resistance. By overaccepting she finds a power unknown to those who strive to block. This power is the way the book of Esther discloses the power of God.

Esther's decision in 4:16 is not the only act of overaccepting in the book of Esther. There are two significant parodies of overaccepting. The first is Memucan's colossal overacceptance of Vashti's refusal to come before the king (1:16–19). Memucan takes Vashti's gesture as the pretext for a decree to pass throughout the empire. The second is Haman's vast overacceptance of Mordecai's refusal to bow down before him (3:6). Haman takes Mordecai's gesture as the pretext for the savage decree invoking the genocide of the entire Jewish people. These two parodies may be taken as analogues of the fall of Adam: *all* are punished for the sin of *one*. By contrast, Esther's decision is an analogue of Christ's turning toward Jerusalem and the way of the cross: *one* accepts danger and likely death for the sake of the salvation of the *many*.

The third trope of improvisation, reincorporation, adds poignancy to Mordecai's words: **Perhaps you have come to royal dignity for just such a time as this**. Reincorporation makes Esther and the reader look back over her life, particularly the events narrated in Esth. 2 and see significance where it might not have appeared before. Every discarded element in the story now has vital power. The king's love of banquets, his reluctance to tolerate anything disagreeable, his pliability under the influence of wine, his inclination toward a compliant spouse, his inattention to detail but somewhat contrary desire always to look good, the tendency of palace politics to have immediate imperial ramifications, the benefit of getting on the right side of the eunuchs, the wisdom of taking advice from those who know the king's proclivities, the importance of getting the timing right for the king's mood, the significance of hiding and revealing, the power of beauty and sexual expertise, and the king's sensitivity and forgetfulness concerning his own well-being—all these things Esther has been party to, and all these things cluster back into the story as ingredients with which she will cook up a recipe for redemption. Once again we see the importance of the sequence of events: Esth. 2 precedes Esth. 3. Esther did not pursue **royal dignity** as a response to a crisis; but when a crisis appears, a whole series of apparently unconnected events finds true significance.

That seems as close as the book of Esther gets to identifying God. There is much debate over whether **another quarter** is a subtle reference to the action of providence. Surely the ambiguity is deliberate. To maintain that this is a clear reference to God is to have to explain why it is not spelled out in words of one syllable. But to contend that there is no inference of divine action is to have to propose what precisely this other quarter might be, and there are few if any alternative candidates. The ambiguity and irony of the book of Esther is epitomized in Mordecai's rhetorical question about the hand behind these events: **Who knows?**

Why the ambiguity? The book of Esther is poised between a firm conviction that the destiny of the Jews is assured and an equally strong insistence that it is for the Jews themselves to bring that destiny about. The heart of faith does not lie in resignation to the divine will, nor in acts of piety that carve the grooves of divine purpose in the regular habits of God's people. Instead faith consists in bold steps that evince confidence in the Jews' place in history. Too much emphasis on God's action is in danger of diminishing the urgency and necessity of courageous contemporary steps from particular Jews. Too much exclusion of the shadowy purposes of God takes away the reason why the Jews are special and the guarantee that their destiny is unique. Mordecai chides Esther to get with the program. But the program is a studied balance between the very present but somewhat tragic efforts of the Jews and the somewhat absent but ultimately decisive ways of God.

This is the heart of the theology and ethics of the book of Esther. On the one hand it is a critique of Torah faith. This is not a religion built around exodus and covenant. There is no decisive action of God. There is no breathless escape. There is no law that binds God to Israel and Israel to God. There is no safe land within whose bounds Israel can know it is in the lap of God. There is no ruler who embodies the purpose of God among the people. There is no special place in which to worship God and find the forgiveness of sins. With this absence of Torah faith comes a degree of bitterness toward the Torah tradition. The hint that Ahasuerus is a parody of God is a playful yet acerbic indication that God's ways seem arbitrary, God's faithfulness seems unreliable, and God's judgment seems fragile. The Feast of Passover is rivaled by the Feast of Purim, a celebration of luck, and chance, and coincidence, and of human endeavor, humor, irony, and wit. These are the new resources of the people of God.

The faith of the exodus is this:

> If it had not been the LORD who was on our side
>   —let Israel now say—
> if it had not been the LORD who was on our side,
>   when our enemies attacked us,
> then they would have swallowed us up alive,
>   when their anger was kindled against us;
> then the flood would have swept us away,
>   the torrent would have gone over us;
> then over us would have gone
>   the raging waters. (Ps. 124:1–5)

But the faith of the Diaspora, the faith of the book of Esther, lies elsewhere. This faith is centered on the role Jews themselves can play in dismantling the impossible odds (what I have called the givens) stacked against them. How do those givens come to be undermined? The end of Esth. 4 is an appropriate time to review and preview this key dimension of the book. There are perhaps four ways.

First, the whole story is written in a carnival style. There is extravagance in every quarter: a colossal empire of 127 provinces, a 180-day banquet for the officials, a seven-day banquet for residents of the citadel of Susa, a decree for the whole empire on domestic politics, a yearlong preparation for the king's bedchamber, a massacre of the entire Jewish population of the empire, and so on. This is spatial and temporal excess on a grand scale. The exaggerated, sometimes absurd, proportions bend the boundaries of possibility, creating a narrative in which wonders may take place. The wonders that chiefly benefit the Jews are extraordinary coincidences and turns of fortune—Esther's accession, Mordecai's knowledge of the assassination plot, the lengthy interim period before the thirteenth day of Adar, the king's insomnia, and many more. The grand sweep of the narrative inspires the Jews to see the details of their survival against the largest possible spatial and temporal backdrop.

Thus if the kingdom of givens is to be subverted, it will have to involve luck, surprise, and accident. These are of course secular terms for providence. When Esther says **if I perish, I perish**, she is embarking on a course of action that she knows will require good fortune if it is to be a success. When the lot is drawn for the date of the destruction of the Jews, it falls out with the greatest delay possible— almost a whole year. The king has a sleepless night. He asks for the annals to be read to him. Haman completely misunderstands Ahasuerus's inquiry about the man the king wishes to honor. These are key turning points in the plot, and they fall outside the conventional logic of intention and action. If givens held sway, every action would have its intended consequence, within a clearly prescribed boundary. But actions have extraordinarily unforeseen consequences, and all works together for good for the Jews. An unseen hand is at work. It is this hand, rather than the conventional pattern of cause and effect, that emerges as the true given. But the Jews discover this hand only when they shoulder their responsibility in shaping their own destiny.

Second, while the social and political systems seem rigid, the characters at the heart of them are mercurial. Ahasuerus commands the world but not his wife. He is persuaded into issuing a ridiculous decree. He faces an assassination plot but forgets about it. He accepts a gigantic bribe from Haman to issue a decree. He orders genocide but again forgets he has done so. He maintains the golden scepter custom but is seduced by Esther into becoming her plaything. Later on he is quite prepared to issue an edict in favor of the Jews that practically counter-mands the previous edict against them. Having once given his signet ring away to a favorite and allowed him to write as he pleases in the name of the king, he later is happy to do so again. Meanwhile Haman jeopardizes his high office by a vendetta against Mordecai's people and is so puffed up with his own position that he cannot see the danger that lies around him. In an empire based on the king's whim, few givens are genuinely secure. It is up to the Jews to navigate the extravagances and opportunities this absurd empire makes available.

Third, in spite of the forces pitted against them, there are a number of things the weak can do. Jews can be part of the royal household. Mordecai can get close enough to public affairs to uncover a plot against the king's life. Esther can become queen. She can use her wit and charm to gain the king's ear (while his scepter stands erect). Together they can win the confidence of the eunuchs who are the oil in the joints of the royal household. Their hand contains no aces—but it does contain one or two jokers.

Fourth, the givens that present themselves in the story are superseded by other givens that emerge as the story proceeds. When Mordecai advises Esther that **relief and deliverance will rise for the Jews from another quarter**, the point is that Mordecai assumes there *will* be help from another quarter. It is a given.

Similarly the narrative truth of the book of Esther is that, as Zeresh later puts it to Haman, "If Mordecai, before whom your downfall has begun, is of the Jewish people, you will not prevail against him, but will surely fall before him" (6:13). This given is so self-evident that even Gentiles perceive it. The Jews will survive. This is the fundamental given of the story. This is the political theology and ethic of the book of Esther.

REVERSAL

ESTHER 5–8

Transformation Begins (5:1–8)

The first scene in Esth. 5 is a lesson in how to acquire power. Levenson summarizes the timing perfectly:

> If Esther's intercession occurs immediately at the conclusion of the three-day fast (4:16), and if the fast immediately followed the issuance of the genocidal decree on the thirteenth of the first month (3:12), then she approached Ahasuerus during Passover (Lev 23:5–6)—a most auspicious date for the Jews. Note the parallel of Esther 5:2 with Exodus 12:36, which reports that the Lord put the people in favor (*hen*) with the Egyptians.[1]

For Christians the opening words of Esth. 5 are drenched in paschal resonance. Esther begins her quest **on the third day**—a key anticipation of Easter. She wears **royal robes** just as Jesus wore a purple robe. She inhabits the **court of the king's palace** just as Jesus wended his way between the high priest's house and the governor's quarters. Most significantly she lays down her life that her people may be saved, embodying within her the failings and hopes of the Jews, yet placed like no other Jew to intercede on their behalf because she has both the trappings of majesty and a body subject to decay and death. She is to be the lamb that brings Passover freedom; she is to discover the miracle that recalls the exodus.

We are about to witness a new kind of exodus, to be celebrated with a different kind of Passover feast.[2] Like God, Passover is in the background of the book

---

1. Levenson, *Esther*, 89.
2. The idea of a new exodus is explored by Gillis Gerlemann, *Esther*, Biblischer Kommentar: Altes Testament 21 (Neukirchen-Vluyn: Neukirchener Verlag, 1973), 11–23, cited in John Goldingay, *Theological Diversity and the Authority of the Old Testament* (Grand Rapids: Eerdmans, 1987), 52.

of Esther, not the foreground. The narrative is an improvisation on the Passover tradition in a new and very different context. And that improvisation places in the foreground not the grand sweep of God's mighty arm but the attention to detail of one isolated woman.

Queen Esther begins Esth. 5 in a parlous state. Her people are in dire jeopardy, and she alone can save them, but she has little hope that she has the resources to do so. The stakes could not be higher. Either she risks dying in advance of her people, or she faces dying among them. Or just possibly, she risks knowing of their annihilation and being the only one to survive, her survival being predicated on her silence—perhaps the worst fate of all. These are the steps she takes to climb from a position of utter weakness to a place of remarkable strength.

First, she harnesses the strength of her own people and tradition. Alone as she is in the court, she is not alone in Persia (hence calling on the Jews of Susa to fast on her behalf) and in history (hence falling back on a practice with long roots in Jewish history). She has taken over from Mordecai as the emblem of her people and the embodiment of their destiny. Her victory will not simply be one of technique and opportunism but one rooted in her community's practices.

Second, she takes full stock of the authority she has gained thus far. Not only does she put on her royal robes—in contrast to the sackcloth Mordecai donned at the start of the previous chapter, as a sign of his powerlessness—but also the references to royalty tumble over one another in the early verses of Esth. 5. There is no inhibition in the book of Esther about Jews using whatever power they have in whatever way they deem most appropriate for whatever benefit they can achieve. Whereas Ahasuerus and Haman seem to have no notion of acting for the common good, except the parody of the common good represented by their two intemperate decrees, Mordecai and Esther operate for the benefit not of themselves, at least from Esth. 4 onward, but of their people.

Third, she uses her full awareness of the character of the man whose power she must turn to her advantage. The same quixotic qualities that made it possible for him to let through a catastrophic decree make it possible for her to hope that she can turn matters to her advantage. Sauce for the goose has potential to become sauce for the gander. Sure enough, when the moment comes, Ahasuerus says, **What is your request? It shall be given you, even to the half of my kingdom**. As we already know and as Esther turns to her advantage, this is a man who loves the trappings of power, loves extravagance, and loves dramatic gestures. The negligence in relation to Haman's decree is culpable, but the recklessness of this offer is worse. Anything is possible with the king, but you can never be sure of what is coming next. All you can rely on is that he will use the passive voice and make out he was not directly responsible. Nonetheless, Esther shows she has the measure of her man. Later she uses obsequious flattery: **If it pleases the king, let the king . . . come today to a banquet that I have prepared for the king**. Mentioning the term **king** three times, she panders to his ego. But she also knows he loves a banquet, and banquets have already emerged as the definitive place where dramatic things happen.

Fourth, she uses her unique and priceless asset—her beauty. This is the intersection of what Esther knows she has, and what Ahasuerus knows he needs—or at least desperately desires. Here the narrative cannot resist a playful indulgence in the directness of Esther's technique. **She won his favor and he held out to her the golden scepter that was in his hand**. Any doubts that the narrator is enjoying the double entendre are dispelled by what follows. **Then Esther approached and touched the top of the scepter**. He is helpless in her hands. The narrative retains no more ambiguity. We already know that from her own capacity, from wisdom received from Hegai, and from her adaptability to Ahasuerus's longings, Esther is a queen in terms of sexual prowess. But there is nothing subtle about the way her power is described on this occasion. Knowing when not to be subtle is clearly part of her armory.

Fifth and finally, she employs delay, suspense, and secrecy. Ahasuerus is being teased. His sexual and gustatory appetites are being alternately gratified and deprived. What kind of person is twice offered half the Persian Empire in one day and finds other things more pressing than to accept? The king's curiosity is, to say the least, aroused. Anybody and everybody is a sucker for a secret. Esther has marshaled every power at her disposal—collective action, personal status, knowledge of her adversary, her own talent, and the trickery of the tease. At the start of the chapter she was facing a tragic but honorable death: now she has the king of the universe at her utter mercy, eating out of her hand.

Hubris (5:9–14)

Like Adam and Eve, Haman may have the whole world and permission to enjoy it, but all he can think about is the one thing he does not have. In Esth. 3 the account of Haman gave us a portrayal of evil: the dressing up of malevolence and perverted purpose and breathtaking poison as if they were good and wise and prudent ("it is not appropriate for the king to tolerate them"). Here in Esth. 5 the account of Haman gives us a portrayal of sin. Haman has abundance, but can see only scarcity. He has the opportunity to live out of joy, but instead lives out of envy and pride and fear. He can recount **the splendor of his riches, the number of his sons, all the promotions with which the king had honored him, and how he had advanced him above the officials and the ministers of the king**, but all that really matters to him is that he sees **the Jew Mordecai sitting at the king's gate**. Haman makes the world smaller than it would otherwise be.

Haman does things the Persian way. Like Ahasuerus, he enjoys counting out his material superiority. Like his mentor, he wavers somewhat when it comes to making decisions, so, as seems to be the custom, he is surrounded with advisers. He accepts the advice—on this occasion, from his wife—that **pleased** him, just as Ahasuerus tends to do—although he misses a trick by following his wife's advice, something no loyal Persian should do lightly after Memucan's decree.[3] The mention of **a gallows fifty cubits high** enhances the association with Ahasuerus on two counts: it is another dimension of absurd proportions, and, if this is to be an instrument of impalement, it is another double entendre.

And yet the appearance of a ghastly instrument of hanging at a moment in the plot before it is likely to be used has a particular resonance in Christian ears. It is not just that the gallows has some resemblance to the cross set up on Golgotha. It is that Jesus three times, in the Synoptic Gospels, predicts his passion with reference to the cross, some time before a cross emerges as his unavoidable destiny. Haman's gallows appears to be, at this stage of the story, the fate of Mordecai and, synechdochally, of the Jewish people. And yet that fate is averted. Just as Christians see God's provision of the ram to Abraham (Gen. 22) as an anticipation of the cross, so they may also see the pattern of a certain kind of redemption in the appearance of a gallows from which Mordecai will come to be delivered. The contrast between the theology of the book of Esther and that of the Synoptic Gospels lies in that in the former it is Haman who goes to the gallows *as a result of* the reversal, whereas in the latter it is Christ himself who goes to the cross *to bring about* the reversal.

Haman's mistake is a ridiculously exaggerated pride. This pride leads him to see matters only as they relate to himself; for example, the invitation to the banquet—where the real conversation is to be between Esther and Ahasuerus—is one of foreboding not affirmation. Pride also leads him to prejudge the outcome of forthcoming events—indeed to take the king's judgment for granted—and so to create a massive landmark dedicated to his self-esteem. Pride leads him to surround himself with admirers and spend his time impressing them with catalogs of his accolades. But pride leaves him vulnerable to the one detail that undermines his centripetal worldview: Mordecai's refusal to have any of it.

Mordecai's conduct is hard to understand. His refusal to bow in Esth. 3 kicked off a series of events that led to him and his people facing almost certain destruction. He has been pleading with Esther for her to risk her life to avert the impending disaster. But here in Esth. 5 he refuses to rise and thus maintains his lone opposition to Haman. Mordecai seems determined to avoid giving Haman any satisfaction. While Esther is employing the extensive improvisatory arts of the weak, Mordecai seems content to continue to use the clumsy instruments of futile blocking. Esther is finding escape while Mordecai is digging a deeper hole. His refusal to tremble is another matter: Haman is entitled to claim respect, but not fear. Nonetheless, Mordecai exhibits either overconfidence in Esther's suit or reckless bravado in the face of likely death.

The overall effect of this passage is to point out that the Gentiles may have all sorts of things—honors, wealth, sons, high office—but the Jews have the only things that really matter. Esther gets to invite the king to a banquet. There is no

3. Reid, *Esther*, 114.

sign Haman has such a right of invitation, even if his wife Zeresh believes he should be in the business of telling Ahasuerus whom he should execute. Haman is delighted to be included in the invitation, which suggests that Esther's status is higher than his. Meanwhile Mordecai's honor is undimmed by Haman's power and glory. And for Haman, honor continues to be what life is all about.

Humiliation (6:1–10)

Several key themes and distinctive features of the book of Esther cluster within this pivotal passage. One is colossal coincidence. Ahasuerus could not sleep. That in itself is not remarkable, but this is not just any night for the Jews. Haman is bent on making this Mordecai's last night before his execution. And Esther has built up to this being the last night before her death-or-glory attempt to persuade the king. The astonishing thing is that a man who has an irresistible wife and countless concubines to draw on, and a regular habit of seeing at least one of them nightly, stretching back breathless year after breathless year, should instead on this portentous occasion choose as his nocturnal entertainment highlights from the **annals** of the kings of Persia, the details of which he has not even taken much interest in while they were taking place live. And within those no doubt voluminous annals, his sleepy ear should settle on **how Mordecai had told about Bigthana and Teresh, two of the king's eunuchs, who guarded the threshold, and who had conspired to assassinate King Ahasuerus**. And that on this occasion he should inquire, **What honor or distinction has been bestowed on Mordecai for this?**—given that Mordecai was apparently no more a part of his world now than he had been at the time of the plot. And that at this very moment, when Ahasuerus is finally moved to exalt Mordecai, Haman's impatience impels him to appear at the palace to sue for Mordecai's execution. And finally that Haman should so misunderstand Ahasuerus that when the king asks, **What shall be done for the man whom the king wishes to honor?** Haman assumes Ahasuerus must be referring to him, Haman, and thus responds accordingly. This is high farce, suffused with irony, in which the intersection of timing and the audience's awareness of things of which the protagonists remain unaware provides merciless humor and excruciating humiliation. Without even speaking—without even rising from slumber—Mordecai triumphs over his ruler and his oppressor. Do not mess with these Jews.

Coincidence in the book of Esther is never just coincidence, of course. And humor is never just humor. Coincidence means that, once the Jews have shown courage and spirit by taking their destiny into their own hands, all kinds of allies begin to appear in the most unlikely of places. This is the diffused notion of providence that is the closest the narrative comes to identifying the ways of God. Humor means the reader is exposed in stark terms to matters that the protagonists have not yet seen (or perhaps never will see) against their true backdrop. The humiliation of Haman in Esth. 6 is funny because it is so massively exacerbated by Haman's own preparations and hubris. He really has only himself to blame. But it is also deliciously satisfying because it anticipates not only the way in which Mordecai and Esther will lead captivity captive, but also the way in which all the enemies of the Jews will one day be exposed and their power dismantled. In the words of Col. 2:15, Jesus "disarmed the rulers and authorities and made a public example of them, triumphing over them." Just as Esth. 1–2 anticipates and paves the way for what is to come, so this vivid scene portrays the narrative truth of the book: that the enemies of the Jews will not prevail.

The narrative includes a disproportionate number of references to clothing, and this episode is a particular example. Clothing affects a number of things. It can celebrate—as the fine hangings do in Esth. 1. It can conceal—as when Esther withholds her true identity from Ahasuerus. It can communicate—as Mordecai's tearing of clothes and putting on of sackcloth speaks of his mourning and bitterness. It can make superficial alterations—as in Esther's facile attempt to send new clothes to Mordecai in Esth. 4. It can proclaim—as Esther's royal robes do at the start of Esth. 5. Here in Esth. 6 it is as if each of these prior meanings of clothing are reincorporated in ironic form. The **royal robes** in which Mordecai is paraded **through the open square of the city** are, for Mordecai, garments of celebration, communication, and proclamation—but still superficial ones, for despite the satisfaction and *Schadenfreude* of Haman's humiliation, Mordecai is still facing impending death. But for Haman, these royal robes might as well be sackcloth: his honor is in tatters.

The book of Esther has a descriptive and a prescriptive purpose. The prescriptive purpose, besides encouraging bold acts of individual and communal assertion of Jewish destiny, includes some specific insights. A notable one concerns the written record. Mordecai's discovery of the plot of **the king's eunuchs** against Ahasuerus was testimony to his range of contacts, his initiative, and his practical wisdom. His lack of reward was testimony to the king's irresponsibility, his inability to gauge the nature and duties of power, and his forgetfulness in the face of perpetual distraction. But his final reward, besides in coincidental elements, was due to the existence of a written record. The book of Esther itself is a written record. Memory is identity, memory is training, memory is power. Memory is part of what the Jews need if they are to survive in the Diaspora. They have few institutions of their own. They thus need other ways of passing on wisdom from past to future.

That the king has an accurate record of the events that saved his life is a vital element in the narrative. It is a basic political lesson to record and remember those deeds and people who have saved you. This is the book's conclusion (9:32). The Jews are to learn from Ahasuerus's uneven example and Esther's good example. Just as Deuteronomy implores its readers to recall the Passover and the exodus, so the book of Esther is an appeal to its readers to record and remember how the Jewish people were saved. The scriptures are full of apparently insignificant particulars that later become part of the story of salvation. Minority communities learn to become acquainted with the power of those particulars.

One can discern in this emphasis on writing an implicit affirmation of the Torah—over, perhaps, the temple and the throne and the land—in the preservation of the Jews' identity through the Diaspora. While the role of law is ambivalent, though widespread, in the narrative, the role of the written record is crucial to the Jews' deliverance. Salvation needs to be written down if it is to save not just the Jews of the present but the Jews of the future.

The events of Esth. 6 are much more about Haman than they are about Mordecai. Mordecai does not even utter a word. We have been given a strong impression that it is all the same to him whether he is fêted or ignored. We have no reason to suppose Mordecai yet knows that Esther's approach to the king has met with initial success. This little adventure gains Mordecai nothing within the big picture. Afterward he simply **returned to the king's gate**. The superficialities of pomp and crown and royal robe and king's horse are not the issue: the issues are securing a position from which the Jews can find deliverance and driving his (and their) enemy into the ground.

By contrast Haman says a great deal; at least, until he discovers what he has talked himself into. Whereupon he says only what he has been commanded to say: **Thus shall it be done for the man whom the king wishes to honor**. The poignancy of Haman's humiliation is twofold. It is not just that he finds himself acting as servant and cheerleader for the man whose execution he had been devising only moments before. But it is also that he has been accumulating the accoutrements of royalty—the signet ring being the most notable—and his ready-made list of **royal robes . . . which the king has worn, a horse that the king has ridden**, and **a royal crown** indicates that he has precisely calibrated what it will take to usurp the throne himself. What he is describing is a coronation. This reversal puts him firmly back in his place. He returns to his house **mourning and with his head covered**. He has already attended his own funeral.

In Christian eyes Mordecai's reward and Haman's humiliation constitute the events of a rather differently shaped Holy Saturday. Esther has laid down her life for her people, and she and her people are about to find resurrection and deliverance. This is the day in between the one and the other. Like Holy Saturday, a great amount has already been done and the final sacrifice has already been made. Yet like Holy Saturday, if events were to stop here, salvation would not have come. It is a pause that looks back and looks forward. But in the playful, exaggerated, slightly absurd world of Esther, this pause is not a silent one. It is a frolic of ridicule and reversal.

Foreboding (6:11–14)

Haman is a man in a hurry. At the start of this brief episode he **hurried to his house**. At the end **the king's eunuchs arrived and hurried Haman off to the**

banquet. He has seen, and his wife names without hesitation, that his **downfall has begun**.

Mordecai identified before Esther that if she kept silence, "relief and deliverance" would "rise for the Jews from another quarter" (4:14). That was one Jew talking to another. But this is a very different conversation. This is two Gentiles in conversation, and the person being addressed is the enemy of the Jews par excellence. Zeresh joins a short but significant list of Gentiles who recognize the power of the God of Israel. In Numbers Balaam says,

> From the top of the crags I see him,
>   from the hills I behold him;
> Here is a people living alone,
>   and not reckoning itself among the nations!
> Who can count the dust of Jacob,
>   or number the dust-cloud of Israel?
> Let me die the death of the upright,
>   and let my end be like his! (Num. 23:9–10)

And later Balaam says, significantly in the light of Haman's ancestry:

> How fair are your tents, O Jacob,
>   your encampments, O Israel!
> Like palm-groves that stretch far away,
>   like gardens beside a river,
> like aloes that the LORD has planted,
>   like cedar trees beside the waters.
> Water shall flow from his buckets,
>   and his seed shall have abundant water,
> his king shall be higher than Agag,
>   and his kingdom shall be exalted.
> God who brings him out of Egypt,
>   is like the horns of a wild ox for him;
> he shall devour the nations that are his foes
>   and break their bones.
> He shall strike with his arrows.
> He crouched, he lay down like a lion,
>   and like a lioness; who will rouse him up?
> Blessed is everyone who blesses you,
>   and cursed is everyone who curses you. (Num. 24:5–9)

Besides the reference to Agag, this speech is interesting because it is addressed, like that of Zeresh, to an intractable foe of Israel—in this case Balak son of Zippor, king of Moab. It also refers to the action of God as like a crouched lion and lioness—which resonates with the combined male and female action of Mordecai and Esther. The destruction of the enemy nations also becomes relevant when we come to Esth. 9. Shortly afterward Balaam goes on to prophesy, "First among the nations was Amalek, / but its end is to perish forever" (Num. 24:20). These words echo through the words of Zeresh: **If Mordecai, before whom your downfall has begun, is of the Jewish people, you will not prevail against him, but will surely fall before him**.

In Jonah 1:14, the sailors say, "Please, O LORD, we pray, do not let us perish on account of this man's life. Do not make us guilty of innocent blood; for you, O LORD, have done as it pleased you." The pertinence of this Gentile plea in relation to Zeresh's remark is the difference in status. Zeresh places herself in high status, able to see what Haman cannot see, speaking as if his downfall is a matter of indifference to her own well-being. Hers is prophecy delivered in the form of dispassionate commentary. The sailors, by contrast, are in low-status imprecatory mode. Theirs is an existential cry of anguish. One might say a little of their humility might have gone a long way in Haman's case, guilty, as he is about to be, of innocent blood.

In Daniel Gentiles repeatedly come to acknowledge the God of Israel. In Dan. 2:46 we read, "King Nebuchadnezzar fell on his face, worshiped Daniel, and commanded that a grain offering and incense be offered to him." In 3:28 we hear Nebuchadnezzar say, "Blessed be the God of Shadrach, Meshach, and Abednego, who has sent his angel and delivered his servants who trusted in him." (Nebuchadnezzar then goes on to issue a decree against blaspheming their God.) In 4:34 he says, "I blessed the Most High, / and praised and honored the one who lives forever. / For his sovereignty is an everlasting sovereignty, / and his kingdom endures from generation to generation." Like the words of the sailors in Jonah, these acknowledgements all come in the form of a direct or reported prayer.

All of these conversations take place outside the promised land. It is not that such acknowledgements are not found close to home—Naaman, after all, comes from Damascus and says, "Now I know that there is no God in all the earth except in Israel" (2 Kgs. 5:15). But the difference between all of them and the declaration of Zeresh is that they all exalt the God of Israel whereas Zeresh exalts *the Jewish people*. Zeresh does not say, "The God of Israel is the true God"; neither does she say, "LORD God of Israel, have mercy upon us and deliver us from the vengeance of the Jewish people." She simply says, "Don't mess with the Jews. You won't win." This sums up the moral of the whole story.

Like a peal of thunder, as soon as powerlessness is revealed, **the king's eunuchs** appear to confirm it. In Ahasuerus's approach to Vashti in Esth. 1, the presence of the eunuchs symbolized the king's impotence. When they appear as individuals, coaching Esther toward sexual conquest and conveying messages between Esther and Mordecai, the eunuchs are oil in the joints of the story, particularly facilitating the well-being of weaker parties. But here again they are in the plural, and that seems to indicate political and personal impotence. Haman is **hurried . . . off to the banquet**, and the seventh and decisive meal in the story is set to begin. Haman is in a fluster; by contrast **Esther** is well **prepared**.

Transformation Enacted (7:1–8:2)

The denouement in Esth. 7 brings together—or, in the language of theatrical improvisation, reincorporates—all the major themes of the plot.

First, it displays the haphazard and reckless nature of Ahasuerus's rule. Whereas the earlier portrayals may be read as parodies of Persian rule as a whole, this chapter is more focused on Ahasuerus himself. The king lurches from **feast** to feast. He scarcely makes a single decision while sober: yet again he is reaching a key moment **as they were drinking wine**. A day after his initial wild offer, he is more than happy to repeat that he will give Esther **even to the half of my kingdom**. His fitful memory is not even jogged by the repetition of the key words of the decree—**to be destroyed, to be killed, and to be annihilated**—which one might have thought would be quite memorable, given that the decree was so freshly minted. He seems to have no idea who passed the decree, even though the only person in the empire who passes decrees is him. Once the declaration is finally made, he disappears into the garden, as if overwhelmed by confusion or responsibility. He then jumps to an immediate—and mistaken—conclusion about the nature of Haman's imprecation to Esther and, true to form, takes advice from a close associate who has a ready-made solution to the problem. Before pausing for breath he has already taken his **signet ring** off again and handed over legislative authority to yet another chief minister. This is a man who learns nothing and forgets everything.

Second, it is a thorough vindication of the tactics commended by the book as a whole. Until this point Esther has employed before the king nothing but the arts in which Hegai trained her. Her power rests on one thing. When she posits the hypothetical **if I have won your favor, O king, and if it pleases the king**, it is not really hypothetical at all: she has full confidence—as much as one could have with such an unpredictable character—that she has him in the palm of her hand. Thus she has not done the two things that might have been expected of an exiled Jew in adverse circumstances: invoke the name of God or refuse to have any dealings with the Gentile culture and power structure.

This is the nature of what I have described in these pages and elsewhere as overaccepting. Esther seems utterly powerless. She is a woman, she is a Jew and thus subject to Haman's decree, she has limited access to the king, and she has no way to defend herself or her people. And yet she does not pathetically block like Vashti or passively accept and give up her heritage and identity. She is a person in a weak position who develops arts and resources the strong never turn to, and she uses the power of her enemies against themselves. Her royal station is not an end in itself or of benefit to her alone, but an element to be fitted into the larger story of her people and their destiny. This is the heart of the political ethics of the book of Esther: life in the Diaspora is not to be passively endured, actively opposed, or dissipated through cultural assimilation. It will continue to present opportunities that must be creatively incorporated into the life of the Jewish people, for immediate or subsequent employment as levers to attain or preserve safety and well-being in the short and long term.

The subtlety of this point may be affirmed in contrast to analyses that assume the options are limited to accepting and blocking. Thus Clines laments that a narrative "promoting racial identity, . . . collective action, experience, and memory" does so by celebrating "a deliverance achieved through *denying* one's Jewishness."[4] This appears to be a problem only if the range of options is limited to the conventional two.

Third, it is typical of the book of Esther in that God is not sought or credited in the dramatic and rapid turnaround of events. If Ahasuerus is taken as a parody of God, this is perhaps the harshest parody yet. But if Zeresh's prophecy is taken as the theme of the narrative as a whole, Haman's downfall is but the most explicit evidence that no one in their right mind should try to stand in the way of the flourishing of the Jews. The irony is underlined by Zeresh knowing all about the indestructibility of the Jews, at the same time as Ahasuerus is unaware that he has consigned them to oblivion.

Fourth, an analysis of the assumption and interaction of status roles offers an illuminating insight into the way Mordecai and Esther get the better of Ahasuerus and Haman. Part of the dynamic arises through the distinction between the status the narrator accords Esther—notably by calling her **Queen Esther** on six of the nine occasions her name appears in this episode—and the status Esther herself chooses to play. At the beginning, Esther is high status, because she is hosting the banquet and Ahasuerus and Haman are eager to come; meanwhile she has a piece of information Ahasuerus is falling over himself to hear, and Haman is rushing to get there—both low-status indicators. Ahasuerus's repeated offer is a delicious mixture of ultrahigh status (he has the ability to dispense with half his kingdom at a stroke) and ultralow status (there is nothing he will not do to find out what the matter is and ingratiate his wife, even at enormous cost to himself and the empire).

Suddenly Esther plunges into low status, pleading with the king and apparently wondering if she has any hold on his affections: **If I have won your favor, O king, and if it pleases the king**. That the king has now three times demonstrated in reckless terms the extent of his affection for her and thus made this low-status language unnecessary just shows what an expert status player she is. She knows she has power over the king, but she knows that the only way she can lose it is by naming that power, particularly in front of a third party. By consistently playing low status she reinforces her hold on Ahasuerus. Finally the teasing is over and she says what she wants: **Let my life be given me—that is my petition**. This is a huge anticlimax—how could the life of the wife of the most powerful man in the

4. David J. A. Clines, "Reading Esther from Left to Right," in *The Bible in Three Dimensions*, ed. David J. A. Clines, Stephen E. Fowl, and Stanley E. Porter; Journal for the Study of the Old Testament Supplement 87 (Sheffield, UK: Sheffield Academic Press, 1990), 31–52 at 47–48.

world be in danger, particularly when he is utterly devoted to her? But because it is such an anticlimax, it is intriguing, particularly when the words **and the lives of my people** are added. Suddenly Esther appears acutely vulnerable and genuinely desperate, and the power differential between the one who can blithely offer half his kingdom and the one who is about to lose her life, together with the lives of all her people, is colossal. She and her people are set **to be destroyed, to be killed, and to be annihilated**. A swinging banquet suddenly loses all its bonhomie.

Now comes Esther's next brilliant status move. **If we had been sold merely as slaves, men and women, I would have held my peace.** She elevates Ahasuerus to astronomically high status, as one who, despite his deep affection for his queen, is not to be troubled by the trifling information that she is to become a slave. She has maneuvered the dialogue into a place of two contrasting status realities, and the contradiction between them is unbearable. On the one hand she is about to be liquidated, as a member of a people surplus to imperial requirements; on the other hand the king adores her and has said he will do anything for her. The problem was hers: it now becomes his.

But she gives him a get-out: **No enemy can compensate for this damage to the king.** In other words, she plays on one consistent feature of the king's personality throughout the book: his inability to see his own agency in the turn of events. It was not the king, she suggests, that brought about this state of affairs—she has no interest in humiliating him. The only sense in which she wants him to be low status is his devotion to her. In all other respects it is about time he really did assume the high-status expectations of his role. It was an enemy who brought this about. The king gobbles down Esther's version of the story, which enables him to be her protector and gives him a chance to assert his high status in a moment of crisis: **Who is he, and where is he, who has presumed to do this?** The word **presumed** is crucial, since it elevates Esther's status and in the process elevates Ahasuerus's own status even further.

Now for the coup de grâce. Esther, while remaining vulnerable and thus low status, makes the most of Ahasuerus's gesture to elevate her status and identifies the source of the threat, which is now not just to her and her people but to the king as well. **A foe and enemy, this wicked Haman!** She and the king are now one like never before, and as a result **Haman was terrified before the king and the queen**. There is no sign that Ahasuerus yet appreciates Esther's true identity—it was only after Haman's death that Esther **told** the king **what** Mordecai **was to her**—but there can be little doubt that Haman now realizes it all. At this point Esther, the expert status player, who knows when to raise and when to lower her status, judges it is time to maintain her status. By contrast the two figures who are obsessed with maintaining high status both make errors of judgment by lowering their status inappropriately. The king shows himself incapable of controlling his emotions, a feature of low-status activity, and leaves the scene, another low-status move. Haman panics and makes a drastic low-status attempt to plead to the queen for his life. By the time the king returns, **Haman had thrown himself on the**

couch where Esther was reclining. Haman has done nothing illegal, and by retaining his status he could have talked his way out of it. But by losing status from his own volition at the key moment he makes himself look guilty, leaving aside the misinterpretation of his advance on the queen. The king, of course, imagines things only in sexual terms. Haman's status plunges further into the abyss, as he is impaled not only in front of his own house but, on account of the height of the gallows, in front of the whole city. The appearance of a **eunuch** again emphasizes Haman's impotence.

The ironies are so satisfying that they hardly need emphasizing in the narrative. This whole crisis began with Mordecai's refusal to do obeisance to Haman, and now it reaches its climax with Haman doing obeisance to Esther. Then Esther is given **Haman's house** and what seems to have been the root of the whole standoff—the enmity between the house of Haman, or Agag, and the house of Mordecai, or Saul—is settled by the decisive act, not of God, nor of Ahasuerus, but of Queen Esther. The Joseph story has been echoed by a misunderstanding over an allegation of sexual assault—this time not a foul cry by Potiphar's wife but a misreading by the king. Now, in yet another echo of the Joseph story, **the king took off his signet ring, which he had taken from Haman, and gave it to Mordecai**. This recalls Gen. 41:41–42:[5] "Pharaoh said to Joseph, 'See, I have set you over all the land of Egypt.' Removing his signet ring from his hand, Pharaoh put it on Joseph's hand." The narrative in Esth. 8:1–2 is very similar, with one striking exception: it concludes with the summary and unambiguous words: **So Esther set Mordecai over the house of Haman**. Ahasuerus may have meant it for a further gesture of flamboyant generosity and arbitrary power: Esther meant it for the salvation of the Jews.

New Law (8:3–17)

In all the drama surrounding Mordecai's parade and Esther's announcement and Haman's downfall one could have been induced into thinking that Haman was the problem and that with his demise salvation had come for the Jews. But Haman was not the problem. The problem was the law. Haman was "sin," but the law he promulgated against the Jews was "death." And the law threatens the Jews as much after Haman's death as it did while he still lived. This is the force of the words **the evil design of Haman the Agagite and the plot that he had devised against the Jews**. The mention of the word **Agagite** highlights that, just as Agag may be long gone but lived in Haman, so Haman is now gone but lives on in his unalterable law.

Once again we can see the bitterness of the account if we see it as a portrayal of the God of Israel through the lens of the mercurial Ahasuerus. The king is slow to realize that, despite his stunning intervention, the Jews are still at death's door.

5. As Fox, *Character and Ideology*, 90, points out.

It is not hard to hear echoes of the God of Israel who has delivered his people from the land of Egypt and has given them the law—but who now seems oblivious to their peril in the Diaspora. Ahasuerus is a king who is greedy for devotion but is desperately short on concentration. He does not seem to be able to see any initiative through to its conclusion. So his people have to resort to manipulation and pleading desperation.

The subsequent scene thus echoes much of what has gone before, reinforcing that vital work remains to be done. The Jews are in just as much jeopardy as they were when Esther first went in search of the golden scepter. Now she must do so again. Once again, her principal asset is her hold on the king's sexual imagination. That she **spoke again to the king** is not striking until one recalls that Haman's death has changed nothing. We are still in the land of absurd laws and an unpredictable monarch, and if Esther initiates a conversation her life is once again in danger. Esther takes to **weeping and pleading**—the only way, it seems, to alert the king to his wife's life being still in mortal peril. But in the end there is one language she can be sure he understands. The reference to the king's **feet** is a somewhat coded sexual allusion; the prompt observation that **the king held out the golden scepter to Esther** is rather less subtle. Esther knows what she needs and she knows exactly how to solicit it, even in public.

But still it is best to pile on the obsequious language: **If it pleases the king, and if I have won his favor, and if the thing seems right before the king, and I have his approval**. Nothing taken for granted here. For the first time, on this platform of flattery and sexual arousal, Esther discloses that she is a Jew. The name of the people was never mentioned by Haman and remained a mystery even in Esther's long-awaited request to the king at her banquet. Now there is no ambiguity. But the tone of voice is different from her earlier request. There she spoke of her own plight—"I and my people" (7:4). Here she is an advocate with the "Father" on behalf of her people, but, perhaps not wanting to seem ungrateful for Ahasuerus's disposal of Haman, she refrains from suggesting her own life is still in danger. Instead she asks the king—a man not noted for his skills of empathy—to enter into her own anguish: **For how can I bear to see the calamity that is coming on my people? Or how can I bear to see the destruction of my kindred?** The change in language is small, but the christological significance is great. Christians may see Esther in Esth. 7 as the one who lays down her life for the salvation of her people, in the process evoking the death of death in Haman's demise; meanwhile here in Esth. 8 Esther is the advocate with the "Father" pleading *on behalf of* her people of whom she is still one, but one explicitly set apart for the purposes of propitiation. Again she reveals herself as an expert status player, weeping and pleading in an ultralow-status manner but setting her own well-being to one side in a high-status move. Esther is displaying the full range of resources available to the downtrodden Jews.

She is **Queen Esther**; her cousin is **the Jew Mordecai**. The difference in status between their respective roles is enhanced at this moment in the narrative. Esther now disappears from the rest of the chapter. It is as if her role is strategic, while Mordecai's is operational. The strategic intervention has been made, and now the decision simply needs to be implemented. Step back Esther; step forward Mordecai. Ahasuerus is somewhat slow on the uptake: his appalling memory has already forgotten why he executed Haman. He recalls it was **because he plotted to lay hands on the Jews**. But the truth is, the words in 7:8 that precipitated the execution were, "Will he even assault the queen in my presence, in my own house?" (Ahasuerus, true to form, in fact never initiated the execution at all: it was Harbona the eunuch who seized the moment when the king was in a rage.)

The great dilemma of the book—how the Jews are to escape once an irrevocable law has been passed that invokes their extermination—is about to be resolved. The law is not to be revoked; seventy days after its passing there is simply to be a new law that runs parallel to and in practice undermines Haman's law.[6] Here, yet again, we see Ahasuerus's inability to focus his mind on the details of any matter whatsoever—even the extermination of a substantial body of his people and the potential death of the queen: he repeats his earlier disastrous habits and simply hands authority over to Mordecai. Echoing his treatment of Haman, this cavalier king says to Mordecai, **You may write as you please with regard to the Jews, in the name of the king, and seal it with the king's ring**. The subsequent words, **for an edict written in the name of the king and sealed with the king's ring cannot be revoked**, when juxtaposed to a reiteration of the king's prodigal delegation of unique authority, conjure up a picture of a cat's cradle of irrevocable and absurd laws passed at the whim of the king's immediate circle. This is of course exactly what the book of Esther mercilessly portrays.

There follows a litany of elements in the passing of the new law, the concatenation of which is principally designed to echo and unravel the doom-laden bell tolling of 3:12–15, albeit with rather better horses and at a somewhat faster pace. The theme is that of reversal.[7] This is demonstrated sartorially: Mordecai, who once tore his clothes and put on sackcloth and ashes, now appears **wearing royal robes of blue and white, with a great golden crown and a mantle of fine linen and purple**. It is demonstrated emotionally: the Jews, among whom there was once great mourning, now express **gladness and joy**. It is demonstrated in food: the Jews, who once neither ate nor drank for three days, night or day, now celebrate **a festival and a holiday**. It is demonstrated by fear: once it was the Jews who had every reason to be terrified; now **many of the peoples of the country professed to be Jews, because the fear of the Jews had fallen upon them**. It is demonstrated linguistically: once use of the Jewish language was a risk; now the new edict is written **also to the Jews in their script and their language**. Once Susa was in confusion at Haman's decree; now at Mordecai's decree Susa is full of glee.

6. Levenson, *Esther*, 110, highlights the significance of the number of days, connecting this satisfying figure to Gen. 46:27; Judg. 9:2, 4; Jer. 29:10; and Ps. 90:10.

7. Linda M. Day, *Esther*, Abingdon Old Testament Commentaries (Nashville: Abingdon, 2005), 130.

Once the dust has settled on the wonder of Esther's achievement, the extent of the reversal, and the absurdity of an empire where even perfidious laws are irrevocable, what are we to make of the content of the new law? **The king allowed the Jews who were in every city to assemble and defend their lives, to destroy, to kill, and to annihilate any armed force of any people or province that might attack them, with their children and women, and to plunder their goods on a single day throughout all the provinces of King Ahasuerus.** Let us first enumerate the problems this decree raises.

First, the book of Esther has been at pains to point out that there is no inherent tension between what is good for the Jews and what is good for the empire as a whole. Haman is dead: Why then should there be any specific **enemies of the Jews?** A sober answer, particularly in the light of the Holocaust, would be to say, That is a question Jews have never had the luxury to ask. There are always enemies of the Jews. Yet the narrative does not give any clue as to any cause of enmity beyond the atavistic enmity with the Agagites. On the contrary, the normal state appears to be general social harmony. One can only assume that Haman's decree created the enmity, by offering an irresistible opportunity to scavenge among the defenseless and dispossessed Jews.

Second, it is not clear that Mordecai is simply concerned with self-defense. We are told that **the Jews were to be ready on that day to take revenge on their enemies.** Why they *had* enemies is still not clear: but the language of revenge does not sit easily with the ethos of self-defense.

Third, while the necessity for the survival and flourishing of the Jews is a continuous thread from what I earlier called the "Passover tradition," significant elements have been lost. One is that Israel should be a people in whom "all the families of the earth shall be blessed" (Gen. 12:3). Another is that Israel should shine in a way that peoples who do not know the Torah should be drawn to it and transformed. And a third is that what makes Israel irresistible in battle is that God fights on Israel's behalf. In the absence of these significant elements it becomes much harder to see the theological dimension in the necessity of Israel's survival. Or, put differently, Esther's achievement constitutes Israel's *survival*, rather than her *salvation*. It is not clear in the book of Esther that God has any further use for Israel as a light to the nations or that Israel has any longer any particular sense of such a unique vocation. The sonorous words of Lev. 11:44, "Be holy, for I am holy," that echo through much of the Old Testament, seem in the book of Esther to have gone seriously out of fashion. Israel's salvation involves no inviolable law, no direct divine action, no return to a promised land, no holiness that imitates the character of God. Instead it involves guile and wits, luck and opportunism, good timing and, when the moment comes, ruthless use of violent force.

These are formidable objections to the content of Mordecai's decree. There are, however, substantial counterarguments. First, the most persuasive is to recognize the narrative shape of the story and the degree of satisfaction that lies in the reincorporation of all the elements of Haman's decree in Mordecai's counteredict. The repetition of the words **to destroy, to kill, and to annihilate** is not a signal to the Jews of the empire to unleash vindictiveness, but a nudge to the listener or reader in later days to take delight in the symmetry of the story's resolution. Zeresh was right: all that Haman had planned against the Jews would rebound on him, no more—but no less. The Jews are galvanized not by an external hand that arbitrarily shifts the pieces on the game board but by an elastic force of natural law somewhat resembling gravity—however high Haman might hoist the Jews, his malevolence would come tumbling down and land on him with equal force. The abiding assumption of the book of Esther is that peace is possible for Jews in the Diaspora. The book does not give extensive details of what this peace entails, but here it offers a picture of peace as equilibrium, a balance of forces canceling one another out. This picture of equilibrium is, however, undermined by the subsequent phrase, **the Jews were to be ready on that day to take revenge on their enemies**, which eradicates the sense of balance established previously and replaces it with revenge.

An extra dimension of this reasoning, which also stays true to the rubrics of the narrative, is, second, to note the exaggerated numbers and details of the burlesque style. When it turns out in Esth. 9 that 75,000 fell in a single day, the enormous number sits more easily alongside the other overblown dimensions of this fairy-tale story than it does in a sober evaluation of how many casualties might be permitted in a just war. The book of Esther is a celebration of what happens when the Jews take their destiny into their own hands; but it is not a strategic evaluation of how Jews may exercise administrative power over the long term. The lesson is not, "Go and do likewise"; it is, "If Mordecai, before whom your downfall has begun, is of the Jewish people, you will not prevail against him, but will surely fall before him."

A less attractive argument—but one still true to the character of the story—would be to recognize, third, that neglect of the practice of *herem* (the total annihilation of the enemy), imposed in the book of Joshua on the Midianites, the Amalekites, and the town of Jericho, lies at the root of the problem faced by the Jews in the book of Esther.[8] Had Saul annihilated the Agagites, not only would he not have lost God's favor, but there would have been no Haman to concoct a devilish plot against the Jews. The instruction to annihilate the enemy takes on a new dimension in this context.

Attention naturally focuses on the extraordinary sequence of events by which the Jews came to overturn their parlous condition and gain a place of perhaps unprecedented stability in the empire. Before leaving the question of Mordecai's decree, however, it is worth speculating on what alternative content one might expect his edict to have. The heart of this question lies in the moral imagination. What *should* Mordecai have done?

8. This point proposed by Day, ibid., 137, but doubted by Bechtel, *Esther*, 75.

Elsewhere I outline three broad strands of ethics.[9] I call these (1) "universal" ("ethics for anybody")—which includes theories that focus on right actions/intentions and theories that focus on right outcomes or consequences; (2) "subversive" ("ethics for the excluded")—which privileges the often suppressed voices arising from social locations relating to race, gender, class, and so forth; and (3) "ecclesial" ("ethics for the church")—reflecting virtue, narrative, and nonviolent perspectives and locating ethics less in the moment of decision than in the formation of character. As is often the case with Old Testament material, universal ethics run into difficulties. What seem like universal injunctions ("you shall not murder [or kill]"; Exod. 20:13) seem to be superseded by specific instructions from the God of Israel, as we have seen in the command to annihilate the Agagites. These specific commands cannot be understood universally, and therefore a Kantian categorical imperative, which enjoins acting such that the principle of one's action could be a universal moral law, is not helpful. If there is a principled theory at work here it is closer to natural law, as reflected in Zeresh's prophecy. By stating that the Jews *cannot* be subdued, without identifying an agent that makes it so, Zeresh articulates what amounts to a principle of natural law.

Indeed this is, in ethical terms, one of the key themes of the book of Esther: the Jews' relationship with God is less a matter of heeding divine commands, as most of the Old Testament assumes, than of acting in step with natural law—the law that states that "relief and deliverance will rise for the Jews from another quarter" (Esth. 4:14). Rather than dwelling on the absence of God from the text of the narrative, it is more fruitful to perceive the book as describing what later came to be known as a natural-law, rather than divine-command, approach to ethics. Ethical approaches rooted in natural law have two dominant characteristics: they are based on observation of the way things are, and they have some teleological anticipation of the way things will ultimately be. The ethics of Esther keep these two dimensions in a fine balance. Haman and Zeresh in different ways embody the way things are: the Jews have enemies but those enemies will never ultimately prevail. And yet there are glimpses of the way things will finally be, in the **gladness and joy among the Jews** and the benefits to the empire of wise Jewish leadership.

Such a reading stays true to the narrative shape of the book in a way that other attempts to elicit or identify a universal ethic do not. For example, the simplest reading from a universal perspective is to see Mordecai's reasoning as consequential—that is, based on a calculation of the likely outcome of the decree. While the desire to learn from and/or critically evaluate the example of great figures in the scriptures is understandable, the impulse to turn Mordecai's edict into an ethic ripe for imitation is putting more weight on it than it can bear. It runs counter to the whole larger-than-life tenor of the story; but it also presumes Mordecai could possibly know what the likely aftermath of Haman's edict might be, given Haman's removal from the scene. The heart of Mordecai's edict lies in

9. Wells and Quash, *Introducing Christian Ethics*.

its reverse symmetry with Haman's edict, not with a political or psychological calculation of the most effective way to offset a series of vigilante attacks. The most satisfying moment comes when **many of the peoples of the country professed to be Jews, because the fear of the Jews had fallen upon them**. In other words, just for a moment, in a story whose background is the overwhelming pressure on Jews to lose their identity and faith and culture and become Persians, there is a window in which Persians long to become Jews.[10]

A subversive reading is more promising, but also risks stepping outside the assumptions of the narrative. On this account, those who have not been at extreme risk of, or subject to, genocidal threats and activity should exercise appropriate humility before hastening to pass judgment on Mordecai's decree. This assumes a universalizability that the spirit of the book of Esther does not easily allow. As we have just seen, the book hinges on what would later be seen as natural law—that seeking to destroy the Jews is like forcing together two identical magnetic poles, which a force beyond the visual imagination will not allow to be drawn together. The Jews are exceptional, even if God's role is not visible. This is not a generalized claim about God being on the side of the oppressed. The subversive reading also has to reckon with Mordecai's decree coming when he and Esther are occupying positions of significant power. The Jews may indeed be in peril, but Mordecai has just been told by Ahasuerus: **You may write as you please . . . in the name of the king, and seal it with the king's ring**. Besides revoking an earlier law, there is nothing whatsoever that Mordecai cannot do. This is not a social location with which subversive ethics is generally familiar.

Perhaps the most vexing dimensions of Mordecai's decree come in relation to ecclesial ethics. According to the understanding of ecclesial approaches to ethics, the decree arose not through a universalizable action or a careful calculation of likely outcomes: it arose through the habits and practices developed by Mordecai over time through his membership of a people living by their tradition and their wits in the Diaspora. This is what Esther falls back on at her moment of crisis in 4:16. She did not have a flash of inspiration: she looked to the habits in which her people had been shaped over centuries. And here is the rub—is that exactly what Mordecai was doing in the wording of his decree? Is Mordecai's edict the sum total of the character formation of the Jews in the Diaspora? The problem for ecclesial ethics is not that there are no habits, no practices, no traditions, and that character has not been formed: it is that these things are all in place but the decree seems to fall short of the witness of a people to the grace of God. In mitigation of Mordecai's actions, it is not just that the peril to his people is real and urgent; it is that no Jew has occupied a position of power like this ever before (or since) in history, and no Jew had, at this juncture, occupied a seat of any power at all for quite some time. The only remote precedent is Joseph, and he had no

---

10. Edward L. Greenstein, "A Jewish Reading of Esther," in *Judaic Perspectives on Ancient Israel*, ed. Jacob Neusner, Baruch A. Levine, and Ernest S. Frerich (Philadelphia: Fortress, 1987), 225–43 at 236.

equivalent of the bare-toothed antagonism of Haman to deal with. The habits of the Jews are the habits honed in the Diaspora: it should perhaps be unsurprising that they do not transfer too well to a sudden and unexpected elevation to global executive authority.

This survey of the ethical dimensions of Mordecai's decree demonstrates, perhaps more vividly than at any other place in the book of Esther, the way the narrative's theology and ethics intersect. God is not going to offer a miraculous rescue; neither should the Jews assume they can simply follow God's commands. There is going to be no promised land to run away to, and "Israel" may no longer be such a significant word in the Jewish vocabulary; but there is no reason why the Jews cannot be at home in the Persian Empire. There will continue to be malevolent individuals, perhaps with historic reasons for enmity with the Jews; but there is no entire people whose identity is predicated on its opposition to the Jews. The Jews may face profound threats to their existence, but a kind of natural law written into the heart of things means the Jews cannot be destroyed. The Jews' survival is thus a theological and political necessity, and hence about more than their own national salvation; but in order to find safety they must continue, like Esther and Mordecai, to pursue paths of courage and imagination that expose them to personal risk but open their people to their true destiny.

OUTCOME

ESTHER 9–10

New Fear (9:1–4)

The aftermath of Mordecai's law makes two points, loud and clear. The first concerns vigilance. The Jews' plight was not ended with the death of Haman, nor even with Mordecai's decree. Only when the Jews had themselves turned the opportunity of Mordecai's edict into the reality of the eradication of their enemies could they begin to see themselves as free of the curse of Haman. The second concerns obedience. Saul's error consigned his descendants into jeopardy; Mordecai and the Jews are not going to make the same mistakes again, even at the risk of seeming brutal and gratuitously vindictive. Both are lessons in thoroughness.

The opening verses of Esth. 9 neatly summarize the plot of the book of Esther. The summary is this: **the very day**, the thirteenth of Adar, when Haman had planned to exterminate the Jews, **had been changed to a day when the Jews would gain power over their foes**. The Jews had turned themselves into an organized fighting force and had the blessing of the king, the prime minister, and all the provincial officials. Formerly their enemies had the power, and they had the fear; step forward Queen Esther, and now their enemies had the fear, and they had the power.

As we have seen in other places, a moment in the drama when one might have anticipated the fear or worship of God becomes a moment squarely directed toward the Jews—and the fear of one Jew in particular, Mordecai: **For Mordecai was powerful in the king's house, and his fame spread throughout all the provinces as the man Mordecai grew more and more powerful**. One thinks of the fear present through the Holy Spirit in the early chapters of Acts. After the death of Ananias and Sapphira we are told "great fear seized the whole church and all who heard of these things" (5:11). Earlier we learn of the "boldness" and "great power" and "great grace" (4:31–33) that characterized the apostles. But this was without question the power and grace of God, and the fear of all was not far from the worship of God. Here, by contrast, the power of the Jews is almost a *substitute* for faith in the power of God; and the fear found among the wider population is not a fear that imagines a people of great grace. Both Levenson and Fox highlight the similarity between the words **for Mordecai was powerful in the king's house, and his fame spread throughout all the provinces as the man Mordecai grew more and more powerful** and the words of Exod. 11:3: "Moses himself was a man of great importance in the land of Egypt, in the sight of Pharaoh's officials and in the sight of the people."[1] The vital difference is that the words in Exod. 11:3 are preceded by these words: "The LORD gave the people favor in the sight of the Egyptians." No such attribution appears in the imagination of the book of Esther. Indeed, even the Jewish identity of Mordecai is obscured for a telling moment: **the man Mordecai grew more and more powerful**; not, as elsewhere, the Jew Mordecai, but just the man.

Once again it is important to highlight the apparent similarities but crucial differences between this story and the accounts of Joseph and Daniel. Joseph, Daniel, and Mordecai all attain high office in Gentile lands. (The apocryphal Judith does too.) Joseph uses his power for the benefit of all; it turns out his own family (it is anachronistic to call them the Jews at this point in the scriptural story) are major beneficiaries, but he did not anticipate that when he embarked upon his plan of action. Daniel also attains high office, although we have no account of how he exercised authority or for whose interests he considered himself obliged to use his power. But the contrast with Mordecai is that Daniel attains power explicitly through the miraculous action of God and his own unwavering obedience to the Torah. Mordecai and Esther have already strayed far from the Torah before their people even find themselves in jeopardy. They employ astonishing wit and courage but at no stage explicitly look to God to visit them in their distress. When they attain power it is not because of their witness to the God of Israel but because of a sequence of blunders by their enemies and their own opportunistic ability to manipulate those around them. And their exercise of power is without question designed to advance and safeguard the Jewish community above all else. This is their *telos*. There is no greater good—not the worship of the God of Israel, not the common benefit of all in the empire, not the restoration of the Jews to the land of Canaan. Moses stands as a stark contrast: one who had a high place of honor in Egypt, but one who found that such a place of honor was incompatible with his identity as a Hebrew. For Moses, the path was not of assimilation or violent assertion of identity: it was the path to the promised land. No such path presents itself in the book of Esther. The word "Israel" never appears.

---

1. Levenson, *Esther*, 121; Fox, *Character and Ideology*, 109.

Battle (9:5–16)

By any standards this is a challenging passage for theological interpretation. At first reading it looks like an abandon of slaughter, with the aforementioned "fear of Mordecai" and of the Jews so overshadowing proceedings that "all the officials of the provinces, the satraps and the governors, and the royal officials were supporting the Jews" and thus the Jews could, almost to their own disbelief, do **as they pleased to those who hated them**. Doing **as they pleased** seems to mean striking **down all their enemies with the sword, slaughtering, and destroying them**.

How to come to terms with such a bloodthirsty conclusion to the book? Most of the strategies were reviewed in the discussion of Mordecai's decree at 8:3–17. Here it is worth noting that what seems to be a bloodbath has a number of dimensions. Perhaps the most significant is disclosed by the threefold refrain of the phrase **but they did not touch the plunder**. This is more than a historical footnote: it is an explicit nudge to the reader or listener. It stands in direct contrast to Haman's decree, which gave "orders to destroy, to kill, and to annihilate all Jews, young and old, women and children, in one day, the thirteenth day of the twelfth month, which is the month of Adar, and to plunder their goods" (4:13). Whatever it is, this dramatic action is not simply about the Jews becoming like other nations. It is saying this slaughter is a principled action, in keeping with what would later be wrapped in the language of the just conduct of war—*ius in bello*.

In the background lies Abram's forbearance in Gen. 14:20–24.[2] Abram gives Melchizedek one tenth of everything: "Then the king of Sodom said to Abram, 'Give me the persons, but take the goods for yourself.' But Abram said to the king of Sodom, 'I have sworn to the LORD, God Most High, maker of heaven and earth, that I would not take a thread or a sandal-thong or anything that is yours, so that you might not say, "I have made Abram rich."' I will take nothing but what the young men have eaten, and the share of the men who went with me—Aner, Eshcol, and Mamre. Let them take their share." Likewise Mordecai and the Jews are concerned to show that this is not about greed and pillage: it is about self-defense and security.

In the foreground is the by-now-familiar legacy of Saul's treatment of Agag and the Amalekites. To understand Esth. 9, we need to examine closely 1 Sam. 15. It begins with Samuel's words to Saul: "Thus says the LORD of hosts, 'I will punish the Amalekites for what they did in opposing the Israelites when they came up out of Egypt. Now go and attack Amalek, and utterly destroy all that they have; do not spare them, but kill both man and woman, child and infant, ox and sheep, camel and donkey'" (15:2–3). Saul carefully extracted the guiltless Kenites from the doomed Amalekites and then "utterly destroyed all the people with the edge of the sword" (15:8). However, crucially, "Saul and the people spared Agag, and

2. Sidnie White Crawford, "Esther," in *The New Interpreter's Study Bible: New Revised Standard Version with the Apocrypha* (Nashville: Abingdon, 2003), 689–701 at 699.

the best of the sheep and of the cattle and of the fatlings, and the lambs, and all
that was valuable, and would not utterly destroy them; all that was despised and
worthless they utterly destroyed" (15:9). Immediately the Lord says, "I regret that
I made Saul king, for he has turned back from following me, and has not carried
out my commands" (15:10). Saul tells Samuel, "I have carried out the command
of the Lord" (15:13). But Samuel replies, "What then is this bleating of sheep
in my ears, and the lowing of cattle that I hear?" (15:14), and adds, crucially,
"*Why did you swoop down on the spoil*, and do what was evil in the sight of the
Lord?" (15:19). Saul protests that the spoil was taken simply to make sacrifices
in Gilgal. But Samuel points out that the Lord desires obedience more than sacrifice. There is no second chance for Saul. And the story ends with these resonant
words: "Then Samuel said, 'Bring Agag king of the Amalekites here to me.' And
Agag came to him haltingly. Agag said, 'Surely this is the bitterness of death.' But
Samuel said, 'As your sword has made women childless, so your mother shall be
childless among women.' And Samuel hewed Agag in pieces before the Lord in
Gilgal" (15:32–33).

It is hard to be critical of Mordecai and Esther and the Jews as described in
Esth. 9 in the light of this uncompromising legacy. The threefold refrain **but they
did not touch the plunder** seems to be an indication that, unlike Saul, they had
every intention of this time finishing the job. The killing of Haman's **ten sons** is
similar: it is both the final confirmation of the demise of Haman (who had boasted
of the number of his sons at Esth. 5:11) and an exhibition of thoroughness.

A further dimension of these gruesome events is that they are from the perspective of the mouse (of a minority religious and ethic people) confronted by the
elephant (of empire and anti-Semitism). This is the perspective assumed throughout the book. The number **seventy-five thousand** seems astronomical; but if it is
taken to represent an approximation of the number of Jews in the empire, then a
certain balance emerges. Haman aimed to kill around that many; by a remarkable
turn of events and remarkable prescience and courage on the part of two Jews,
the punishment Haman plotted for Mordecai and the fate Haman plotted on the
Jews was turned on their enemies. Undue moralizing misses the sense of reversal
that lies at the heart of the book: slaughter seemed to be the fate of the Jews,
but it turned out it became the fate of the Persians. Banqueting and outrageous
partying seemed to be the habit of the Persians, but by a remarkable reversal it
became the regular habit of the Jews. Since the identity of **the enemies** of the
Jews is never revealed, it is not unduly fanciful to regard them as placeholders for
the Amalekites, just as Haman is a placeholder for King Agag of the Amalekites.

This is the land of exaggerated numbers and burlesque plotting. The only precision involved is the meticulous concern to lift the curse on Saul and for once
follow the instructions of Samuel to the letter. Esther 9 soon opens out into the
celebration of Purim, and the participatory nature of Purim feasting is particularly suited to the adversarial and vivid divisions made in this chapter between
the good, who can do no wrong, and the bad, who deserve extermination or

worse. But the emphasis, throughout, remains on the astonishing reversal. The litany of the names of Haman's sons illustrates this acutely: previously the lists of eunuchs and kinds of royal officials had been overblown trumpetings of the majestic pomposity of the empire: now the litany becomes a song of rejoicing in the wondrous nature of the Jews' achievement. The account carries the force of wish-fulfillment, much as the psalms of lament articulate visceral longings for the crushing of enemies. The book of Esther in some ways represents the sentiment of those psalms in narrative form: it is almost like a dream. The message is, do not give up, do not slacken, do not despair: there is a future for the Jews, and it includes days of almost unbelievable rescue and triumph, but if you are to enjoy it you must strain your imagination and your courage to discover it. The Bible offers many accounts of peoples wiped out by their enemies: here is a view from the other side, from a people like a ball bearing in its indestructibility and like a star in its inspirational quality.

And this explains the relish with which yet another new law comes into being. This time Ahasuerus himself takes the initiative and approaches **Queen Esther**: there is no need for the clumsy and dangerous shenanigans with the scepter. Things really have changed. Ahasuerus, true to form, is little troubled by the evidence of civil war across the length and breadth of his domains. He makes an uncharacteristically long speech, which seems to share the awe of the Jews now widespread in the land. But his only concern is the one that has dominated the second half of the book: the peace of mind of his queen. **What is your petition? It shall be granted you. And what further is your request? It shall be fulfilled**. In fact, she has not on this occasion suggested that she had a further petition. But she knows her man, and she has one to hand just in case. The point is that this is the new status quo in the empire. Esther sets the policy and the king turns it into law. She is truly the one in charge. Like Deborah in the book of Judges, she is a woman who knows how to lead and finds the opportunity to do so.

However, as with Mordecai's decree, there are elements that do not fit the Amalekite/underdog reading of this bloodthirsty account quite so well. One is the observation that the Jews who had "gathered in their cities throughout all the provinces" (9:2), and thus turned themselves into a military force, **did as they pleased to those who hated them**. There is again the satisfaction of reversal, for the first decree in Esth. 1 was that each palace official should do as he desired, and now each Jew does as he desires. But there is something here of the negative connotation of the book of Judges, where we are summarily told that "all the people did what was right in their own eyes" (Judg. 21:25). Doing as one pleases may be a sign of a certain kind power, particularly the wish-fulfillment kind, but outside the world of Esth. 1 it hardly corresponds to obedience, and it was obedience that emerged from our earlier discussion as the most plausible rationale for the slaughter. The sense of excess is enhanced by Esther's petition. Haman's decree had applied for one day only, the thirteenth of Adar. Esther wants an extra day. One can of course take this as a sign of the extent of violent anti-Semitism in the empire: but the narrative does not elsewhere support that. That **the ten sons of Haman were hanged . . . on the fourteenth day of the month of Adar** is an indication of utter humiliation; but obedience to the Saul legacy and protection against endemic enmity need not include imposing this level of public ignominy. This comes more from the thrill of the mouse overcoming the elephant than it does from any handbook of how Diaspora Jews may exercise such power as they may from time to time attain.

And finally among the abiding discordant elements, a familiar theme. Samuel's instructions to Saul constituted a divine command ethic: the classic quandary—is it good because God commands it or does God command it because it is good?—is answered decisively in favor of the former. The book as a whole seems to embody a kind of natural-law ethic: the Jews are indestructible, and anyone who supposes otherwise will get their comeuppance, provided the Jews act according to their destiny. But the material surrounding Saul's legacy is of a different character. This is divine-command territory. Annihilating Agag and the Amalekites is a matter not of universally invariable duty, nor of universalizable principle, nor of a calculation of beneficial outcomes: it is a matter of simple obedience to God. This is the test that Saul fails. But here lies the problem: what does a divine-command ethic mean in the virtual absence of a divine character to the story? In 1 Samuel there is an ethical problem, and it lies in the character (or description) of God, who seems brutal, vindictive, and utterly inflexible. But in the book of Esther the ethical problem cannot be placed on God, since God is not an explicit character in the story. So Esther and Mordecai's obedience is less obedience to God than obedience to their people and the tradition of their people. There seems, in this book, to be no higher ideal.

Celebration (9:17–19)

Here are the final two banquets of a story of many banquets. Throughout the book there has been a sense that **Susa** is a kernel of the empire, that things were different but somehow more focused there. Susa got its own banquet at the beginning of the story and had its own recognition in the promulgating of both the key decrees. Now **the Jews who were in Susa** have a celebration slightly different from those of **the Jews of the villages, who live in the open towns**. The celebration alleviates some of the more uncomfortable aspects of the battle that preceded it. This is a time of **gladness and feasting**. The note of revenge in Mordecai's decree and the gratuitous dimension in the hanging of Haman's sons is by now laid to rest. All focuses on the wonder of deliverance.

Here we have gifts of **food**, but no prayers of blessing. We have **feasting**, but no story of what God has done. We have **gladness**, but no songs of praise. We have a Sabbath, when the Jews **rested**, but as a respite from battle rather than as a sign of God's grace or a faithful keeping of the Torah. We have celebration, evacuated of worship. At no stage in the book does the notion of the Purim festival as a parody of the Passover seem more striking than now. We have a tale of countless absurd and sometimes destructive laws, but no Torah. We have fantastic descriptions of magnificent buildings, but no temple. We have a special city where the fate of the Jews is decided, but it is not Jerusalem.

Here we see drawn together the themes of the book of Esther. This is a fairy story of wondrous fantasies and an existential crisis of murderous realities. Here is a stupendously wealthy king, a parody of God: but when we reach the heart of the story, it lies in a conversation (between Mordecai and Esther) and a celebration (of **gladness and feasting**) where God is not mentioned and the king is not present. The people called to be a blessing to all peoples are here portrayed, in the exchange of gifts, as a blessing to one another. The Jews are delivered from catastrophe; but the nature of the mystery by which they are saved either goes without saying or has ceased to have a transcendent dimension.

Recording (9:20–10:3)

Perhaps the greatest moral injunction of the book of Esther coincides with the habits enjoined by Deuteronomy: *remember*. Again, the irony lies in the difference of precisely what is being remembered. In Deuteronomy the memory is that you were once slaves in Egypt but that God led you out by a powerful hand; remember that the Lord led you forty years in the wilderness to test what was in your heart and whether you would keep his commandments, his statutes, and his ordinances. Here the memory is that **the Jews gained relief from their enemies**, and that **Haman son of Hammedatha the Agagite, the enemy of all the Jews, had plotted against the Jews to destroy them, and had cast Pur—that is "the lot"—to crush and destroy them; but when Esther came before the king, he gave orders in writing that the wicked plot that he had devised against the Jews should come upon his own head, and that he and his sons should be hanged on the gallows.** Besides being a somewhat selective (and in a small degree) revised version of the story, this constitutes a very different kind of remembering from Deuteronomy. The remembering is not fundamentally about love, about nurture, about the longsuffering and painstaking faithfulness of God; it is about individuals taking the initiative and their people coming out on top after an enemy tried to destroy them.

The story comes to be among the scrolls incorporated in the canon because both accounts are true. God did bring the children of Israel out by a mighty hand; but in later times, particularly in the Diaspora, God's hand was somewhat less easy to perceive, and Jews who took matters into their own hands could well imagine they were being faithful to their people. And yet there are hints in these very last verses that the remembering constituted by Purim has a place alongside other practices of remembering, other dimensions of the tradition of God's people.

The instruction from **Queen Esther** and **the Jew Mordecai is that these days of Purim should be observed at their appointed seasons . . . just as they had laid down for themselves and for their descendants regulations concerning their fasts and their lamentations**.[3] True to the solemn message and teasing playfulness of the book, there are laws about both feasting and fasting. This ties the remembrance not just to the wondrous moment of reversal, but to the carefully fostered practices of the Jews that Esther had drawn upon in her hour of greatest need in 4:16. Whether such practices explicitly direct the people to God's mercy, there is no doubt from this story that they galvanize an apparently powerless population into a formidable force.

The second habit to be embodied is like unto the first: *record*. It is of the highest importance to record and remember those deeds and people who have saved you. If Mordecai's intervention to save the king's life in the face of assassination had not been recorded in the book of the annals, there would have been no parade through the streets of Susa and probably no elevation to high office. The last verses of Esth. 9 emphasize this need to record the saving deeds of your people. The Bible as a whole is a record of apparently insignificant particulars that later become part of the story of salvation. Each must have been recorded by a people who did not yet know that what they were recording would become the Bible.

Clines has a more skeptical view of writing. He notes that for the Persians "reality . . . attains its true quality only when written down."[4] It is writing, rather than whim or law, that truly threatens the Jews. There is no writing between Esth. 4 and Esth. 7, "because nothing there is settled or finalized." Clines is troubled by "the Jewish adoption of Persian writing." Using the legal system is one thing, but making it their own when **Mordecai recorded these things, and sent letters to all the Jews who were in all the provinces of King Ahasuerus**, is quite another. Clines regards this as "a crisis for Jewish identity," because Persian writing is a symbol of Persian lugubrious bureaucracy, whose typical use is to put the king to sleep (6:1), whereas the Jews are one people, sustained by folk memory. The numerous mistakes in the final record in 9:24–25 (Clines counts seven errors) show the high price of committing a Jewish story to Persian chroniclers; and the stockpile of paperwork in the closing verses shows Esther's fusion into Persian administrative culture. Clines also points out that writing in the story is primarily the writing of law, which is everywhere proclaimed to be unalterable, but whose irreversibility turns out to be a myth. The question left unresolved by Clines's healthy critique is whether the book of Esther itself is brought down by the same tokens or whether the book as a whole is precisely a response to such concerns. The canonical place of the book seems to me to address Clines's anxiety: here the book is never restricted to the written word, but always surrounded by a larger story

3. Day, *Esther*, 162, spots a pleasing irony, that the first letter in the book seeks to reduce the power of women, whereas this final letter is from a woman—a woman who has shown clearheadedness for government that the king never displays.

4. Clines, "Reading Esther from Left to Right," 48–51.

and enacted in worship and celebration; nonetheless the indispensable authority and importance of the written word are honored and cherished.

The third habit requiring embodiment follows: *repeat*. Repeat again and again. The book of Esther is a training school that works by being repeated again and again, at least annually. It is a rehearsal for reversal. It is to be repeated until its lessons become habits, its gestures become practices, its givens become trusted, and its transformation becomes expected. The final part of Esth. 9 performs what it advises: that the record of saving deeds is best remembered through repetition. Hence the Jews established and accepted as a custom for themselves and their descendants and all who joined them, that without fail they would continue to observe these two days every year, as it was written and at the time appointed. At every juncture the themes remember, record, repeat are reiterated.

In case it is not yet clear, the text goes on in similar vein: **These days should be remembered and kept throughout every generation, in every family, province, and city; and these days of Purim should never fall into disuse among the Jews, nor should the commemoration of these days cease among their descendants**. Again—remember, record, repeat. And once Mordecai has done his best to impress these things upon the Jews, Queen Esther takes over and underlines the same three themes, giving orders that **these days of Purim should be observed at their appointed seasons**. Esther, it is repeated once again, **fixed these practices of Purim, and it was recorded in writing**.

And the fourth habit to be embodied involves *reading* the story aloud and interactively. The reading of "the scroll" at the Feast of Purim has become a suitably riotous community event, with an atmosphere to suit the burlesque plot and dimensions of the narrative. This is not primarily a text for private meditation or a manual for political ethics, but a script for public performance. Memory is not a matter of memorizing tablets of stone, but of letting a covenant be inscribed on the heart. Ritual and community enactment ensure that **these days of Purim should never fall into disuse among the Jews, nor should the commemoration of these days cease among their descendants**. The liturgical year is important to bear in mind at this point. Purim comes before Passover, the great feast of God's miraculous deliverance. But it comes after Hanukkah, the great celebration of Jewish violent resistance. The cycle of all three festivals keeps a sense of balance between the three and offers a further perspective in which to read the book of Esther.

The fifth embodied habit is to *relish* in the context of eating food together. The book of Esther is all about ten interconnected banquets—lavish, sensuous, enticing, surprising, joyous.[5] The banquet is the transforming moment. An invitation to a banquet is an invitation to a political reversal. Here the implications for Christian liturgy become evident. It begs the question, is the Christian Eucharist such a banquet—such a repeated, interactive, reading-and-performing rehearsal

5. Fox, *Character and Ideology*, 157.

of reversal? The Eucharist should be the place and time where Christians recall that God has put down the mighty from their seats and exalted the humble and meek—and that God, the mighty, has come down from that seat and become humble and meek so that we, if we are humble and meek, might, through the power of his Spirit, become mighty. This should be the place and time where Christians celebrate that greatest of all reversals and where they reenact the death and resurrection of Christ, the definitive reversal gently anticipated in the mission of Esther.

But is it, truly, such a place and time? Reading Esther in the context of the Eucharist and particularly in the context of Purim highlights one significant query in relation to Christian liturgy. Why is it, particularly in the West, so obsessed with imposing order on chaos? Why is it so sober, so measured, so modest in its emotional engagement and inhibited in its passionate display? There is a place for the carefully planned banquet of the thoughtful Esther, and there is clearly little place for the mindlessly extravagant 180-day banquet of the king: but does Christian liturgy speak sufficiently of the sheer joy of being released from the sentence of death—*does eucharistic worship feel like discovering the fearsome edict has been overturned*? Do Christians realize that if Haman's decree had not been overcome it would have meant no Christianity? Is there a sufficient sense that the world has been turned upside down, and now anything is possible with God? Perhaps, among more deprived and oppressed peoples, it does. But maybe in the West the banquet feels disturbingly like one of a people who never believed that the fearsome edict really applied to them. And this is perhaps the real heart of the church's alienation from the Jews.

The final words of the book return to a theme underlying the whole narrative. When the Jews flourish, there is room for all to flourish. Ahasuerus is back in his heaven, and all is well with the world. In a lightheaded moment Ahasuerus had remitted taxes when Esther became queen;[6] now normal service is resumed, and the remission is reversed. Permanent deliverance from famine is marked in the Joseph story by a sweeping levy of taxation: "Joseph made it a statute concerning the land of Egypt, and it stands to this day, that Pharaoh should have the fifth" (Gen. 47:26). Like Joseph, Mordecai's influence on government is good for the population and good for the king's treasury.[7] If only Ahasuerus had realized sooner who his true friends were! And yet Mordecai's greatest legacy is not to the king and the empire but to his own people: he has shown it is possible and necessary for his people's continued deliverance to be **powerful among the Jews and popular with his many kindred**. And this is brought about by the way **he sought the good of his people and interceded for the welfare of all his descendants**. Esther has disappeared from the story: Mordecai is now the one who intercedes at the right hand of power. **The king advanced** Mordecai—exactly (and in the same words)[8]

---

6. As Levenson, *Esther*, 132, notes.
7. Fox, *Character and Ideology*, 130.
8. Ze'ev Weisman, *Political Satire in the Bible*, Semeia Studies 32 (Atlanta: Scholars Press, 1998), 144.

---

as he had promoted Haman at Esth. 3:1. This epitomizes the Jews' achievement and precariousness. They now hold the power that their enemy so recently held: but if he was toppled so dramatically, so could they be.

The irony and satire of the book's underlying message are underlined by reference in the final verses to **all the acts of his power and might**. This has not been, it need hardly be recalled, a conventional account of the acts of the **power and might** of the God of Israel. Neither has the great reversal brought about by Esther and Mordecai been a transformation enforced by **power and might**. And to laud the **power and might** of Ahasuerus is really to poke further fun at him, because it hints that at the end of the story he still thinks it has been a story about him, whereas Esther and Mordecai know better. The interplay between the sham power of Ahasuerus, the absent power of the God of Israel, and the ability of Esther and Mordecai to manipulate the former and substitute for the latter are all focused in these ironic words. God should be the central character, but is not. That is the paradox and tragedy of this period of Jewish history. Ahasuerus is the central character, the only person to appear at every stage of the story; but he is an ironic main character because he is oblivious to many of the most significant developments in the plot. Esther and Mordecai are the keys to the transformation the story retells; but the whole point of the story is that they become so without ever being in a position to call themselves central.

Finally, lest the fate that befell Joseph's descendents befall the descendents of Esther and Mordecai, the best insurance available is put to work: **the full account of the high honor of Mordecai, to which the king advanced him** is duly **written in the annals of the kings of Media and Persia**. Remember, record, repeat, read, relish: it seems that even Ahasuerus himself is learning from the example of the Jews. Perhaps God may too.

DANIEL

by George Sumner

AUTHOR'S PREFACE

Theologians sometimes talk about a "canon within a canon," a portion of the scripture privileged for interpreting the whole of scripture. When my son Samuel was seven, that passage was the description of the monster with the iron teeth in Dan. 7! Sam knows a vivid symbol and a dramatic conflict when he hears them. Daniel puts these elements to work in the service of wisdom about living in exile and insight into the coming end of all things. Thus it has preserved the power and strangeness of the Bible's message and guarded against its domestication, even as it has sometimes fallen prey to the extreme and the controlling.

But the more we study Daniel, the more we realize that it is not just a fascinating and sometimes dreamlike outlier in scripture. It is a key source of the idea of the kingdom of God. Resurrection, Son of Man, powers and principalities, the ascension—these Danielic ideas are central to the New Testament studies. Eschatology moved to center stage in twentieth-century New Testament; after the Second World War systematic theology followed suit. Our own era of worry and foreboding on a global scale contributes not a little. For all these reasons the interpretation of Daniel matters for theology and practice today.

This commentary is part of a series devoted to theological interpretation, for which a major issue is finding the right place for modern historical criticism. I am with respect to historical criticism an amateur, and I have sought in a positive spirit to learn what it has to teach. But it is a mistake to suppose that what a text means is exhausted by its origins, and so this commentary seeks to listen to passages in relation to the book as a whole, the Old Testament as a whole, and finally the Christian Bible as a whole. This involves a trust that tensions in the text have something to teach us too. Likewise (and perhaps more debatably), I will suggest that contending interpretations of passages may point to a trajectory toward a christological interpretation. The latter is not necessary, but, when articulated, does seem fitting.

In keeping with this approach, the detailed introduction to the commentary proper begins with a survey of the classic historical-critical problems: Why does the book of Daniel begin with six chapters of fables with a moral followed by six chapters of apocalyptic vision? Why a book set in sixth-century BC Babylon whose historical details are those of second-century BC Judea? And what are we to do with the welter of predictive numbers with which the book is filled? The introduction then moves into more substantive theological areas, for these historical questions lead me to put my cards on the table interpretively. For me, the central question of the book is the place of the Gentiles in God's plan of salvation (ironically raised by the displacement of the Jews). The center of the book, then, is the ascension of Christ and the coming of the nations, as presented (so I argue) in Dan. 7. Seeing the center in this way will determine the approach I take to interpreting eschatological statements. Finally, the calling of the Gentiles in the wake of the ascension is what Christians call "mission," and so I will pay attention to what guidance the book offers to this field. In keeping with this approach, the commentary is sprinkled with examples from the history of the *missio ad gentes*, not at all arbitrarily, but because the book of Daniel is really about just this history. The commentary, because of this, finally gives rise to a brief postscript, in which I focus on the virtue of hope that the book would instill in Christian missioners.

But the commentary itself is the real substance of this volume. It follows each chapter of Daniel in order, sometimes reflecting individual verses, sometimes taking several verses together. On this score, I should mention some of my modes of operation relevant to theological interpretation. I pay attention to the theological issues that premodern commentators identified. I engage contemporary systematic theologians and their interest in apocalyptic. I consider the reception of the book in other parts of the worldwide church, where passages seem occluded to Westerners. The reader will, I hope, forgive occasional forays into pessimistic culture critique—Daniel, after all, has something to say about this. Finally, I consider the opinions of the rabbis and try to remember that Daniel is scripture for Jewish readers as well.

In the course of writing this commentary, I had a helpful exchange with my friend John Goldingay of Fuller Seminary, a renowned expert on Daniel, about the nature of such an undertaking. He did not consider what I have written exegesis, though he is perfectly willing to agree with some of my conclusions under the rubric of application, as a reflection on the book from the perspective of mission theology. One could debate whether there is really a debate here! Daniel is full of types, which have a meaning in their first setting and point to another meaning as well. While the Christian community chooses to read the one in the stories and visions of Daniel, in fact he has chosen us, Gentiles that we are: on this we are gratefully agreed.

I want to express my gratitude to my editors, Ephraim Radner, Rusty Reno, and Robert Jenson, and to the kind offices of Tyndale House, Cambridge, when I worked on the book during a sabbatical. Stan Walters offered expert advice and encouragement. Over the years, Karen Baker, Deane Patchett, and Jonathan Turtle gave aid at Wycliffe. My Brazos reference editor was invaluable.

INTRODUCTION TO DANIEL

Critical Knots and Historical Cul-de-Sacs

Daniel offers as many gnarled critical problems for the historical critic as any book in the Bible. It is written in both Hebrew (Dan. 1, 8–12) and Aramaic (Dan. 2–7) and presents both fables (Dan. 2–6) and apocalyptic visions (Dan. 7–8, 10–11); as one can readily see, languages and genres do not line up neatly. The work bears the name of a legendary Hebrew figure of wisdom, the same name found in Babylonian inscriptions. The early material is written in the third person, while in the later chapters the visions are relayed in the first person. What relation might exist between an earlier writer and Daniel, and so how we are to understand this figure, are not clear.[1]

We may simplify the numerous, complex historical-critical questions about the book under three rubrics. The first question concerns the *unity* (or lack thereof) of the work. How did its different sources come to be collected into one work? What were the original *Sitzen im Leben* and the purpose of each? Critics often point out that the stances toward the ruling, sometimes persecuting, Gentile rulers seem to be different in the earlier chapters from the later. Wise and courageous strategies toward periodically accommodating rulers give way to patient endurance in the face of monstrous oppression.

Closely related to the unity question is the *when* question. To what oppressive ruler is each section referring, and who had the last editorial say? The nettle of the matter is that the predictions found in Dan. 7–12, tracking as they do the events surrounding the reign of Antiochus Epiphanes and the Maccabean revolt, are by consensus understood to be *vaticinia ex eventu*, composed so as to fit those historical events. What does this thesis do to the credibility of the work as a whole? Here traditional conservative interpretation took its stand in opposition, for it

1. Aaron Hebbard, *Reading Daniel as a Text in Theological Hermeneutics* (Eugene, OR: Pickwick, 2009), has separate designations for Daniel the character and Daniel the author.

sees the revisionist account of the original context as a fatal betrayal of the divine inspiration of the work.

Interpretation cannot but assume the historical-critical consensus on the *ex eventu* reference to Antiochus. But the redactional history of the book is complex, and this casts the *ex eventu* conclusion in an altered light. The negative judgment should not be assumed too quickly. For example, Brevard Childs agrees with the *ex eventu* conclusion, but points out that Dan. 2, with its vision of the kingly statue of the four empires, preceded the Antiochean era, and its nub may even date back to the Persian era.[2] Daniel 7 deliberately picks up this fourfold schema and applies a new version of it to a later era, including the Antiochean situation. In other words, seeing the work as a tradition is not so simple as an either/or choice between prospective and retrospective reference. It implies both predictive and consequential elements. Similarly some readily hypothesize that the fable material in the early chapters may have a prehistory that stretches back even to the Babylonian era. If this is so, then the material and its redaction would have a series of origins across all the empires referred to in the prophecies. Redaction history and canonical formation helps to cast the "when" question in a new light.

The third standard historical-critical worry derives from the *genre* of the later material, which is an early example of what is called "apocalyptic literature." Massive critical energy has been devoted to delving into the sociological conditions of such writings. One key factor has been a claim of determinism in Dan. 7–12. History is already set, and all that the faithful can and must do is wait for its determined outcome. In the meantime the forces of evil are seemingly in control. Such an outlook is seen as a devolution from the classically prophetic sense of God's full and ongoing involvement with human history.[3] This critique is derived from an assessment of texts considered apocalyptic as a whole and from the specifics of Daniel itself. It assumes a radical discontinuity between the two sections of the book with their contrasting genres. Reading the text as a whole serves to mitigate this deterministic effect. For example, the moral exhortation of Dan. 9 presents strong counterevidence to this concern about two ill-fitting halves.

The fourth major critical issue has to do not with the text itself, but what interpreters have traditionally done with it. In the history of Christian interpretation the import of Daniel has been understood in very different ways: the exhortation to martyrdom of Hippolytus, the refutation of Jewish claims in Theodoret,[4] the relation to philosophy in Jerome, the hope of the Tudor exiles for a Protestant England, the lessons of justification in Melanchthon, and so on. A vast, perhaps disproportionate, amount of energy is devoted by commentators to identifying who, for example, the beast with the little horn, the ruler setting up the abomination of desolation, might be. With equal intensity interpreters worry over

2. Brevard Childs, *Introduction to the Old Testament as Scripture* (Philadelphia: Fortress, 1979), 616.

3. E.g., Paul Hanson, *The Dawn of Apocalyptic* (Philadelphia: Fortress, 1975).

4. Kenneth Stevenson and Michael Glerup, *Ezekiel, Daniel*, Ancient Christian Commentary: Old Testament 12 (Downers Grove, IL: InterVarsity, 2008), 152.

elaborate arithmetic schemes to make sense of Daniel's various and sometimes contrasting numerological passages. To the historical-critical ear, all this sounds forced and eisegetical.

Here we can see in relief both the contribution and the limits of modern historical-critical interpretation. To say that application to Nero or to the Ottoman Empire cannot be the original reference is, in a sense, tautological. If one rules out typology from the start, then criticizing typological readings adds nothing. But, as we shall see, forbidding interpretation beyond the immediate limits of the text in its original contexts will bring a book like Daniel up against the clear intent of the New Testament, and hence the canon as a whole, to understand unfolding history in its specificity to be in the hand of God. We must see both the validity and the self-imposed limits of the critical project and so see the way in which it is itself addressed by the very message of Daniel itself. The variety of its genres and the complexity of its approach to time show the richness of the work and encourage us to take a broader view of the task of criticism.

The contribution of historical criticism is related to its limitation, for by narrowing the focus to original contexts and by privileging meanings in those contexts one creates a gulf between those meanings and contemporary applications. One is left with the bifurcation of "what it meant" and "what it means,"[5] without a clear way to relate the two. As with any science, the assumptions that historical criticism makes define the parameters of its possible answers. We could equally well focus on the way meanings are conveyed between settings within a tradition at its various stages, for this is an equally historical inquiry, though of a different sort. That is the option to which Childs is pointing with respect to the reference to Antiochus. The reception of material within the scriptural tradition is a historical inquiry that lends itself naturally to the hermeneutical question, as I will argue in more detail in the next section. It suffices to point out that, while historical criticism offers insight into individual passages, due to the predetermined confines of the historical-critical enterprise, it offers surprisingly little help in the interpretation of the meaning of the book as a whole.

On the subject of the intellectual presuppositions, and so the limits, of historical criticism, let us bear one further observation in mind. Entailed within this discipline is a sociological interest. As Dan. 1–2 illustrates, what one will or won't eat, and what one will and won't worship, are directly related to the maintenance of a community's boundaries. Likewise the ideology of apocalyptic, as we find in Dan. 7–12, serves to maintain the hope of the oppressed community and so to maintain identity in the face of such suffering. Resurrection in Dan. 12 provides a theodicy after the loss of "the righteous" of the Maccabees and so overcomes communal despair. In all three cases sociology has its say. These

---

5. The classic example of this is the hard distinction made by Krister Stendahl in his article on contemporary biblical theology in the 1962 edition of *The Interpreter's Dictionary of the Bible*, ed. G. A. Buttrick et al. (New York: Abingdon, 1962), 1.418–32.

examples are observations on the role of passages from a perspective outside that of the community's own reading of the text. Such observations are presented as value free and, as such, assume a relativistic perspective. Jew and Babylonian, Jew and Seleucid, they are each in their own way involved in "boundary definition" and "social identity construction."

Sociology offers helpful explanatory insight, especially into the exilic condition. But it needs the complement of a reading that moves from the sympathy and identification derived from a shared and ongoing tradition of interpretation, for in Dan. 1 and Dan. 7 the issues of boundary and identity are anything but value free; they are matters of life and death. "By the waters of Babylon— / there we sat down and there we wept. . . . / How could we sing the LORD's song / in a foreign land?" (Ps. 137:1, 4) is at the end of the day no social-scientific observation.

One could make the same kind of observation about the concept of culture, which has become the central concept for understanding religious practices. Appeals to contextualization in contemporary culture suffer from this very same confusion about the limits of sociological observation. Daniel can provide insight into the relationship between such observations about identities and cultures in theological discourse and the life-or-death judgments between them that conflicts like those in Babylon and Jerusalem entail.

All this being said, sociology does raise one most apposite question. As indicated, the original settings of much of Daniel involved suffering and danger for believers. While all are required to make their witness, situations threatening the martyrdom of blood are distinctive. Here sociology provokes a hermeneutical question that is the inverse of Ps. 137: how may the message of Daniel be heard in a church at ease? Are there times and situations in the church's life that, due to hardship, are simply more open to hearing Daniel? We might ask a similar question about eschatological texts such as Dan. 12. The faith of the church is that the whole of the scripture speaks to the whole of human history, but some churches whose circumstances resemble Daniel's suffering may have a "preferential option" in its interpretation.

Christians Reading Daniel: Exegetical Assumptions

What is theological exegesis? This commentary on Daniel is part of a deliberate series of theological commentaries, though it may be easiest at the outset to say what these volumes are not. This work makes no claim whatsoever to expertise in the voluminous and specialized field of historical criticism of the book; I am myself a grateful student of the best recent commentaries in this vein. Theological interpretation, however, implies more than technical modesty. Theological exegesis, while open to the insights of the historical-critical method, at the same time feels free to pick those fruits judiciously and to place the whole of the tree in a larger garden—namely, interpretation at the service of the Christian church.

100

That latter service in turn involves two related, material assumptions. First, it requires interpretation in a canonical mode. The most obvious and persuasive are cases in which New Testament texts actually offer interpretations of Danielic passages—for example, in the treatment of the "abomination of desolations" in 2 Thess. 2. More generally, we assume that, for all its redactional history, Daniel is a single work, within a coherent collection called the Old Testament, within the wider unity that is the whole Bible as Christians know it. Childs, a pioneer in the reclamation of this venerable way of reading, always balanced this emphasis on coherence with an admonition to respect the seams within a work, its stress points, and the distinctive message each book conveys; I aim to honor this advice. For early catholic Christianity, and for us as well, the canonical assumption entailed a christological (i.e., creedal) assumption. For orthodox Christianity, theological exegesis is simply the assumption that the one God referred to in the text is Father, Son, and Spirit, though the implications of such an assumption are anything but simple.

These starting points are not arbitrary, but represent the reclaiming of a way of reading that characterized the norm for most of the church's history. It entails paying more attention than is customary these days to commentators prior to the modern period. These voices of the great tradition are hardly in agreement, as the fiercely polemical interpretations of the abomination in Daniel will remind us. A careful friendship with historical criticism, canon, Christology, and listening to the premoderns are the fundaments of theological exegesis, though how the resulting confections appear will vary, as this series will attest.

Surely the determined historical critic would not contest the freedom of believers to read the book in a manner serviceable for their own community. The retort would be, however, that this is arbitrarily to impose a meaning on an ancient text and so to make of the church an intellectual ghetto, a hermetically sealed post-modern subworld. The most obvious reply is that the Christian reader believes himself or herself actually to stand in continuity with the people of Israel who first heard the story of Shadrach, Meshach, and Abednego (contested though this claim too would be).

Second, the Christian reader does not disregard the conclusions of historical criticism, nor does he or she impose meanings arbitrarily superimposed on the text. For it is at the very points of ambiguity and interpretive impasse that an explicitly Christian interpretation often sets to work. How are we to understand Nebuchadnezzar, who appears in stories written in contexts later than his historical home? What is the relationship between the Chaldean mantic arts and Daniel's wisdom? And what place then do they have in Yahweh's world rule? How do Daniel's moral exhortations relate to its set schemas of history? Who is the fourth who appears in the fire? Who is "one like the Son of Man"? What is his relation to the "saints of the most high"? And what is the scope of the "resurrection" spoken of? The ongoing process of editing and internal interpretation is included in what theology means by "inspiration." The meaning of a passage is enhanced by what follows: tension between passages can be fruitful; ambiguities can open a direction for interpretation. Taking the whole book seriously takes nothing away from criticism, but rather makes it historical in a deeper and more extended sense.

We can go a step further. The Christian exegete must make good on this most basic claim by making an overarching argument that the book and its interpretation shows an inherent trajectory. The "one like the Son of Man"[6] coming to "the Ancient of Days"[7] in Dan. 7 may have had one reference in its original form, yet another in the completed book, yet another in its decisive reception into Rev. 5, and yet another when the church came to articulate its doctrine of the Trinity. The task of the commentator is to show how each stage invites the next, how all the stages together form such a trajectory.

This manner of reading has an obvious affinity to theories of interpretation that have built on the idea of "the history of effects," especially as found in philosopher Hans-Georg Gadamer. What a passage means is not encased in its original setting and intention, but possibilities are opened up by the ongoing history of interpretations. While something similar is assumed here, in this project one particular stream of effects is being privileged, accompanied by an implied claim that reading the world through its lens gives the best account of reality. This implies another kind of trajectory, from the task of the exegete to that of the systematician.

As Gadamer himself would agree, however, it is an error to suppose that the "how" of exegesis, interpretive method, can be worked out in an introduction and then applied to the text. In the act of reading as a Christian and for the church, these issues become crises or resolutions. Daniel itself has been a prime battlefield for the very issues at hand. Edward Pusey thought the abandonment of Babylonian dating of the book to be the Rubicon of interpretation's battle with modernism. His assumption was that a denial of the Babylonian origins of the book rendered its witness untrustworthy.[8] While he was mistaken to draw the line in the sand there, he was surely right to see an issue of life-or-death importance for the health of the church at stake in the reading of a book like Daniel, though the location of the decisive battle line has to be determined.[9] Key questions for theological exegesis are found dramatically and repeatedly in Daniel: What are we to do with debates over dating? What are we to do with passages traditionally understood as messianic? What is the relationship between resurrection as it appears in Dan. 12 and what Christians have come to say about it? In other words, it is as we answer

---

6. The NRSV translates this phrase "one like a human being," with "one like the son of man" in the margin. Out of deference to tradition, I use "one like the Son of Man" throughout this commentary.

7. The NRSV translates this phrase as "the Ancient One," with "the Ancient of Days" in the margin. Out of deference to tradition, I use "the Ancient of Days" throughout this commentary.

8. Edward Pusey, *Daniel the Prophet* (Oxford: Parker, 1864). The recent commentary by Andrew Steinman, *Daniel* (St. Louis: Concordia, 2008), revives Pusey's tack by arguing that the denial of Daniel's Babylonian context undercuts the claim that the God of Israel truly rules history.

9. Christopher Seitz, *Figured Out: Typology and Providence in Christian Scripture* (Louisville: Westminster John Knox, 2001), 16–18.

some of these concrete exegetical questions that the methodological questions will come into better focus.

Contemporary Christians Reading Daniel: A Unique Point of View

The opening verses of 1 Peter state: "Peter, an apostle of Jesus Christ, To the exiles of the Dispersion in Pontus, Galatia, Cappadocia, Asia, and Bithynia, who have been chosen and destined by God the Father and sanctified by the Spirit to be obedient to Jesus Christ." The strange thing about the New Testament as a whole is that its audience, these chosen exiles, included Gentiles. How do we hear the scriptures when we are by faith Israel and by blood Gentiles among whom Israel is dispersed? To put the matter in Danielic terms, the Gentile believer who hears the New Testament is both kin to Daniel the Jew, who must be faithful amid hostile and uncomprehending peoples, and a Gentile now drawn into worship of the one true God. He or she occupies several locations in the story at the same time. The faithful Gentile is now in the train of victory and praise of the nations for King Jesus, and the dual hearing this will require makes Daniel complex and fruitful.

Matters get more complex still for the contemporary Christian. We might easily suppose that references to Israel are simply references to the church without remainder. Surely the Gentile Christian is meant to hear Dan. 1 as an exhortation to preserve the distinctiveness of his or her faith in an alien environment and to hear Dan. 12 as a reassurance that on the last day he or she will find that faithfulness rewarded. But it would be a mistake to elide the continuing Jewish people as a possible referent. Paul's speculation about the final restoration of Israel in Rom. 11 takes Dan. 12 as one of its starting points. Though it adds another layer of complexity, keeping Judaism in the picture as a referent is one way that the book has its own contribution to make, whose Jewish reading cannot be supposed to be superfluous now that the "one like a Son of Man" has come.

Christian witness to God and his reign among the nations, what we call "mission," and resulting conversion have produced this unique perspective on the believing Gentiles. A precondition for this mission was the dispersion of Israel among the nations, on whose perils and opportunities Daniel reflects. Since witness, kingship, and dispersion among the Gentiles are the abiding concerns of the book, Daniel has a particular relevance to the subject of Christian mission. Nebuchadnezzar is a sporadically violent idolater, and yet he enjoys listening to Daniel: How should faithful Israel of the last times relate itself to the Gentile world prone to such mood swings? What is the relationship between active witnessing and "sealing the scrolls"? One could multiply the questions. A pervasive objective of this commentary, then, will be to relate its Christian reading of Daniel to the history and theory of Christian mission.

This additional interest suggests a way of understanding the interpretive task. I will offer a way of reading eschatological texts that amounts to a reworking of the traditional medieval fourfold senses, though one would not want to be compelled to find all four senses in every passage. The flexibility of the earlier method that accompanied the *lectio divina* is appealing.[10] The stage of *explicatio* begins by considering the literal sense, which involves assessing the gains and quandaries of historical-critical debates as well as the trajectory that suggests itself from the series of interpretations of the canonical tradition. The stage of *meditatio* involves the free play of the imagination once the doctrinal and salvation-historical assumptions of the Christian community are brought to bear upon the passage. What echoes resound, and what intratextual developments suggest themselves in books of the New Testament? What would Christian midrash, in the same spirit as the midrash found within Daniel itself, look like? Finally, in the stage of *applicatio* I will suggest moments in the history of the Christian witness among the nations that illustrate points made in Daniel or that can be better understood when Daniel's light is brought to bear.

Gentiles in the Old Testament

Most Christians who are not recent converts do not think of themselves as Gentiles, and so, first and most obviously, to read Daniel is to recall this aspect of our identity. This leads us to ask what the Old Testament's assumptions about Gentiles are, for these assumptions form an essential background to the book's message. The verdict of the early chapters of Genesis is mixed. All are made in the image of God, and all share a single ancestor, Adam. All prove rebellious and are punished by the flood. Still, the various descendants of Noah have a variety of languages, lands, and skills, and nothing in Gen. 10 suggests that these differences are in themselves the consequences of their sin. A vision of "one world," this protoimperialism, is linked to hubris against God's sole overlordship: the relevance to the Gentile dreams of world domination in Daniel is apparent. The multiplicity of nations is not itself sinful, rather there is something in the heart of the nations that, in overvaunting this difference, would overvaunt God as well.

As an aside, I note that beginning with the descendants of Noah, both Jewish and Christian commentators and theologians have acknowledged a modicum of justice among the Gentiles. In rabbinic tradition the Noachide covenant provided a road to relationship with the God of Israel scaled to the more limited capacity of the Gentiles.[11] In both traditions righteous Gentiles are identified in the subsequent history, figures such as Melchizedek and Job, who "implicitly" (to use the technical Latin theological term) display the theological virtues of believers. Both traditions were careful to find in the Gentiles a complex and (at

10. It is described appealingly in Jean Leclerq's *The Love of Learning and the Desire for God: A Study of Monastic Culture* (New York: American Library, 1962).
11. A good source is Michael Novak, *Jewish-Christian Dialogue: A Jewish Justification* (New York: Oxford University Press, 1989), chap. 1.

least) two-sided reality. This ambivalence also provides a backdrop for Daniel interpretation.

With the rebellion at Babel (which, let the reader note, is also Daniel's exilic home), the purpose of the story as a whole, the restoration of the sons and daughters of Adam and Eve to right relationship to the one God of all creation, is endangered. So in the very next chapter the divine strategy is unveiled, the calling of faithful Abram out from his people (the Chaldeans). He is to journey he knows not where, and the purpose of that journey is so that "all the families of the earth shall be blessed" (Gen. 12:3). His purpose is the biblical story's purpose, hence Abraham's archetypical role (Rom. 3; Heb. 11). So in the remaining chapters of Genesis the promise sojourns among the nations, often at great peril (not least because of Israel's own unfaithfulness). In the final section of the book, we learn of Joseph, an Israelite who finds himself abandoned and thrown in the midst of a powerful and hostile Gentile kingdom, Egypt. Combining cleverness with faithfulness, he survives, indeed rises to power. Possessed of wisdom, especially in the interpretation of dreams, he provides saving insight for his own people. Commentators throughout Christian history have pointed out that Daniel is presented as an exilic Joseph.

Joseph is an exemplar of wisdom, *hochmah*, that insight into how the world really is and works that allows him to prevail while maintaining his integrity. The Old Testament canon bears a considerable debt to the Gentiles in the area of wisdom. Historical criticism shows actual borrowing from its neighbors; considerable sections of Proverbs seem devoted to secular know-how, with no apparent reliance upon belief in the one true God. Yet the message of that book, with its repeated insistence that "the fear of the LORD is the beginning of knowledge," is that true wisdom sees that all reality is the creation of the one true God. This same rooting of wisdom in faith in God is the point of the nestling of wisdom literature within the canon itself. Joseph again serves as an exemplar, for he proves himself adept in a worldly sense, though the reader learns that what matters most is what the God in whom he trusts is doing through him.

Daniel as the exilic Joseph is also an exemplar of the real wisdom that knows its origin—and in Daniel's case, its end—in the purposes of the God of Israel. At this point too, debates among historical critics prove theologically suggestive. Some question the relationship between classical prophecy and the emergence of apocalyptic literature. Others, following especially Gerhard von Rad,[12] offer conjectures about possible roots of apocalyptic literature in wisdom literature. Daniel is a key text. It is included in the prophetic books; it is considered the first biblical example of apocalyptic.[13] Daniel himself is preeminently "versed in every

---

12. Gerhard von Rad, *Old Testament Theology*, trans. D. M. G. Stalker, 2 vols. (New York: Harper & Row, 1962–65), 2.306.

13. Michael Shepherd, *Daniel in the Context of the Hebrew Bible* (New York: Peter Lang, 2009), cites Joseph Blenkinsopp's view that both the Law and the Prophets conclude with the expectation of the "prophet to come" (Moses, Elijah). Shepherd also cites John Sailhamer, who shows how at the outset

branch of wisdom" (1:4, 17), one who has the Joseph-like wisdom to interpret dreams. It is as if these categories were fused and surpassed in the book of Daniel itself. For our present purposes of setting out the background concerning the Gentiles, it suffices to show Gentile wisdom even in its worldliness is to be borrowed but reframed. It amounts, as we shall see, to a kind of canonical archetype of what contemporary jargon calls "contextualization."

The significance of the Gentiles cannot be captured simply under the category of what we call "culture." Daniel is a book about kings, and the central dynamic of its plot is the question: Who is the true king of the whole world? It is neither incidental nor innocent that the nations have kings, as Samuel was at pains to point out to Saul and God's people (1 Sam. 8:10–18). The presumption and consolidation of power that is kingship are constitutive aspects of the nations. If, then, we are providing an overview of the role of the nations in the Old Testament, pride of place must go to Pharaoh. The exodus of the people of Israel away from his cruel domination is the paradigm in relation to which the exilic prophets would understand God's deliverance of the people once more from among the nations, only this time yet more gloriously (see, as examples among many, Isa. 40; Jer. 32; Ezek. 34).

Pharaoh functions as a foil to Moses and as the occasion, in the story of the exodus, for the display of Yahweh's glory. One purpose of the saving act is so that "the Egyptians shall know that I am the LORD" (Exod. 7:5). The goal of the story is glory, the acknowledgement of Yahweh in praise, and it is toward this end that Pharaoh's heart must be hardened (in spite of the conundrums this would create for later Christian theologians worrying over the relationship between free will and election). One could offer the same estimation of the purpose of the book of Daniel as a whole: the rightful offering of glory and praise to the God of Israel by the nations, beginning with the prideful king himself. Only now the scope of this Gentile praise is much wider, as the book imagines a comprehensive act of praise as history itself is summed up. In this universal expansion of the scope of Gentile praise, Daniel may be seen as a continuation and development of a theme found in the exilic chapters of Isaiah. In both cases a preexisting prophetic theme in relation to the Gentiles is developed, for already in Isa. 2 we find the hope for the "latter days" that the nations would flow into Zion, which exists for the praise of the God of Israel.

The repeated prophetic theme of the new exodus points out another way in which Gentile material was appropriated yet changed. Von Rad placed at the heart of his Old Testament theology the "historicizing" of myth.[14] Cosmogony, the mythic origins of the world in the divine slaying of the monster of chaos, is

---

of the Prophets and Writings the wise scribe meditates on Torah, whose most recent witness was that very prophet. Taken together, these witnesses, as Shepherd sees it, show that "the composition of the Hebrew Scriptures at critical junctures is messianic, eschatological, and faith-oriented" (5–6). No matter whether Daniel's roots are prophetic or wisdom related, or both, the two now present, within the Old Testament canon, a framework of meaning within which we can see the importance of Daniel's message about the one coming on the clouds in the end time.

14. Von Rad, *Old Testament Theology*, 1.136–65.

tamed and transformed in the splitting of the Red Sea, though one can still see evidence of the appropriation in verses like Ps. 74:12–13: "Yet God my king is from of old, / working salvation in the earth. / You divided the sea by your might; / you broke the heads of the dragons in the waters." A divine victory is at the heart of Israel's identity, as also with the nations, but the difference is that Israel's victory has taken place in the realm of human events, and its main actor is the God of Israel who created and rules the world. The victory from the middle of the nations, about which Daniel, like the other exilic prophets, speaks, is patterned in the same way, though now the exodus has become the type of something greater. (And so the line of interpretation is opened for reading the canon of the two Testaments together.) As we shall see, this insight is an important element of the background for Daniel, since the book will allude to the older cosmogonic themes—for example, in the emergence of the beasts of Dan. 7 from the raging waters. This should not be seen as an attempt to remythologize, but rather it alludes to other Israelite texts as it reinforces the scope of the Lord's coming act.

The primal chaos raged, the Red Sea raged, and in a similar way in Daniel the kings' rage expresses that of the nations in general. This rage includes the violence and disorder of that which does not know the rule of the God of creation. For this reason, when the world finally comes to obey and praise the Lord, even the seas will, with their roaring, praise him (e.g., Ps. 96:11; 98:7). In the imagination of Israel rage was associated with the turbulence of Sheol and the bestiality of the subhuman, animal order. Bulls, wild dogs, and boars run wild and destroy in the Psalms, as do the nations who resist God and would destroy his appointed ones: "Why do the nations conspire / and the peoples plot in vain? / The kings of the earth set themselves, / and the rulers take counsel together, / against the LORD and his anointed" (Ps. 2:1–2). Clearly this passage forms an important part of the allusive background for Daniel, especially for the insane, bestial rage of Nebuchadnezzar in Dan. 3. In fact one could compare this chapter to the bestial rage of the creatures crawling from the primal lagoon in Dan. 7; this rage is a leitmotif for the book as a whole. For Daniel the Gentile world is revealed as disordered madness, and its kings display this most vividly.

The message of Daniel is that, though the nations rage and their rulers descend to the bestial, all remains within the hand of God. So our account of the theme of uncontrollable rage must be tempered in two ways. First, the nations are "the rod of [the Lord's] anger" (Isa. 10:5), which he, who rules the nations and human history, uses to chastise Israel for its sins. But when this chastisement is done, the Lord is free to judge those same nations for their own pride (as the oracles against the nations in the prophets remind us in profusion). And second, as we have seen, this raging is matched by a yearning in the Gentile heart. Nebuchadnezzar enjoys listening to Daniel, rewards his wisdom, and finally repents of his evil in order to be healed of his madness. Even the evil Belshazzar rewards him when he prophesies woe, though Daniel forswears the honor from such a king's hand. Raging and longing: Daniel's interactions with kings will display this twofold reality repeatedly.

Canonical Reading: Arteries Running to the "Little Apocalypse" and to Revelation

Canonical reading requires reading each book within the larger body of the canon as a whole. This task is aided by the vast "circulatory system" of allusion to earlier texts. Behind virtually every chapter of Daniel is some text that the author is re-applying in a manner that has come generally to be called "midrashic." Likewise, while references and allusions in the New Testament to the Old are ubiquitous, the relationship between Daniel and two New Testament texts deserves special mention, since we find there explicit borrowing from and appeal to Daniel.

Concerning the book of Revelation, Richard Bauckham goes so far as to say "a consistent and complete exegesis of Daniel 7 lies behind [John's] work."[15] Bauckham understands Revelation as a traditional *testimonium*, a defense of the faith by appeal to assembled texts of scripture, in this case a series of Danielic-style visions. In other words, within the intratextual system of scripture, a major artery runs directly from Daniel to Revelation, the book that closes the canon. We are invited to interpret the two books in relation to one another and to bring our conclusions to bear on our understanding of the whole. To demonstrate this close and telling connection I will follow Bauckham's lead in three areas of direct dependence.

Daniel closes with the angelic command to seal the scroll. Daniel has done his duty and may now rest (12:9–13). The determined time must come to completion, while the faithful and the evil each go their ways. Presumably at some undisclosed time the scroll can be opened. Revelation refers directly to this passage, for, just as the angel raised his arm to heaven in Dan. 12:7 at the time of sealing, so in Rev. 10:5 he raises it once again as he tells John to "take the scroll that is open" (10:8). In other words, Revelation picks up the suspended action in order to interpret and complete the Danielic oracles. Revelation 10:5 answers not only the "when" question, but also the "what" question. What is written on the scroll now unsealed? The angel of Rev. 10 tells us that, with the seventh trumpet blast, "the mystery of God would be fulfilled." *Mystērion*, here as elsewhere in the New Testament, should be understood as the salvific deeds of God hidden from eternity but now enacted and revealed (compare, e.g., its use in Eph. 1:9–10: "the mystery of his will . . . as a plan for the fullness of time"). As in Daniel, so in Revelation, that mystery is the coming of the kingship of the God of Israel, though now the identity of Christ, who has brought it about, is revealed.[16] The saving deed sealed in Daniel is opened in Revelation.

15. Richard Bauckham, *The Climax of Prophecy: Studies in the Book of Revelation* (Edinburgh: T&T Clark, 1993), 329.
16. It is worth noting that this is the second appearance of the scroll in Revelation. John has wept that it is still sealed in 5:4–6 and is reassured by the angel that the Lion of Judah, the wounded Lamb, Jesus Christ, has come to open it. Then the seven seals are opened and the seven trumpets sounded, which commences the process of opening that comes to its culmination with the opening in Rev. 10. I take the chapters' account together as a single, ritually and symbolically ornate, opening of the Danielic scroll.

The second direct and extended appeal to Daniel is of course the coming of the one like the Son of Man to the Ancient of Days at the coming of his kingdom, found in both Dan. 7:13–14 and Rev. 5:6–10. In the latter account we find additions: the Lamb with the seven horns and eyes, the living creatures, the twenty-four elders, the blood of ransom, and the nations now providing a new priesthood for the earth (note a fusing of elements from Daniel and from Exod. 19 and Exod. 24, the other major imaginative source for the vision). More will be said in the commentary itself, but the point is simply this: the great opening vision of Revelation is the Danielic scene embellished and interpreted. The stage for Dan. 7 and Revelation is one and the same. The connection is so close that the two books must be interpreted canonically in tandem, each with an eye to the other.

The third direct appeal to Daniel may be found in Revelation's focus, beginning in the throne scene itself, on the destiny of the Gentiles. In both books the coming of the Son of Man to the Ancient of Days is the occasion for the delivery of the nations to the throne in order that they might serve and worship the true God. Here too Revelation adds even as it borrows. In Revelation God brings in the kingdom by means of the Gentile mission, in the wake of the victory of the wounded Lamb. Mission causes neither the victory nor the coming of the kingdom, but it is their effective sign. While in Daniel the faithful must patiently endure suffering, in Revelation martyrdom takes on an added importance in obedience to the crucified Lord. Oscar Cullmann convincingly argues that the rider on the white horse in Rev. 6:2, coming "conquering and to conquer," is in fact Christian mission.[17] The victory of the Lamb, martyrdom, and eschatological watchfulness are here inextricably bound up with mission, and as I shall argue below, their nexus washes back on our understanding of its precursor, Daniel.

In Daniel the nations will be delivered to God as his kingdom comes in spite of the crushing of God's own people in history. In the scenes that follow the unsealing of the scroll in Rev. 10, this delivery and this crushing are related directly to Christian mission. Even as the holy ground is marked out in 11:1, the "trampl[ing]" (11:2) of the faithful has begun. So far the picture is fully Danielic. The added missionary dimension may be seen clearly in the following chapters: when the Danielic Son of Man appears on the clouds, he now has a sickle in hand, to bring in the harvest (14:14).[18]

The witness of believers drawn from the nations who are ready to suffer as their Lord did is an important new element that the open scroll reveals. With this added element comes a more developed picture of what the inclusion of the nations in the worship of the God of Israel will look like. Recall that the diversity

---

17. Oscar Cullmann would have us read the verse in conjunction with 19:11, where we are reminded that the victory is Christ's and the conquest not of a sort that the world of power and violence understands; "Eschatology and Missions in the New Testament," in *The Background of the New Testament and Its Eschatology: In Honour of Charles Harold Dodd*, ed. W. D. Davies and D. Daube (Cambridge: Cambridge University Press, 1956), 415–16.

18. Bauckham, *Climax of Prophecy*, 294–96.

of the nations was not the problem in Gen. 10, but rather the imperial hubris of the tower of Babel. With the fall of "Babylon" (Rev. 18), here representing Rome and symbolizing all presumptions of empire, the nations in their diversity can be restored to their rightful dignity. So the light of the Lamb in the new Jerusalem will bring into it "the glory and the honor of the nations" (21:26). A few lines later the waters of life, reminiscent of the springs of the new temple in Ezek. 47, now flowing in the streets of the city, supply the tree of life, and so now serve for "the healing of the nations" (Rev. 22:2). The contrast with the presumptuous tree of Dan. 4 cannot be accidental. As the nations are gathered for God's rightful praise by Christian mission, they are healed and restored to the state intended in creation.

The New Testament concludes with the vision of the kingdom, which also cannot be understood without reference to Daniel. Revelation offers explicit answers to both the "when" and "what" questions about the kingdom, and to these is added a new answer to the "how" question—namely, mission—along with a more robust account of the final destiny of the nations.

The second direct, arterial New Testament reference to Daniel is found in the passage called by scholars the "Little Apocalypse," found in Mark 13 and redacted in both Matt. 24 and Luke 21. I will consider the latter, fuller accounts. Jesus, sitting on the Mount of Olives (so as to remind us of the eschatological prophecy of the battle with the Gentiles in Zech. 14), foretells the coming final distress (in a manner allusive of his own distress and death in the coming hours). He combines his Danielic interpretation with an allusion to the judgment against Babylon at the hands of the Medes in Isa. 13: the tumult of nations, agony as a woman in childbirth, and the darkening of the sun, moon, and the stars. In this context our Lord's discourse offers two direct interpretations of Daniel: "So when you see the desolating sacrilege standing in the holy place, as was spoken of by the prophet Daniel (let the reader understand), then those in Judea must flee to the mountains" (Matt. 24:15–16). The incomparable distress of Dan. 12:1 will accompany this disaster (Matt. 24:21), until, in fulfillment of Dan. 7:13–14, the Son of Man comes on the clouds in glory and summons his elect. Clearly for Jesus both Dan. 7 and Dan. 9 have future references relevant to his disciples.[19]

Other verses in the Little Apocalypse also assume a Danielic background, even as they counsel what we might call "hermeneutical reserve." We are encouraged to learn "from the fig tree" that the season of fulfillment, of flowering, is coming (Matt. 24:32). In fact Jesus's words, and the words of scripture he interprets, such as those from Daniel, are more lasting than "heaven and earth" themselves, and so history must be conformed to them (24:35). At the same time, we are warned against following false Christs or prophets (24:23). We are told that it is out of mercy that God has shortened the days (24:22), for otherwise no one could have survived. As some in the history of Daniel's interpretation pointed out, this cutting

---

19. To this we may add the direct references to Dan. 8–9 in Jesus's prediction of the nations' assault on Jerusalem in Luke 21:20, 24.

short may mean that the number schemes offered by Daniel have been changed, out of mercy, by God himself.[20] This is a salutary warning against excessive interest in this aspect of Daniel to the exclusion of its larger purpose. In a similar vein, we are warned against too much attention to knowing "that day and hour" (Matt. 24:36).[21] Suddenness and surprise accompany his lordship. Instead Jesus places the emphasis on the virtue of watchfulness: "You also must be ready, for the Son of Man is coming at an expected hour" (24:44). As I shall describe in more detail in the commentary itself, the reception of Daniel in the Gospels offers specific guidance especially for reading the numerology of the former.

Central Thesis: The Interpretive Center and Structure of the Book

When it comes to the exegesis of scripture, we ought to be distrustful of interpretive centers, lest we impose a principle on the varied messages of the book and render ourselves deaf to how the text itself goes. And at the same time, one might criticize a christological hermeneutical key as so self-evident as to contribute little. Undeterred by these warnings, I offer the following thesis as a way to order and focus our observations. The thematic center (and almost the actual center of the text) of Daniel is the coming of the "one like a Son of Man" to the Ancient of Days in Dan. 7, to whom is delivered "all peoples, nations, and languages" (7:14) in a triumphal procession to his praise. The image of the nations delivered over to Christ confirms Ps. 68's reference to "leading captives in your train" and is then received in Paul's Epistle to the Ephesians, where it is connected to Paul's ministry to the Gentiles, the need for unity, all in service to the ascended lordship of Christ (4:4–10).

Of equal importance are the ways in which Daniel, read through this lens of an ascension Christology, fills out the picture on other fronts. First, the place of the Gentiles and the mission to them are knit irrevocably to Christology. The Gentile mission is given a particular location in salvation history, and so a particular motive: the nations are to be gathered for triumphal praise. Second, the witness of Daniel insists that this center be understood as the converse of the "other story" in human history, the seeming triumph of the kingly beasts, their anomic rage, and the resulting destructive exile of the people of God. The breaking down of the elect and their scattering is a precondition for this triumph. We might even speak, in imitation of Luther, of a "history of glory" and a "history of the cross" with two simultaneous and opposite senses of "victory." A procession of worldly glory by the kingdom of oppression is the occasion for the real procession of the

20. E.g., George Joye, *The Exposicion of Daniel the Proheete Gatherd oute of P. Melanchthon, Iohan Ecolamadius, Chronrade Prllciane and out of Iohan Draconite* (London: J. Daie and W., 1550), 240–41, on cutting short the days as with Noah.

21. The suggestion, first heard from William Tyndale, that we cannot know day and hour but can reckon month and year, gives rise to end-time speculation to this day, but surely misses the point of the verse!

glory of the coming kingdom of God. There is no missiology without Christology (and vice versa), even as there is no Christology without staurology.

In Dan. 7–12 the Son of Man is representative of and, so, inclusive of the elect people in a way that informs a Christian understanding of the church as the *totus Christus*, the whole reality that is Christ. We will also see the important role of the angelic realm, of the "powers and principalities," in ways that were familiar to both the New Testament and many global Christians, but have been occluded from the view of many Western Christians. To follow this pattern, there can be no missiology and Christology without ecclesiology and cosmology. It will be the business of the commentary as a whole to give a fuller theological account of these gnomic utterances.

The ascension Christology of Dan. 7 as the hermeneutical key for the book is reinforced by the structure of the chapters. In other words, this claim is not arbitrarily dropped upon the work, but makes sense of its own ordering. The first chapter introduces the work as a whole, as it opens with the historical and theological premise of all that will follow: exile. The action is set firmly among the Gentiles, who are to be led captive in praise. The last chapter, by contrast, establishes where not only Daniel's story, but the whole human story, is going. It insists on an eschatological horizon for all history. Exile and final judgment, problem and solution, are firmly in God's hand, and both involve a salvation history that no longer depends on Zion in an earthly sense.[22] The chaos that follows is bounded by God in both time and place.

Within these bounds, the house is built around the twin beams of Dan. 2, which lays out the vision of the four beastly kingdoms, and Dan. 7, which recapitulates the vision and adds its dramatic resolution. The chapters that follow each amplify themes found in the two. Daniel 2's picture of a confused, raging, searching Gentile king is followed by traditions involving similar accounts of Nebuchadnezzar or his successors. The chapters following Dan. 7 offer theme and variations on its periodized and symbolic account of persecution.

Concerning the question of the unity of Daniel as a whole, christological references have traditionally been found in virtually all the moral tales (Dan. 2–6), as well as references to the Son of Man and Messiah in the night visions (Dan. 8–12). Modern critics complain that the two halves sit uneasily together since they offer contrasting strategies to the "resident alien": in the first half accommodation, and in the second waiting for the predetermined end. But these two summaries are partial and unfair: in the first half the young men are ready to resist unto death, and, in the second half, Dan. 9 amounts to an exhortation to penitence and a return to faithfulness, hardly a recipe for determinism! We should not paper over the distinct differences in the two halves. But reading them together, with the

22. Here it is worth noting that at the conclusion of Revelation the new Jerusalem has no temple, since it has the Lamb at its center. This is in a sense the final working out of the exilic problem; i.e., how can the God of Israel be with us without Zion?

grain of the book's ordering as a whole, leads to greater insight. The whole offers two complementary approaches to exilic persecution, one involving how to act and the other how to think about the situation in which the Danielic believer finds himself or herself.

I can offer one more conclusion from my interpretive center of the book. Several of the abiding critical knots are related to some form of the "when" question. Was the book written in the Babylon of Nebuchadnezzar or the Jerusalem of Antiochus? Is the abomination to be located in the time of Nero, or Saladin, or Saddam Hussein? Without evacuating the valid place of critical work, the Christian interpreter somehow wants to say "all and none." The hermeneutical power of the work is related to the manner in which it illumines all those settings and more. Yet each setting threatens to become a straitjacket imposed over the text. We need a more specifically Christian account of time, one that again is not laid upon the text but grows out from it and the canon as a whole. In other words, the "when" question should be asked within the context of the question of "Christ and time,"[23] the impact of the ascended Christ on our understanding of the shape of history. Otherwise all the critical perplexities simply slip in through the backdoor of history sevenfold. The answer to the "when" question must be first the death, resurrection, and ascension of Jesus in fulfillment of the prophets; then, second, the end of time that those events anticipate. Third, it must be the continuous flow of events of human history, which are not simply blotted out or leveled by the event of Christ. Fourth, within that flow, the answer to "when" questions must include special times when, as it were, human history has bumped up against the final tribulation more directly than others. For all times are not the same; some convey that christological-eschatological reality behind and ahead of all history more powerfully than others. Only such an account of history, itself drawn in part from a Christian reading of Daniel, can make it possible for us fully to answer "when" questions. Here too we are reminded that content and method cannot be cleaved apart in biblical interpretation or theology.

A commentary ought not to have an argument, for it should follow the text itself where it goes, but it may have a perspective. As should now be clear, I intend to read Daniel as a whole, and as part of the whole canon. Daniel is a work in the apocalyptic genre; reading it whole overcomes some of the genre's problems. And reading the book in the canon contributes the strengths of that genre to the whole. Apocalyptic reminds us of the urgency of the faith and the sovereignty of our Lord, both of which we as church are in desperate need, and it acts as a challenge to the captivity of our own cultural assumptions.

Biblical scholarship rediscovered the apocalyptic strain in the nineteenth century, only to draw back, resolving apocalyptic into either historical-philosophical schemata or a history-dissolving existential immediacy. To avoid these pitfalls, we should read the book with the material center of the ascended Jesus Christ

23. Oscar Cullmann, *Christ and Time* (London: SCM, 1962).

constantly in view. Apocalyptic was the natural habitat of his historical first-century setting, and yet, ironically, it was systematic theology in the present era that awakened to the apocalyptic theme.[24] So we will also read the book in conversation with the voices of systematic theology in the past generation. Finally, we must read against the horizon of the question our own late-modern age has about the meaning and *telos* of history. This is ultimately the question of the possibility of a single destiny for, and so of the reconciliation of, the nations in history, whose false form, Daniel reminds us, is empire, its true form the *missio ad Gentes*. All the while, we seek not to forget that these are Judaism's questions too and that Daniel is the book of our cousins, from whom we can learn about exile and expectation.

On Interpreting Eschatological Texts

Who is the "little horn" of Dan. 7, or the "anointed one . . . cut off" in Dan. 9? And how do references to the impending end of all things affect our answers? Reading Daniel in a way that is at once cognizant of the historical criticism, of the canon as a whole, and of the ongoing tradition of interpretation, especially if we lend interpretive weight to Dan. 7–12, leads inevitably to the more general question of how we are to understand eschatological statements. What assumptions should reasonably be brought to the text? To ask this question is to bring one's reading of Daniel into conversation with systematic theology. What we find in the field of theology on this topic is highly conflicted. Some reinterpret future statements as existential states or as moments of glaring oppression. No less conflicted is how to relate eschatological claims to christological claims. We should not imagine theology dictating to the exegete how to interpret. Our reading of Daniel should also challenge and inform our doctrine of eschatology. A conversation between the two, with the tradition of interpretation as a horizon for both, is required to foster understanding.[25]

Let us begin with the plain sense of the text, informed by the results of historical criticism, but bearing in mind the ongoing tradition of postexilic reception and interpretation. What that tradition presents to us is a multilayered context of exile. From the original Babylonian setting through the succeeding kingdoms, down to the Maccabean setting, and on to the context in which Jesus himself spoke,[26] that is the category shared by all. (And this category works backward as well, so that Moses in Egypt or Adam expelled from the garden are exiles too in their own ways.) From the very first line of the book, that is the atmosphere for

---

24. Klaus Koch, *The Rediscovery of Apocalyptic* (London: SCM, 1972), rehearses how systematic theologians rediscovered apocalyptic when biblical scholars disregarded the theme (for their own reasons).

25. So Hans Georg Gadamer, *Truth and Method* (New York: Continuum, 1975), esp. 267–74.

26. For N. T. Wright's concept of the exile, see, e.g., his *Jesus and the Victory of God* (Minneapolis: Fortress, 1996), 123–31.

the whole work. Let us call this first horizon of interpretation *historical* in the widest and most variegated sense.

Growing in part out of this interpretation of the exilic context of hearing Daniel in the first century AD is the *christological* reading, according to which Dan. 7 refers to the risen and ascended Jesus Christ with the worshipful Gentile churches in his train. The strong relationship we have seen within the canon between Daniel and passages such as Mark 13 as well as the whole of Revelation confirms this second horizon. In this light his death, resurrection, and ascension are in a sense the end of the age toward which Daniel looks expectantly. A Christian and canonical reading of Daniel is, most fundamentally, this christological reading. This, however, does not mean that the usefulness of Daniel in its Old Testament context is left behind once we come to attain this christological fulfillment. The latter requires the former, in order for there to be a sense of what the exile, in its fullest sense, Christ has come to end, means. The fusion of these two horizons is entailed in canonical reading.

It is precisely this enduring importance of the witness of Daniel that leads to the third horizon in which the book must be read *eschatologically* in the proper sense, and the rest of the canon so read in light of the witness of Daniel. We must read Dan. 7–11 in light of Dan. 12 and its witness to a final and encompassing resurrection of the dead. Likewise all these chapters are heard repeatedly in the New Testament writings in relation to future and conclusive events—for example, in the later chapters of Revelation or in Jesus's advice to his followers, members of the persecuted church, and so on. Daniel as a whole and its reception serve to ensure the fully cosmic and future-oriented dimension of the interpretation of passages such as Dan. 7, and so of the canon as a whole. Understanding the ascension of Jesus, and the church that lives in its wake, from Daniel within the canon as a whole means preserving the truly future[27] aspect of eschatology. Here we may appeal to the hoary categories of "already" and "not yet," for they point to the meaningfulness of the claims about Jesus in light of the language of scripture found in Daniel (as well as elsewhere) depending precisely on the interplay between these two time frames. We cannot collapse interpretation into either history or Christology. There must remain a genuine third horizon. But this third cannot stray too far from the context of exile from which it is derived, nor can it devolve into speculation independent of our claims about Jesus Christ. The horizons impinge on one another. The last day is precisely the working out on a wider canvass of what we see in him, though "we see in a mirror, dimly" (1 Cor. 13:12) and "what we will be has not yet been revealed" (1 John 3:2).

So far we have been considering the interpretation in and between canonical texts. But there has been a strong reminder in contemporary theological hermeneutics of the act of interpreting itself. This may take a more *existential* or a more

---

27. This should include what I would call a future perfect sense, since, for some, futurity seems ever to remain tantalizingly ahead.

performative turn,[28] but in either case the meaning of the text cannot be abstracted from its utterance and enactment. The hearer is in some sort of exile of his or her own, is called to fall into the ascended Christ's train, and must confront his or her own death and judgment. This fourth horizon interacts, then, with each of the other three; it does not empty them into a mere subjectivity, but rather reminds us that their import is grasped only as we recall their *pro nobis* dimension. Otherwise Daniel declines into a source of information about second-century BC Jerusalem, or calculations of the end time by some historical scheme, or an example in the history of doctrine, and so on.

To understand eschatological statements in general, and passages of Daniel in particular, we need to consider them against these four horizons: the exilic/historical, the christological, the cosmic/futurist, and the existential/performative. I am not claiming that each verse's meaning may be confected by the amalgam of all four, nor that each passage has four meanings. But I am saying that rightly reading passages one might call eschatological bears all four in mind, implicitly or explicitly. They form a kind of interpretative field within which the Christian exegete must operate. They lend our readings grounding (the exilic), focus (the christological), scope (the cosmic), and import (the performative). As a result, a helpful heuristic test for a particular way of reading eschatological passages is to ask whether it is understood in some way or other against each of these four horizons.

Thinking about interpretation in light of eschatology is appropriate both to the doctrine's centrality to theology and New Testament studies in the past century, as well as its comportment with Daniel itself. But in fact these four horizons are closely aligned to a more traditional hermeneutic—namely the fourfold sense of scripture. The historical sense, especially in relation to the exile, corresponds to the literal sense, and christological interpretation falls under the rubric of typology. The performative is related to what the tradition called the tropological, and the eschatological proper is a subset of anagogical interpretation.

The Lens of Christian Mission

Within these four horizons or parameters, Daniel has a decisive influence on the nature of Christian mission. Most definitions of Christian mission are derived from what one would primarily have the enterprise do—save souls, work for justice, share cultures, and so on. Each of these activities is requisite in certain ways and at the right moments. But, in light of a reading of Daniel centered on Dan. 7, we may say that Christian mission per se is actually this: the gathering of the Gentiles in obedience at the end of time so as to praise the ascended Son of Man. Performative actions such as sharing the faith, working for justice, and so on are best defined christologically and eschatologically. Meanwhile the nations who are

28. In the terms of the philosophy of language, I refer here to what is called the "illocutionary sense."

being gathered are to understand themselves as "the exiles of the Dispersion" (1 Pet. 1:1), though they are to understand themselves as the children of Nebuchadnezzar too! Daniel 7 defines nothing less than the stage[29] on which mission is to take place. What is the import of this identity? First, its eschatological bearings serve as a check against overemphasis on accomplishments—works do not save, and our actions do not bring in the kingdom.[30] Second, the eschatological dimension is the guardian against all domestication and technologizing of Christian mission. The doxological *telos* serves to put other ends in their rightful order. Third and finally, it offers encouragement. Though it would seem that history is one long tale of woe, not least for and in the churches of Christ, what matters most, and is most telling, is the gathering in of the Gentiles taking place amid that travail. On this score we may think of the crushing of the church by whose martyrdom the gospel was spread—the rapid growth of the church in China confirms Tertullian's proclamation that the "blood of the martyrs is the seed of the church." Obviously disaster itself cannot then be turned into a vehicle of deliverance, for Dan. 7's unleashing of the monsters on the world is real, but so is the triumphant gathering in it.

My argument is that Daniel is an extended theological reflection on the status, purpose, and destiny of the Gentiles. The considerable range in their portrayal is suggested already in a passage like Ps. 2 ("the kings . . . take counsel . . . against the LORD" [2:2], until "the nations [are made God's] heritage" [2:8], and in the meantime "kings [should] be wise" [2:10]) but worked out in greater detail in Daniel. This question of what then to "do" theologically with the nations defines exilic and postexilic life and itself receives a range of answers in the scriptures, with the surprising salvific possibility of Isa. 40–55 and the exhortation to courage and wisdom of Esther exhibiting thematic resemblances. What is Israel to make theologically of the nations? Incomprehensible raging to articulate praise: this is at once the explanatory arc running from origins to eschaton, as well as present hope of the people of God. Rage and praise in Dan. 7 come into a surprising kind of relationship, the first creating the conditions, by the "left hand of God" as it were, for the second. Here we may find a trajectory all the way to the killing of the Son of Man Jesus at the hands of the Gentile beast Pilate, which was necessary so that he might be ascended and summon the nations to himself.[31]

In Daniel the "greatness and misery" (Pascal) of the Gentiles is revealed, both their "beastly" rebellion and their worshipful inclusion in the train of the ascended

29. On defining a *theatrum* for Christian mission, see Karl Barth, *Church Dogmatics*, vol. 4: *The Doctrine of Reconciliation* (Edinburgh: T&T Clark, 1961), 3/1.152–53, following Calvin. The idea of the stage on which the drama of salvation is played out is equally important in contemporary hermeneutics; see Kevin Vanhoozer, *The Drama of Doctrine* (Knoxville: Westminster, 2007).

30. Here we may include even some evangelical suggestions that the bringing in of members of the last "unreached people" will usher in the end—"it is not for you to know the times" (Acts 1:7). A technological version of the idea may be found in the writings of noted global mission demographer David Barrett.

31. C. H. Dodd, *The Apostolic Preaching and Its Development* (London: SCM, 1939), chap. 1.

Son of Man. This calling of the Gentiles is the purpose for what the Christian tradition calls "mission." We should be wary of finding a full-blown theology of mission in Daniel itself, where the centripetal theme may be found, but not yet the New Testament's full account of the centrifugal dynamic.[32] Still, if we listen to the book canonically, it can inform our own mission-related interests and impulses and so contribute toward such a theology of mission.

At this point a detour through some contemporary issues in missiology will illustrate how much the witness of Daniel has to contribute. I can summarize the contemporary movement in thinking about mission in the following way. There has been a desire to overcome mission's isolation, both from the rest of church life and to particular locales. Mission should be thought of as holistic—that is, involving the whole of the activities God calls us to—and inherent—that is, "built into" to the very nature of the Christian life—so that engagement in it should not be thought of as optional. (Hence the famous quotation from Emil Brunner that the church is for mission as a fire is for burning.) In churches in the West this has been combined with a dissatisfaction with the institutional church that seems obsessed with its own survival, in conjunction with a call to be a more self-consciously post-Constantinian and exilic community. The holistic and inherent impulses came to fullest expression in the 1950s and 1960s, when the idea of the *missio Dei*, of God's own mission (as opposed to ours), was prominent. We may find various contemporary expressions that return to this idea, most often appealing for a missional church. That the focus should be on God's will cannot be denied, and the desire to turn attention to his action in history strikes a note with the witness of Dan. 7–12.[33]

While the desire to perceive the missionary nature of the church is laudable, it entails certain problematic aspects. First, *missio* came to mean something like "God's will for the world," which comes to work itself out as "what God wants us to do in the world." As history teaches us, this can readily be equated with what we ourselves advocate.[34] Second, the language of mission as constitutive of God's

32. The classic case for Old Testament mission is H. H. Rowley's *Israel's Mission to the World* (London: SCM, 1939), while Johannes Blauw's *Missionary Nature of the Church* (London: Lutterworth, 1962) maintains the centrifugal versus centripetal contrast.

33. On the narrative and its relation to mission in the widest sense, see Lesslie Newbigin, *The Gospel in a Pluralist Society* (Grand Rapids: Eerdmans, 1989), chap. 8, and then, under his influence, Chris Wright's *Mission of God* (Downers Grove, IL: InterVarsity, 2006), a popular textbook that represents a theologically solid example of the missional idea. But it is so because it consistently maintains its salvation-historical bearings as well as the *pro nobis* thrust of the message. Wright takes seriously sin, spiritual struggle, the end, even as he espouses mission in what I have called its inherent and holistic dimensions. In so doing he offers a good example of a missiology that preserves what is desirable and eschews the flaws of such a *missio Dei* approach. His presentation in short respects the parameters for a mission theology that the witness of Daniel sets out.

34. This decline in the use of the *missio Dei* was opposed vigorously by Newbigin himself. See H. H. Rosin's *Missio Dei* (Leiden: Interuniversity, 1972) for the way the idea of the *missio Dei* degenerated into a tag for ideological causes in the 1960s, precisely because the mooring to the scriptural framework, as found in Dan. 7, was missing.

nature, and our participating in his mission, has its own systematic temptations.[35] Related to this problem is the tendency to see this mission in relation to God's triune nature (which is in fact where talk of *missiones* began); here missiology inherits the risks of abstract Trinity talk so prevalent in contemporary theology. Third and finally, the movement at times supposes that it can circumvent the question of the church, an impulse certainly not borne out in the whole witness of Daniel.

The major themes of mission appear in reflection on the witness of Daniel: divine providence, powers and principalities, political theology, cultural inter-action and diversity, and end-time expectation. But the book has something more important to offer than thematic fodder, for these themes need to be held together within an ascension framework or else one of them predominates and a lopsided account of mission results. Such a framework best enables us to see mission in the vista of human history under God's control. Such a framework is grounded not in an abstract concept, but in the specifics of the claim about the ascended Jesus in light of the Old Testament witness. Such a framework is the way to theologize mission and to missionize theology. To think through issues in such a Danielic and ascension-oriented framework means that the doctrines of Christology, cross, ecclesiology, and eschatology must all be brought together in a matrix in which the mission to the Gentiles can be thought through in relation to questions of history, theology, and global catastrophe, as well as an ongoing role for Israel. Here we find clearer and more trustworthy parameters for a mission that is holistic and inherent than in accounts based on abstract themes.

What is to be gained from such a perspective? The ascension is an event in the life of Jesus that draws the church of the nations to itself. As such it cannot be seen as simply separate from the history of the world, nor reducible to it: Dan. 7 reinforces this point. Engagement with the world is foremost the drawing of the Gentiles into the people of God, even as their shattering continues. Mission cannot be isolated as political ameliorization or organizational growth or indi-vidual redemption, but is first of all a dimension of that ascension plot. Likewise the nations cannot be eliminated, or spiritualized, or historicized, but remain the diverse strains of the single voice confessing the ascended Christ at once in history and eternity.[36]

---

35. One may note here one source of the conflation of God's mission and ours that we are worrying about. While it was understandable in modern Trinitarian theology to stress that the economic and the immanent referred to one and the same divine agent, the equation comes readily (perhaps as a result of an underlying Hegelian influence) to conduce toward a collapse of the latter into the former. This creates a climate of thought for authors at a remove from the Trinitarian debate itself, which lends itself to the erosion of the distinction between divine and human action. Systematic decisions do matter once their effects work their way into the food chain.

36. Particularly on this point I have benefited from Douglas Farrow's eloquent account of an ascen-sion theology in *Ascension and Ecclesia* (Grand Rapids: Eerdmans, 1999).

I have already shown how Daniel comes to be heard through, and so interpreted in light of, passages such as Mark 13.[37] The latter shows us Christian mission among the dire signs of the end of the world, an insight consonant with, but additional to, Daniel itself. Both Daniel and Mark 13 are safeguards against the activism and the Pelagianism that tempt Christian mission. (To be sure, one could conclude, as did the great Reformers, for example, that the divine initiative means that actual sending and calling are not required. But this is surely to misunderstand, from a different direction, what it means to say that God's action has priority; the right conclusion is not quietism.) Our own action is not the heart of our calling amidst the Gentiles; Daniel remains in its incompleteness and partiality a word awaiting the gospel fulfillment.

The witness of Daniel, then, is offered from the perspective simply of exiled Israel. It shows us the victory train of the Gentiles, but we do not yet understand fully its summons to salvation. Israel survives, and with the denouement the nations follow along in obedience to the one who truly reigns over them. But what we lack in Daniel may be seen most clearly if we consider the contrast with Isa. 40–55. There, albeit mysteriously, we are offered both the means of that offer, the Suffering Servant, and the occasion of their attraction, their being amazed at his death and return. Daniel tells us that the Gentiles are to come and worship, but how they are to be drawn is left an open question. In this way it serves as prelude to Christian mission as a part of the Old Testament canon, but only in concert with other voices. For this reason it seems apropos, as the commentary progresses, to offer examples from the history of Christian mission that illustrate and fill out our more general missiological observations.

---

37. On the connection with Daniel of Mark 13, as well as supplementary prophetic allusions, see Lars Hartmann, *Prophecy Interpreted* (Lund: Gleerup, 1966).

DANIEL 1

1:1 in the third year—The very first verse of Daniel asserts, in a straightforward manner, the fall of Jerusalem and, by implication, the Babylonian exile to come. It dates the events that follow by the reigning king, for we are dealing with a fact in the history of world powers and politics. But this verse serves a wider purpose, for that event is the premise for all that follows. From the outset, exile is the pervasive reality in which Daniel and his countrymen will have to find their way. Once we reach Dan. 7, the events foreseen in the night vision will pertain to Jerusalem of the future, and so subsequent to the exile. But then they will, in a sense, be even more under the thrall of Gentile kings yet more hostile than Nebuchadnezzar. So even those chapters are "exilic," for "exile" comes to describe the life for God's people "repairing breaches" and finding "a way in the desert" after the cataclysm, wherever they may find themselves.

For cataclysm it was. Some scholars argue that in historical terms it involved fewer people and less social disruption than the scriptures give us an impression of. But this misunderstands what we are being told, for it was a shattering of religious identity and spiritual hope, in the face of which the prophetic literature as a whole was eventually marshaled in order to explain and encourage. How could the Gentiles prevail against God's own city and temple?

Exile begins as a historical fact, but ripples outward in widening circles. It is easy to see Israel's prior history as a preexile, the expulsion from the garden, the patriarchs sojourning, servitude in Egypt, and the apostasy of kingship. It is as if only with this event can Israel see the full distress of the state of their relationship to Yahweh; as such it bears to them a terrible gift of insight. N. T. Wright is particularly persuasive in arguing that "exile" was the continuing category under which Jews of Jesus's time understood their own oppressed existence. Jesus himself is drawn to exilic references to explain his own ministry.[1] The category is so pervasive in the subsequent history of Judaism that one of its most renowned scholars understands all of its different groups as alternate understandings of the term.[2]

The history of Christian interpretation has tracked this trajectory of extended senses of exile. "O come, O come Emmanuel, and ransom captive Israel, who mourns in lonely exile here," cries the sixth-century hymn of Fortunatus, in what we might call exile's soteriological sense. As with the sixth-century exiles, our sins have driven us far from the state for which God intended us.

Distance is now something that the people of God share with their Gentile captors, who are "without God" (Eph. 2:12), the difference being that God's people know of the home they have lost. Exile is, properly speaking, something that the faithful undergo. But by an imaginative act of sympathy we may see all of humanity as a kind of exile.[3] We hear of the "homeless mind" of modernity or of "alienation" as the outcome of economic or political distortion.[4] These more general descriptions of our existential state implicitly ask for a home from which humans are now distant.[5] The task of the church is to name this alienation as sin.

Accompanying the soteriological is what we might call an ecclesiological sense. Part of the unfaithfulness of God's people is their excessive accommodation to their surrounding Gentile culture, whether noticed or not. As we shall see, this is the danger that looms over Dan. 1. At the end of the first Christian millennium the church was at risk of being submerged in claims of blood and clan, and in the sixteenth century Luther decried the "Babylonian captivity" to works of religious merit.[6] Contemporary critics find new kinds of captivity in post-Enlightenment rationality or in Constantinian settlements with cultural privilege, civic religiosity, or bourgeois contentment. By contrast the church needs to come to an understanding of itself as a "resident alien" community.[7] As a warrant in the New Testament, Phil. 3:20 tell us that, in contrast to the self-obsessed of every age, "our

1. As one can see in the work of Bruce Chilton and Craig Evans; e.g., the latter's "Aspects of Exile and Restoration in the Proclamation of Jesus and the Gospels," in Chilton and Evans, *Jesus in Context* (Leiden: Brill, 1997), 267–96.

2. This is the central thesis of Jacob Neusner's *Self-Fulfilling Prophecy* (Boston: Beacon, 1987).

3. For a reflection on exile as the root metaphor for human alienation, see Arnold Eisen's *Galut* (Bloomington: Indiana University Press, 1987).

4. Peter Berger, with the influence of Marx on alienation, extends the idea to the modern consciousness in Peter Berger, Brigitte Berger, and Hansfried Kellner, *The Homeless Mind* (New York: Random, 1973).

5. Frank Kermode describes the postmodern state in secularized and yet Danielic terms: "This is the modern apotheosis of Joachism. The belief that one's own age is transitional between two periods turns into a belief that the transition itself becomes an age, a speculum. We strip the three-and-a-half years of the Beast . . . of all its 'primitive' number associations, and are left with eternal transition, perpetual crisis"; *The Sense of an Ending* (London: Oxford University Press, 1968), 101.

6. Martin Luther, *Basic Theological Writings of Martin Luther*, ed. Timothy Lull (Minneapolis: Fortress, 1989), 4.16.

7. E.g., Walter Brueggemann, *Hopeful Imagination: Prophetic Voices of Exile* (Minneapolis: Fortress, 1986); and Stanley Hauerwas and William H. Willimon, *Resident Aliens: Life in the Christian Colony* (Nashville: Abingdon, 1989).

citizenship is in heaven." This self-assessment about cultural exile has the problem of success; so many have come to claim it that its teeth have been dulled. We need help from Dan. 1 to know what such an ecclesiology requires of us.

These ramifying senses of exile help to put one critical question into context. The third year of Jehoiakim's rule (Dan. 1) is after the second of Nebuchadnezzar (Dan. 2): how are we to reconcile the two dates? Calvin, worrying over this, reckons that two kings, father and son, are referred to (1993: 19–20). The difficulty is diminished when we see that Nebuchadnezzar, himself a historical figure, undergoes a similar expansion of significance. He becomes an archetype for the conquering imperial ruler. He is the ruler who corresponds to captivity and so blends with the series of kings who will follow. He personifies "the kings of the earth."

1:2 the Lord let King Jehoiakim . . . fall into his power—Though one could perceive it only by faith, this is fundamental to all that will follow. The exile is the doing of the Lord and as such is no testament to his weakness, injustice, or abandonment of his people: God is free and powerful to protect and to send into exile as well. Daniel's message is consonant with the chorus of prophets interpreting the exile for Israel. God has done this, and even when the situation for Daniel and his compatriots becomes repeatedly grim, God's control is never lost sight of. The exile is the result of a *felix culpa*, for through it the reach of Yahweh's arm, even on alien ground, will be displayed. Exile as the Lord's "strange . . . deed" (Isa. 28:21) requires explication, which Daniel, taken as a whole, provides.

1:2, 4 the vessels of the house of God . . . young men without physical blemish—For the Israelite the worst part of the exilic cataclysm was not personal humiliation, but rather the humiliation of the temple of the Lord. For there God's glory flashed, there his word was heard, there the sacrifice brought them close to him, and there his promises were affixed. Personal pain expressed cultic and national agony. At the heart of exile is distance from the sanctuary: "By the rivers of Babylon / . . . we wept / when we remembered Zion" (Ps. 137:1).

Exile may be seen as the victory of godlessness over godliness, but it also involves the making of a rival claim about the God of Babylon. Even if we are dealing with an avowed atheism or with a nondescript conflict of "ultimate concerns" (to borrow Tillich's whitewash), Daniel tells us that in fact conflicting claims about gods are at issue and that the pagan claim has within it this element of arrogance. The temple cups are taken into the storehouse of the pagan god. (This verse is a foreshadowing of the blatantly blasphemous use of those vessels coming in the bacchanal of Belshazzar in 5:3–4; it may also hint at the removal of the vessels under Antiochus Epiphanes seen in 1 Maccabees 1:20–24.)

And it is not only cups that serve the veiled arrogance of this rival temple. Nebuchadnezzar shrewdly recruits, so as to coopt, able and elite young men of Judah. Perhaps he wants only the unblemished so that they will reflect his own greatness and be impressive to the onlooker. But there is also an allusion to the priests of Zion, who likewise must be without blemish so as to stand, not before some pagan king, but before the Lord of hosts. To be sure, the Babylonians did offer the children of Israel some kindnesses and accommodations—we shall see one such from the chief eunuch in the following verses. Jeremiah could argue that the Israelites should serve the Babylonians and pray for their welfare during the allotted time of the exile (although he is careful to warn them against putting any stock in their diviners; 29:4). But underlying these mitigations are the challenge and affront of this rival "temple" that they are serving. Already we have an inkling of the struggle over rival worship in Dan. 3.

1:4 taught the literature and language of the Chaldeans—In brief and artful strokes this verse goes to the very heart of the colonial enterprise throughout the ages. The goal is to assimilate the next generation of leadership, to subordinate them to the king's interests. Nebuchadnezzar, an intelligent man, knows that only as he takes over the minds of the young elite has he accomplished the real captivity. Daniel 1 offers a subtle picture of the Babylonians as generous and, in their own way, inclusive. The best of the defeated Israelites deserve a place in the Babylonian elite. They are deemed capable of all the learning the imperial culture has to offer. We might compare the great expense and effort of French colonialists in the nineteenth century to bring their subjects to France and there to inculcate their charges in the grandeur of French culture. From their point of view this was anything but cruelty and servitude. Those captors went so far as to offer paeans to *Negritude*, as long as it was in the wider frame of a Francophile worldview. Such is the enlightened colonialism of the Babylonians. At the same time, with the bestowal of resources and effort goes a will to absorb and redefine, all the more insidious for its generosity. Israel's young leaders will bear Chaldean names, with Chaldean words on their lips. Their feeding and education spare no expense, all in order for them to **be stationed in the king's court** (1:5)—that is, to serve him. With the greatest economy of action, with the utmost enticement, the verse names the essential features of the redefinition of identity. And yet, as the coming chapters will show, behind the velvet is an iron fist, should rebellion ensue.[8] The chief eunuch is under no illusions about his boss's potential for cruelty.

It is worth noting the importance of young men of the court in the history of the defense of the faith in situations of cultural conflict. In the history of mission a chapter like that of the Bugandan martyrs in the 1870s comes to mind, among others.[9] The young courtiers heard the Christian gospel, heard its vision of a new kind of kingdom, and were converted. When the Kabaka tried to abuse them sexually, they refused and proved willing to pay the price of martyrdom. There too we find the dynamics of mutual encouragement, courage in the face of pain and possible death, and intellectual defense in the face of rival claim to truth. With them too the future of a people was decided, after some went to their fiery deaths, like the threatened death of Dan. 3, with Christian hymns on their

8. Walter Luethi, *The Church to Come* (London: Hodder & Stoughton, 1939), 18.
9. E.g., Elizabeth Isichei, *A History of Christianity in Africa* (Grand Rapids: Eerdmans, 1995), 146–50.

lips. Where else might young elites be locked in a contest of faith in the face of enticements to assimilate?[10]

1:8 but Daniel resolved that he would not defile himself with the royal rations of food and wine—Our first reaction is that the laws of kosher eating and drinking are at stake, and this interpretation would be consistent with the problem of defilement. While this may have been true with regard to the food, it is hard to see how that would be the issue with the wine. At the least we can say that this does not capture the whole issue here. Kashrut was the sign of God's lordship over creation and over the life of the son or daughter of Israel, down to the very details of their bodily life. In this way what is at stake in kashrut and what is at stake here are the same. To eat at the king's table is to be in his thrall (Goldingay 1989: 18–19), for at that table the most intense and subtle inculcation will take place. In that privilege, making its recipients at once favored and indebted, Daniel perceives the most dangerous cord binding him to the king. Daniel will be his respectful subject, but he will not be his son.

It makes sense that the danger should take place around sharing the king's table, especially if kashrut was involved. But there was no certainty in advance that the crisis would crop up here, nor a rule by which one could predict it, and so determine the proper response. Some collision is bound to take place between the claims of the rival kings and rival sacral orders, but where and how it will occur varies. It requires of us, as of Daniel, discernment. In the theological parlance of the Reformation tradition, we are speaking of the *status confessionis*, the moment in which, upon the occasion of some issue or other, the very nerve of the gospel is exposed and at risk of being severed. We do know that such moments do occur and that in such moments much more is at stake than the presenting problem would seem to indicate.

We can apply this insight to the realm of missionary encounter, for its history consists of such collisions. There too one cannot say in advance whether some custom inherited from the local past must be retained or not. We are reminded of Paul's dialectical treatment of meat sacrificed to idols in 1 Corinthians, where he alternates between affirming, in Christian freedom, that idols are nothing (1 Cor. 8) and insisting that demons are all too real and the Christian conscience constrained by the need to protect the weaker brother and witness to the unbeliever (10:20–30). In this case too, "it depends." In the same vein, Max Warren reminds readers wondering about the seeming legalism of the east African revivalists that the battle line between faith and unfaith keeps reforming itself.[11] We can be sure that there will be such a line, together with a way of escape and an accompanying cost.

It is no accident that the issue is food, even as it is no accident that the Torah builds faithfulness into eating. "We are what we eat," as Feuerbach taught us, a

---

10. Displacement, refugees, and emigration are at present the most germane issues in global missiology. See especially Jehu Hanciles, *Beyond Christendom* (Maryknoll, NY: Orbis, 2008).

11. Max Warren, *Revival: An Enquiry* (London: SCM, 1954), chap. 1.

sentiment with which Paul, in his meditation on communion and a common table, would have concurred. The temptation to assimilate takes a concrete form and is worked out in a practical way, in this case around the question "with whom will we eat?" In a similar way the abstractions of faith and culture work themselves out concretely in relation to the integrity of the distinctive practices of the church. Consider the intellectual quandaries with which mission to India struggled for centuries around permissible accommodations to Hindu religious practices involving caste. The question came down to whether Brahmin Christians would share the eucharistic bread and cup with lower caste, or outcaste, believers. This concrete line of discrimination and discernment cuts through the intellectual mist, though it made the matter no easier.[12]

1:15 at the end of ten days it was observed that they appeared better—Daniel and his compatriots escape both the king's table and its danger, and the chapter leaves no doubt why: God's miraculous care, working here in the quiet form of preserving their health and even improving their appearance. By this action God delivers the believer when he or she, faced with such a crisis of faithfulness or capitulation, takes a stand for the former. Daniel's stratagems were at work, for he is shown to be a young man who is bold, clever, and persuasive, but these qualities are put to use by his God. He can work through our stratagems or without them. He has sent his servants into exile, and he is fully capable of preserving them there and using them to purposes he has determined.

Purposes he has, as the book will attest by the remaining chapters. But here the perspective of God (which the reader will share, as he or she is shown the vista of history) and the perspective of Daniel and the three young men could not be more different. God can use the cataclysm to further his ends. One might compare the observation that modern global mission, which commenced in earnest in the nineteenth century, with its surprising "time release" harvest, emerged at the very moment that skepticism began to lengthen the shadows in the culture of the West, whence the missionaries came. The pod, dried and split open, sends its seeds to the four winds.[13] Israel is crushed, and with its exile the conditions for a universal mission of the gospel is set in motion. But in Dan. 1 we do not yet see any of this, and the consolation of such a vista is precisely what the young men do not have. Daniel and the three are feeling their way forward in a moment without a spiritual map. The narrative they knew of divine faithfulness in history has come to an end, and all they can do is improvise acts of faithfulness in a land where they cannot see the old monuments. As with the spiritual writers, this feeling their way forward in a dark night implies a maturity of faith, though it cannot have seemed so to them.

1:17 to these four young men God gave knowledge and skill in every aspect of literature and wisdom; Daniel also had insight into all visions and

---

12. For the earlier Catholic experience, see Stephen Neill, *A History of Christianity in India*, vol. 1 (Cambridge: Cambridge University Press, 1984); on the Protestant side, Duncan Forrester, *Caste and Christianity* (London: Curzon, 1980).

13. Andrew Walls, *The Missionary Movement in Christian History* (London: T&T Clark, 1996), 21–22.

dreams—We have already seen how the beginning of the chapter, introducing us to the fact and the theme of exile, sets the stage for all to come. As the chapter ends, we are given the key to the unity of the diverse material that will follow in the book. Generally, the first half of the book is preoccupied with wisdom, and the second with visions and dreams. Daniel is a master of both, and both are tied together, since those visions require the real wisdom that comes from God for their interpretation. They will also require the intervention of God through the wise skill of Daniel, just as we have seen in the quiet miracle of the first chapter. God is the one who rules and provides through all the coming chapters. The wisdom that he provides will be **ten times better than all the magicians and enchanters** (1:20). But this deeper wisdom does not mean that Daniel is set at odds with the pagan king and his court. We are shown in Dan. 1 that Daniel is both subtle and faithful, "wise as serpents and innocent as doves" (Matt. 10:16). He stands before the king (Dan. 1:19) as his advisor, yet when it most counts he retains his integrity. He will maintain this quality of faithful skill even in the labyrinthine life of magi and court over the long haul (1:21).

DANIEL 2

2:1 **Nebuchadnezzar dreamed such dreams that his spirit was troubled**—The end of Dan. 1 left Daniel in place among the magi of Babylon, indeed in premier position. From the outset a question is implied: what is the relationship between Daniel and his gifts and the Babylonian magicians and theirs?

With this question before us we hear of the king's dream.[1] No role would be more traditional and appropriate for diviners than the interpretation of divine dreams. Since the king held a privileged place in relation to the gods, his dreams enjoyed special status. In this case, however, the king cannot remember the dream itself, and so he demands from his magi both the dream and its interpretation, much to their surprise and shock. The bar is raised, and the feat expected of them exceeds merely competing interpretations or dueling hermeneutics. Rather, in the face of royal rage and possible death, nothing less than a miracle will be required.

2:2 **the king commanded that the magicians . . . tell the king his dreams**—As will be so repeatedly, the implied background of Dan. 2 is the story of Joseph, who in Gen. 41 correctly interprets the dream that troubles the sleep of another, earlier king, namely Pharaoh. Both are men of wisdom in whom "the spirit of God" is found (41:38). The interpretive wisdom of Joseph, as of Daniel, helps to save Israel from disaster. At the same time, Daniel uses this background as a foil: of Joseph the summoning up of the king's dream itself was not required, and, through the correct interpretation, no wise intervention is offered by Daniel to Nebuchadnezzar.

A central theme of Dan. 2 as a whole has already emerged. As humans we are not surprised to find Joseph the dream reader among the Egyptian adepts, nor Daniel the wise among the magi. But between the wisdom that comes from Yahweh and human insight there is simply no comparison. They are incommensurable because

1. For parallels in African traditional history relevant to Christian mission, see Tokunboh Adeyemo's note in *Africa Bible Commentary* (Nairobi: Word Alive, 2006), 993.

the Creator is incommensurable with the creation. This does not mean that the gospel has no use for such wisdom in a limited way. Jerome finds an analogy to the gospel's relationship to pagan philosophy (1958: 20, 24–26). Earlier, in Dan. 1, Jerome found in the vessels of the temple a similar type for the portions of the truth found in pagan philosophy (though, strictly speaking, the vessels in the story are in that case moving in the wrong direction!). Here in Dan. 2 he compares the magicians to the magi who come to worship the Christ-child.[2] In both cases, for Jerome the point is that God alone provides the wisdom that saves.

We can restate what is at stake in a more contemporary theological way. Since the 1930s, missiology has deployed the terms "continuous" and "discontinuous"[3] to describe the possible relationships between the knowledge that magi of all sorts—mantic, philosophical, and so on—can attain and the knowledge that is revealed by the God of Israel. Missiologists are describing, in an abstract way, the kind of contest going on in Dan. 2. The answer here is more complex than simply a vindication of discontinuity, though this is surely the direction in which the chapter tilts, for at a descriptive level, the players are comparable and appear on the same stage upon which God has placed them.[4] Yet they are incomparable as well: the magi do not even know what they are to interpret until the wise man of the Lord gives it to them; they need him even for the question! Far from being their opponent, the man of God saves their skin in the face of the frightened and impotent rage of the king himself.

2:19 then the mystery was revealed to Daniel in a vision of the night—There is a close connection between Dan. 2 and Dan. 7. Both are based on visions of the night given in dreams that render mysteries. Another similarity is found in the fourfold pattern of the kingdoms of human history. As I suggested in the introduction, this supports the unified structure of the book as a whole, even amid different genres.

2:21 he changes times and seasons, / deposes kings and sets up kings— When Daniel is shown the mystery by God, he offers this short hymn of doxology. Its theme runs throughout the book as a whole: doxology is the end for which all wisdom and revelation are given.

The visions of ages and kingships in Dan. 2–3 and Dan. 7–12 are variations on this same theme. Even when God seems to have taken a backseat and the pagan nations are gnashing and grasping, we are reminded that he is the one who changes

2. Raymond Brown, *An Adult Christ at Christmas* (Collegeville, MN: Liturgical, 1977), finds a kind of *praeparatio evangelica* in the story, for the pagan wisdom can get one close to the child, but only the scriptures can enable one to find him. But from another point of view, close is of no help, since everything depends on what God wills, which is Christ and the finding of him. It is this insistence on starting where God starts that governs our passage.

3. The terms are derived from the debate around Hendrik Kraemer's *The Christian Message in a Non-Christian World* (London: Edinburgh, 1938), at Tambaram and afterward.

4. Karl Barth stresses that at a human level Christianity is one religion among others; see *Church Dogmatics* (Edinburgh: T&T Clark, 1956), 1/2.17.

times and removes kings. Only the fool could conclude from the successive regimes of history that power tells the tale or that history runs by its own immanent laws. These thoughts of the nations are eventually to be cast down and removed.

To be sure, with respect to the succession of kingdoms, it is humanly possible to lay out a schema. We can offer generalizations about *Geist* or the moral life cycle of empire or the clash of civilizations. These notions reflect the volatile, hybrid reality of the Gentiles, which is bound to be cast down and removed. History may indeed have its own laws and patterns. Empires have a natural tendency toward disintegration. The descent of empires in the vision presented a few verses later corresponds to a common ancient trope about the decline of the ages of humankind, most famously in Hesiod (Collins 1993: 162–65). The real meaning and end of kingdoms, however, are not immanent in themselves. For Daniel, the very transience of the changes underlines the rule of God behind them, an insight beyond what pagan authors or seers could imagine. Nor could they see in that rising and falling a cause for praise. This is what sets Israelite wisdom, for all the superficial resemblances, apart from that of other nations (so, e.g., Job 12).

2:28 there is a God in heaven who reveals mysteries—There is no assertion of power, no *technē*, that can answer the fears of Nebuchadnezzar's mind. All his regal power and resources are stymied, and the answer has to come from outside himself, from the social margins of his empire: **I have found among the exiles . . . a man who can tell the king the interpretation** (2:25). Nor does Daniel attribute to himself any wisdom whereby the riddle of the dream can be solved and the magi overcome (2:30); he is only a divine instrument by which the reality of things might be made known to the nations. Daniel points to the real center of the story of the dream and its interpretation, God, and in so doing exhibits an extraordinary freedom to act, in contrast to the frightened maneuvering of the magi: **Daniel went in and requested that the king give him time** (2:16). Chrysostom finds here the *parrhēssia*, the freedom of speech and action even in the face of danger, that the New Testament considered distinctive of Christians (1856: 242).

2:31–33 you were looking, O king, and lo! there was a great statue. This statue was huge, its brilliance extraordinary; it was standing before you. . . . The head of that statue was of fine gold, its chest and arms of silver, its middle and thighs of bronze, its legs of iron, and its feet partly of iron and partly of clay—The image is at once of the king, of the empire, and of the awe that both evoke. At the heart of the vision is this nexus between ruler, empire, and the claim to worship. That is the fatal flaw, the sickness within, the visible illustration of that original sin that would be "like gods" (Gen. 3:5 NRSV margin). Not only is kingship inevitably prideful and presumptuous, but this presumption drives it to usurp the place of God.

This madness is found egregiously and completely in empire, *imperium*, the rule that would unite and organize all of the races of humankind under one banner. This was the nature of the sin of Babel in Gen. 11, to establish a single human power over all the peoples of the earth and so to build a tower reaching to the heavens. This point was made eloquently in the last decades of the twentieth century by the most seminal of missiologists, Lesslie Newbigin. The gospel is one account among other competing accounts seeking to draw all nations to itself. Each offers some competing basis of world unity or rule. But the gospel's universal claim is different, for it would bring the nations together around something other than the ruler himself in his presumption. Furthermore, under the rule of the one Creator of the world, the gospel has within it a principle of the catholicity of the church that stands in contrast to totalizing human claims. Christianity in its mission can be humble about its flaws, its epistemic limits, and its share of human wisdom, but it cannot be humble about the one around whom the nations will be gathered. Though the gospel's opponents may hide behind a feigned relativism, or the irony of postmodernism, still they are hiding from view the absolute nature of their unifying claim.[5] This rival inner imperial nature of opposing accounts shows why they inevitably come to claim worship, as Dan. 3 will show in great dramatic detail.

The bulk of the interpretive energy in the history of the Christian tradition has been to assign identities to the nations of gold, silver, bronze, and iron/clay. The first is clearly the Babylonian Empire. Modern critical commentators often see in the last the divided empire that succeeded Alexander the Great, though traditional accounts placed the Romans in this category. The interpretation of the vision does not actually assign a nation to each, but rather leaves some free play for varied interpretation.[6] Part of the power of the vision is that it had an original application and yet invites new application.

The passage invites new candidates for these roles in new eras. Luethi, writing in the lengthening shadows of the late 1930s with its own idols and beasts, said that he was not sure to whom the four metals corresponded and wasn't sure it mattered, since he couldn't think of a regime to which the passage didn't refer![7] The point of the dream is that the kingdoms are different, yet they are all part of one reality, one body. (This generalizing line of interpretation is helped by the traditional association of the number four with the world—the four kingdoms then fit the natural digression that is "the way of the world.") They are bright and glorious to the eye, and yet they are all vanity of vanity.

partly of iron and partly of clay—Doug Farrow's larger argument, offering an ascension ecclesiology, supports the approach of this commentary. On this verse his comment has a caustic pertinence; he writes that Irenaeus was able

> to look ahead following the pointing finger of Jesus and the prophets in order to warn us against the deceptive character of our age, which today more than ever gives the

---

5. This theme is found in Newbigin's *Open Secret* (Grand Rapids: Eerdmans, 1978).

6. Paul Ricoeur, in his foreword to Lacocque 1976, sees the dynamic of the book's own interpretation and reinterpretation of visions such as this an invitation to our own application, and he links this to his own ideas of "free play" and "symbolic expansion," here of the type given in apocalyptic.

7. Luethi, *Church to Come*, 29.

impression of mingling without cohesion. What Irenaeus did not foresee, however, and would have been mortified to learn, was the extent to which the church itself would take on the look of iron mixed with clay or the extent to which it would covet the sham catholicity at which worldly institutions and empires aim. In that self-controverting development the doctrine of the ascension, or another doctrine of ascension, had a role to play.[8]

2:34 as you looked on, a stone was cut out, not by human hands, and it struck the statue on its feet of iron and clay and broke them to pieces—Though at one level the vision invites differentiation and identification of the four kingdoms, at another level the kingdoms are as one, in particular as they are compared to that which is utterly different and arrives suddenly and surprisingly from beyond, this rock falling from above. As is so often true in Daniel, the image, with its appropriately dreamlike quality (stone turning into mountains), is developed as a kind of running midrash on various passages from the prophet Isaiah.[9] The rock, the metaphor for the Lord's steadfastness in the Psalms, can become the rock over which people stumble. The key reference, Isa. 8:14,[10] imagines faithless (and soon to be exiled) Israel and Judah, in the face of the Gentiles onslaught, whereas here the stumbling recoils back on the captors themselves in their manifold guises. The stone is combined imagistically with the preceding lines (Isa. 8:9–10) in which the nations in their pride are given this word of judgment: "Band together, you peoples, and be dismayed. / . . . Take counsel together, but it shall be brought to naught; / . . . for God is with us." God's sudden act will turn on the nations themselves. As is often true in Daniel, ambiguity toward the nations lies hidden in the Isaianic allusions. The rock becomes a mountain, and that mountain comes to fill the world. (Here we may compare Nebuchadnezzar's second dream, found in Dan. 4:11, in which the tree grows to fill the whole world.) Given the symbolic background of the temple and its loss lying behind the whole of Daniel, we should combine the aforementioned references with Isa. 2:3, in which the nations flow to Zion, the mountain of the Lord, and with 6:3, in which the glory of Zion is proclaimed by the seraphim to fill the earth. Stone, breaking, mountain, filled earth—all may be found in Isaiah as a way to describe the decisive act of judgment and transformation by the God of Zion in the face of the Gentiles.

2:37 you, O king, the king of kings—to whom the God of heaven has given the kingdom, the power, the might, and the glory, into whose hand he has given human beings, wherever they live, the wild animals of the field, and the birds of the air—The authority of these kings is not all pride and usurpation. On the contrary God has given them their rule. The crucial thing, however, is

8. Farrow, *Ascension and Ecclesia*, 85.

9. On the midrashic nature of the work as "charismatic exegesis" by a community of wisdom interpreters, see Stephen Cook, *Apocalyptic Literature* (Nashville: Abingdon, 2003).

10. It is significant that the reference to "sealing up the scrolls," which is borrowed in Dan. 12, appears in this passage as well.

the echo of Gen. 1:26–31. The human being is the rightful image (*eikōn*) of God and as such is given a rightful kind of stewardly dominion over the creation in its various orders. This stands in implicit contrast to the presumptuous image of the empires here in Dan. 2 and to the way in which dominion is exercised in empire. The real dominion intended by God the creator understands that the human being, like the rest of creation, is simply formed of the clay (Gen. 2:7). As we shall see dramatically in Dan. 3, the key difference has to do with whose glory receives worship. The only glory that Nebuchadnezzar has is derived from the king of heaven.

2:44–45 the God of heaven will set up a kingdom that shall never be destroyed, nor shall this kingdom be left to another people . . . just as you saw that a stone was cut from the mountain not by hands—We have already heard that this vision pertains to the "latter days" (Dan. 2:28; cf. Isa. 2:2). The "infinite qualitative difference" (Kierkegaard) between the kings that naturally decline and inevitably pass away and the permanent kingdom derives from the realms' different authors, on the one hand human and on the other divine (so, the **stone . . . cut from the mountain not by humans**). This difference corresponds to the distinction between limited duration and eschatological finality: **a kingdom that shall never be destroyed**. The eternal God's act is permanent, and so it alone in the created world of time and space can bring into being what is permanent and final. This takes place in human history, **in the days of those kings**, and it yet stands at the last when they are all long gone. But given that the kingdoms of the Gentiles continue to appear and to oppress, how can there be such an unbreakable kingdom amid and yet beyond these insolent kingdoms? Daniel 2 gives us the promise that such a kingdom will come to be, but we do not yet see how. Daniel 2 points us toward the greater clarity of Dan. 7 and Dan. 12; theologically, the promise of God's kingdom, the central theme of the work as a whole, drives us on toward Christology and the doctrine of the resurrection as the answers to the perplexities of time and eternity.

In this verse the stone falls vertically from above.[11] This is an event in history with a tangible effect on the empires of history, but nothing earthly brings it. So it stands in contrast to human efforts to bring in God's kingdom. The stone epitomizes Daniel's radical stance of prophetic critique against all human ameliorative or revolutionary interpretations of Christian life.[12] This vertical dimension is the premise for what the passage tells us about the relationship of divine and human agency.

This does not mean, however, that there is nothing earthly to remind us of that contrast of divine and human or to serve as an instrument of that divine agency. In commenting on this verse, Melanchthon, predictably and consistently appealing

11. Karl Barth, *The Epistle to the Romans*, trans. E. C. Hoskyns (Oxford: Oxford University Press, 1968), 30 (the German is *senkrecht von Oben*, "vertically, from above").
12. Childs, *Introduction to the Old Testament as Scripture*, 622.

to Reformation categories, interprets this unbreakable kingdom here and now as God's reign *per verbum*. Like the Word incarnate, the word of God heard and preached also comes surprisingly to us from outside and above us. It is through this word of God that we are related to Christ the Word and learn to hope in the kingdom of the last day. That word, preached and heard, is indeed unbreakable, though it remains in humility and affliction amid what Melanchthon calls the "hardened kingdoms" of this world (1543: 36).

The other doctrine to which Melanchthon appeals here is grace, which is a promising avenue for teaching and preaching on Dan. 2. Its prevenience corresponds to the verticality we have seen. God is the active agent behind the rise and fall of empires, even in their apparent power and glory. We find here no divine withdrawal, even before the stone arrives. Nor did Melanchthon find any shred of determinism in this passage, but rather the active arranging of all things by God (1543: 35).[13] The freedom and flexibility to work through or upon creation is entailed in divine transcendence. This divine relationship to human power and history is the same, whether the biblical work in question is prophetic, apocalyptic, or something else.

The question of divine and human agency leads us naturally to the question of Christology. Christian interpreters throughout the centuries are united in finding in the rock that descends from above a reference to Jesus Christ. It is a type, by which is meant a figure or image that has an original reference according to the literal sense, but has a further reference to coming Christian realities. The latter emerges in the trajectory of the passage, the convergence of themes, outstanding questions, and prior interpretations in the tradition, which lend a direction to later understandings. Consider the themes present in the passage: the decisive act of God in the middle of a successive empire, the coming of the glory of the Lord on the mountain of Zion, the stone of stumbling of Ps. 118, the one who will live after death, about whom the people say "blessed is he who comes in the name of the LORD," the breaking and gathering of the nations, the question of an everlasting kingdom, the resolution of the mystery of divine and human agency, the true *eikōn* of the invisible God, and so on. These themes are left by the intervening interpreters suspended in midair, and that suspension lends itself to the eventual interpretation of the rock as Christ. The New Testament interprets Christ as the stone that the builders rejected (1 Pet. 2:7), as the rock from which water flowed in the desert (1 Cor. 10:4), as the rock of the kingdom on which a house can safely be built (Matt. 7:24). We shall find in virtually every chapter in the first half of Daniel a similar convergence of themes and questions driving toward a christological interpretation.

13. For the main argument about divine and human agency, see Kathryn Tanner, *God and Creation in Christian Theology* (Oxford: Blackwell, 1988).

DANIEL 3

The dramatic action of the book of Daniel centers on the coming of the kingship of God in the context of the loss of his city. There is no more profound Christian meditation on its themes than *The City of God* by St. Augustine,[1] and a summary of its main thesis provides a fitting introduction to this chapter. There run throughout human history two cities, which is to say, two movements, two principles, two loves. They are rooted in the story of creation and rebellion: the love of self and the love of God. There is for Augustine no neutrality, because human life not submitted to the divine rule organizes itself in mimicry of that rule according to a contrasting, ingrown love. And where there are two loves there are naturally two worships, "worth-ships," the ultimate expression of the direction and commitment of our heart and mind.

Daniel 3 follows naturally on Dan. 2. Having had the dream of empire in his own image, Nebuchadnezzar now erects a physical image of himself to be worshiped by his subjects. Historians tell us that Babylonian kings, for example, Nabonidus, erected just such images (Collins 1993: 180–82). Theologically this behavior exemplified something much wider, the worship following on the self-love of the city of this world. The echo is of the idolatry condemned in the second commandment and the story of the golden calf that follows it.

3:1 King Nebuchadnezzar made a golden statue—The creature defined by *amor sui* cannot rest content in himself. He needs to project and objectify this self-admiration in the world. He needs an idol of himself. The image is an exertion of his will, as is underscored by the threefold repetition of the clause **that Nebuchadnezzar had set up**. The phenomenologist of religion tells us that its worship is really a window leading on to the transcendent and so deserves a better estimation than theology has usually given it. But a self-abnegating window on the beyond is precisely what *amor sui* is not.

1. Augustine, *The City of God*, trans. Marcus Dods (New York: Modern Library, 1950).

The drawing of the world toward an image of oneself outside oneself is inherently unstable. We may contrast this with the life of the Trinity according to the traditional Christian account, for it alone can rest in the inner life of the persons and draw others to itself in freedom and love.[2] The world is not a projection or objectification of the needs of its inner life (pace Hegel and all his offspring), but rather gift, and for this reason real worship, borne of gratitude and praise, is possible only toward the triune God.

3:4–5 you are commanded, O peoples, nations, and languages, that when you hear the sound of the horn, pipe, lyre, trigon, harp, drum, and entire musical ensemble, you are to fall down and worship the golden statue—The chapter's argument is built on an implied contrast. The **peoples, nations, and languages** are gathered as one for the worship of the image, in contrast to the true gathering of the nations that is the hope of Israel for the latter days. The music of the instruments of the subject peoples supplies this worship, representing as they do the cultures whose expressive diversity is affirmed only in the subjugation to the self-love of Nebuchadnezzar, the maximum leader. In this temple of power, what Augustine called the *libido dominandi*, the military and apparatchiks parody the ranks of priest and choir. The end, a counter-*telos*, is not the fire of love that is the vision of God, but the terror of the fiery furnace in which traditional interpreters see a type of the fire in hell.

It is a chilling scene, the laying bare of the real logic and motive of *imperium* behind the schemas laid out so rationally in the previous chapter. The author's artistry is found in the black humor with which the terror is subtly presented. The Gentiles in their pretension are as foolish as Il Duce strutting before the orchestrated masses, even as the furnace is heated in the background. The repeated lists of officials (mimicking the bombast of government missives) and the lists of instruments (mimicking the lavishness of court liturgical language) bring across the point that self-worship in the end is silly in its self-importance, banal in its evil.

Most appositely for our present cultural moment, this scene of imperial vanity casts a shadow over our sense of the diversity and unity of cultures. The empire wishes to celebrate this diversity precisely as it seeks to draw them all together in subservience. Every kind of global music from all the nations of the earth is called forth in worship of the great idol. This is an ersatz diversity that cannot last or matter. What would a real celebration of the diversity of cultures look like? This is a question in which Daniel is deeply interested, though in these early chapters it seems preoccupied with the survival of one threatened nation among the *goyim*. The two are connected, for the presence of the singularity that is Judaism throughout history has at once stirred up the rage of the nations, even as it has served as a signpost of what real ethnic and cultural particularity could mean in the service of God.

2. Barth, *Church Dogmatics* (Edinburgh: T&T Clark, 1957), 2/1.297.

3:6 whoever does not fall down and worship shall immediately be thrown into a furnace of blazing fire—Once again we must read Daniel against the background of other scriptural passages. We hear the resonance of Isa. 43, also written in the context of Babylonian captivity. The Lord gathers the nations to hear his case: "Let all the nations gather together. . . . / Let them bring their witnesses. . . . / I am the LORD, / and besides me there is no savior" (43:9–11). Nebuchadnezzar may think he is holding court and can play the savior from death, but matters are in fact quite the other way around. The Lord is actually doing a new thing, the salvation of his people out of the wasteland in which they find themselves, so that even "the wild animals will honor me" (43:20) (as the king is soon to do). In this context we hear the apposite verse: "When you walk through fire you shall not be burned, / and the flame shall not consume you" (43:2). The furnace, hearkening back to that of Egypt, evokes the whole of the exilic experience. Life in exile is always at risk of violence and destruction, and the promise of Dan. 3 is that the courage to stand against the idol will be provided, miracle that it is, as will the means for the continued existence of Israel on its way back to Zion.

3:12 there are certain Jews whom you have appointed over the affairs of the province of Babylon: Shadrach, Meshach, and Abednego . . . they do not serve your gods and they do not worship the golden statue—Nock points out that in the culturally pluralistic Hellenistic world, the notion of exclusivity belonged only to the children of Israel and the Christians.[3] Neither sought out martyrdom, and both would seek "the welfare of Babylon" as they were able, as did the three young men in the service of Nebuchadnezzar's court. But where the moment of public confession could not be avoided, both traditions required that it be faced with fortitude. At this very moment the identity of Israel is formed: they are the ones who will not have any other gods but the Lord. They are to provide a witness to the nations, and as a result some may see it and be converted. But confessing their God alone ultimately has no other purpose or function. It is not strategy toward anything, even conversion. It is simply who they are marked out to be by God by his call to them.

In the history of mission there have been clarion moments when pagan powers have used the demand for public worship as a means of flushing out and exterminating Christians. As they gather on the Lord's Day, believers who do not live in such a moment should be cognizant that this itself is a blessing; their ease is not to be taken for granted.[4] This moment of saying no to idolatry shows the true relationship of the two loves and the two kingdoms. During the third-century persecutions under Decius and Diocletian, those who stood up for the faith helped to assure the eventual victory of the faith over the empire, and those who did not created the occasion for the Donatist struggle that would bedevil the church for the next two centuries. In sixteenth-century Japan, after a period

---

3. Arthur Darby Nock, *Conversion* (London: Oxford University Press, 1933).
4. Dietrich Bonhoeffer, *Life Together* (London: SCM, 1954), chap. 1.

of cautious welcome, the emperor outlawed the faith and tortured those who would not tread an image of Christ underfoot. This terrible demand to stand and die cannot be avoided under any circumstances, cultural or otherwise.[5] The line between acceptable accommodation and the need, finally, to stand and confess has often been disputed in history, most recently in communist China and Russia.

This moment of contrasting the true God from the false gods lays bare the nature of the struggle of the two cities, which is human history. Augustine does not claim that the two are separate and distinct for the observer to see. They are intertwined, one with the other, like that net of good fish and flotsam in the parable of Jesus. Only on the last day will the two be clear and separate, except for moments of terrible clarity such as the one we find in Dan. 3. This is especially apparent in the Christian era in the case of rulers who have shown the traits of Nebuchadnezzar. To kings in the Christian dispensation the gospel of the coming of the kingdom of God must be preached, and so their manner of rule must also be changed.[6] A Christian reading of Dan. 3, in the strange position we find ourselves in between the times, requires us to identify Nebuchadnezzar and the three young men among us. Nor can we simply divide matters between church and state, since in the former too we find the machinations, the pride, and the false will to unity of the great king.

3:17–18 If our God whom we serve is able to deliver us from the furnace of blazing fire and out of your hand, O king, let him deliver us. But if not, be it known to you, O king, that we will not serve your gods—Some modern commentators interpret the expression **but if not** to mean that the young men will remain faithful even if their God proves unable to deliver them. Given the wider context and the theological assumptions of the whole book, this cannot be the meaning. A pervasive theme of Daniel is God's rule over the nations and his power to direct events by plan and by intervention. The God of Daniel is able. The line should be taken to refer to the clause about his deliverance: even if he should *choose* not to deliver them, they will still refuse to worship the idol. In either case, the faithful would be delivered out of the hand of the king, whether to continued life or eternal life.

This does not mean that Christian commentators have not worried over why and by what criterion God decided to spare one and allow another to be sacrificed. Melanchthon acknowledges that, unless we answer this question, the faith of believers may be vexed. His answers are the expected one. He cites Ps. 50:15: "I will deliver you, and you shall glorify me." Even in the deliverance of the persecuted believer the focus is on God and his praise. A little later he reflects, in keeping with Paul's advice in 1 Cor. 10:13, that "when we cannot

5. E.g., Shusaku Endo's *Silence* (London: Quartet, 1978).
6. E.g., Oliver O'Donovan, *Desire of the Nations* (Cambridge: Cambridge University Press, 1996), chap. 6.

bear the present calamity, he adds consolation" (1543: 50). The goal is that the believer might continue in ministry so as to witness for the sake of God's glory. Who is and is not delivered in worldly terms follows these ultimately doxological criteria.

The emphasis on witness in this passage opens the more general question of the relationship between martyrdom and mission, which is implied by the word *martyria* ("witness") itself. Christian mission, like the individual believer, does not go in search of suffering, for we pray to be delivered from the "great trial" (*peirasmos*). Christian mission is not a cult of suffering. Nor can we reduce the role of martyrdom to its effect, though the pagans of the Roman Empire and their successors since have been impressed by it. We have seen that the witness of the young men in the face of the idol unveils the essential nature of the struggle in human history. Further connections between martyrdom and mission are revealed as Daniel proceeds. The conflict in which the *martyria* takes place is a sign of the latter days, so that hope of the consummation joins mission and suffering together. Finally the existential immediacy of mission in the face of the possibility of suffering lends a moral seriousness. Mission cannot be reduced, as often happens, to a technology of growth, a cause of social improvement, or a theory of intercultural relations. All the other issues that mission might be interested in come into focus against a horizon of witness at a cost.

3:19 Nebuchadnezzar was so filled with rage . . . that his face was distorted. He ordered the furnace heated up seven times more than was customary—The overheated state of the ruler is reflected in the overheated state of the oven. Both are out of control and kill their own. The rage of Nebuchadnezzar, a continual theme in the book, exemplifies the irrational side of the nations. Their rage is like that of a wild beast (see introduction), to which state the king is soon to be reduced. This rage is its own immolation. Once we abandon that orientation to God for which we were created, the disordered passions of the soul are enflamed. Even so, Nebuchadnezzar will also prove a sympathetic and occasionally faithful figure. The Gentile is not simply abandoned by God to bestiality. There is a limit to the rage allowed to be meted out to the three young men.

3:25 and the fourth has the appearance of a god—There is a considerable debate in modern scholarship about the figures variously described as "one like a Son of Man," "one with the appearance of a man," "one like a human being," and so on (7:13; 8:15; 10:16, 18). The discussion centers on the relationship between human beings, so described, and the angelic beings who also appear in the narrative. It is at least clear that the figure in Dan. 3 should be understood in some relationship to the later figures. Reading the book as a thematic whole is helpful here. In this passage, as well as in later examples, the ambiguity about the identity of these figures, whether human or more-than-human, whether individual or identified with the heavenly host, opens a trajectory toward the Christian interpretation. We find a similar tension within intertestamental Judaism over the God who is at once transcendent and immanent, a tension that cannot be resolved properly by layers of intermediary beings.[7] The ambiguity points toward the Son of Man who is also Son of God. To be sure, such suggestive ambiguities are no proofs; they assume that the reader has already seen that toward which the different readings seem to move. Nor is ambiguity per se a convincing argument. As in this case, where we find a debate about a figure's identity, it can have a certain power of suggestion.

Theologically the vision of the fourth affirms that even in the fiery trial the God of Israel is present with his people (so Isa. 43:2, as we have seen). Jerome doubted that the pagan Nebuchadnezzar could see the Son of God, and so split the interpretive difference by suggesting that the fourth is an angel who is a type of God-with-us yet to come (1958: 46). For most Christian interpretation the fourth is clearly the Son of God, Jesus Christ. He who is fully revealed in the flesh and on the cross is elusively and suggestively present in Israel's faithful and hopeful suffering.

Even within the present dispensation Christians experience this sense of an elusive yet palpable presence of Christ. In the middle of persecution, Christians of Matthew's church knew him present wherever two or three are gathered together. In the alienated existence of modern society, God himself may seem exiled from the center of ordinary life, and yet here too he appears as if a fourth appearing at the limits of our capacities.[8] Strained out from the rest of what Daniel would say about this fourth, the feeling of an elusive presence is too thin an account of God. Yet in a society that would grasp, analyze, and use everything by its designs, the fourth in the middle of suffering remains suggestively uncontrolled and mysterious.

3:27 the hair of their heads was not singed, their tunics were not harmed, and not even the smell of fire came from them—The plain sense refers to the young men themselves in their trial. But traditional Christian interpretation finds here other senses as well. The creation of an inferno in which the evil ones themselves are destroyed is a type of hell. According to the spiritual sense, the restoration of the young men in the integrity of their bodily form presages the resurrection of the dead on the last day. Hippolytus offers this divine miracle as a proof of the plausibility of the resurrection: the God who can do this even for the perishable can preserve us from the final fire (2000: 110). Chrysostom emphasizes the tropological sense: to be in the church is to be in the fiery furnace that seems

7. This is evident not least in the florid angelology of the literature following from the Daniel tradition, e.g., the Enoch literature.

8. In T. S. Eliot's "The Wasteland," evoking for a whole generation the alienation of Western society after the First World War, we find the following allusion to this line in Daniel (as well as to the Emmaus story): "Who is this third who always walks beside you?" (line 360). To this Eliot added the following note: "The following lines were stimulated by the account of one of the Antarctic expeditions (I forget which, but I think one of Shackleton's): it was related that the party of explorers, at the extremity of their strength, had the constant delusion that there was one more member than could actually be counted." On the banishment of God to the margins of modern life, see Dietrich Bonhoeffer's *Letters and Papers from Prison* (London: SCM, 1956), e.g., in the poem "Christians and Heathens" or in "Outline of a Book." The existentialist idea of boundary situations, e.g., in Karl Jaspers (see *Philosophy II* [Chicago: University of Chicago Press, 1970]) and in theologians influenced by this movement (Tillich, Bultmann, MacQuarrie), has been important in accounts of the experience of the reality of God for alienated moderns.

to the believer as if it were heaven to come (1856: 253). This church is led by the risen Christ who is, in contrast to the false icon, the "pure and spotless *eikōn*" who shows them the life to come in the present trials.

In the generations after the Holocaust, as we hear the story of the young Jews in the furnace, we cannot help but be reminded of that terrible chapter, in which the delivering hand of God did not appear. It is a humbling and vivid reminder that we cannot subsume this story under a christological rubric. The Holocaust is the most horrific chapter of a longer history of Jewish suffering in the furnace of Gentile, and nominally Christian, devising. The verse must refer not only to the church's savior, but also to that Israel that "will be saved" in spite of the present mystery of the "partial hardening" (Rom. 11:26).

As an aside, we do well to consider the place of Israel "after the flesh" in the reading of Daniel. My typological reading of the fiery furnace, the lion's den, the Son of Man, and other tropes, is obviously a Christian one, though the Jewish nature of the historical sense throughout is no less clear. There remains an important argument for a second reading with ongoing reference to the Jewish people. First, the eschatological scenario included a role for Israel "after the flesh" (Rom. 11). Second, both the nature of peoplehood and the horrors of the pit and the beasts can be fully understood by Christians only as we consider our cousins, Israel. In the French Revolution, the new regime proclaimed the emancipation of the Jews, but only *qua* human beings. *Qua* Jews they had no existence or status whatsoever. So secular modernity seems to promise the end of the furnace, but its tolerance proves false. Christians should bear in mind this cautionary tale. Third and finally, this abiding witness coheres with our understanding of the canon—namely that the book of Daniel must be heard as a part of the whole, but also as an individual book in its own right. Part of this individual voice involves continuing to hear Daniel as it speaks of and for Jews.

Excursus

"The Song of the Three Young Men" is not part of the canon for Protestants, but as an apocryphal addition (between 3:23 and 3:24) it deserves brief mention. Its extended note of doxology dovetails well with the ultimate purpose of the passage (and of the book) as we see it in the opening of Dan. 4. In the history of the liturgy its use in Holy Week underlines the christological dimensions of the story that I have noted.[9] While three young men of Israel are doing the praising, their exultation is over the great deeds of the Lord in all creation (open to Jew and Gentile alike), which are seamlessly one with his deeds of salvation. (In the Anglican tradition this emphasis on creation's praise is consonant with its role as a canticle in the daily office.) In this sense the addition is a most edifying midrash of its own on the theological import of our passage.

9. S. A. J. Bradley, *Anglo-Saxon Poetry* (London: Dent, 1982), 66–67.

DANIEL 4

4:1–3 **King Nebuchadnezzar to all peoples, nations, and languages . . . : May you have abundant prosperity! The signs and wonders that the Most High God has worked for me I am pleased to recount. . . . His kingdom is an everlasting kingdom**—We have seen how the idolatrous nations worshiped an evil parody of the true God. The second point of the passage is more positive. Even in these hard circumstances, the God of Israel has the power to call forth from the nations, even from kings as wrathful and proud as Nebuchadnezzar, praise of his righteous rule over all the earth. This is the end for which creation was made. This was the goal that, by Hegel's "cunning of (divine) history," the exile of Israel has helped to bring about. As with Joseph, out of what was intended for ill God can bring forth good, and so a blessing for all the nations. The purpose of the **Most High God** (note the name used, one open to all peoples) is beginning to be realized—namely, that all the peoples of the earth would confess in praise the universal kingship of God. This is the fulfillment of the hope expressed, for example, in the Psalms (an instance of which is 72:10–12). This is *in nuce* the gospel, the proclamation of the coming of God's rule through the appearing of the Son of God, about which we will hear in the opening passage of the Gospel of Mark. In this "divine comedy," for all its darkness, both Gentile rage and Jewish suffering play their roles in the gathering of all the nations at the proclamation of God's reign.

4:1 **to all peoples, nations, and languages**—Why do we find this chapter here? Daniel 3–6 follows on the vision of the succession of kingdoms set out in Dan. 2, whose bookend is Dan. 7, the development and transformation of the fourfold scheme. So Dan. 4 grows out of Dan. 2, for it too contains a successive vision of a fall of a Gentile king in his pride. The connection to the preceding chapter is easy to see, since Dan. 4 also presents a troubling royal dream requiring interpretation. In the chiasmic structure of Dan. 2–7, it also offers a matched set with the chapter that follows, since both Dan. 3 and Dan. 6 have trials for the Israelites, and both Dan. 4 and Dan. 5 have judgments executed on Babylonian kings.[1] Daniel 4 shares with its predecessor and Dan. 6 what we do not find in Dan. 5—namely, a conclusion extolling the true God. The troubling night vision here (as in the preceding chapter) anticipates not only Dan. 7 but the later chapters as well. We can see in this intricate set of thematic relations the careful hand of the redactor and the architecture of the work as a whole.

4:6 so I made a decree that all the wise men of Babylon should be brought before me—The contest of divine against earthly wisdom is the backdrop for the dream's interpretation, as in the preceding chapter, though here the theme, now assumed, does not need to be developed to the same extent.

4:10–12 there was a tree at the center of the earth, / and its height was great. . . . / Its foliage was beautiful, its fruit abundant. . . . / The animals of the field found shade under it—The images offered in Dan. 4 are bivalent, with resonances both with ancient Babylonian kingly metaphor on the one hand and with scripture on the other. Whatever the later redaction, the kernel of the story originated in the Babylonian exilic setting, probably in some relation to mad King Nabonidus. We know of Babylonian comparisons of kingly rule to great trees, as well as curses wishing that their opponents might be reduced to beasts of the field (Lacocque 1976: 75; Collins 1993: 218). The image emphasizes both the fecundity and protection associated with the ancient pagan king. The material has been reworked with later pagan kingly abuses in mind. The power of the image is in part in the reworking of these associations that shows its symbolic range, open to new applications. We find here, in the deep structure of the biblical metaphor, an example of the contextualization of a symbol borrowed from a pagan neighbor.

4:13 I continued looking, in the visions of my head as I lay in bed, and there was a holy watcher, coming down from heaven—The role of the angelic realm and the nature of the interaction between these divine messengers and Daniel will become a major issue in the second half of the book. It suffices to note their appearance here in Dan. 4, another indication of the thematic and dramatic unity of the book.[2]

4:15 leave its stump . . . in the ground, / with a band of iron and bronze, / in the tender grass of the field—As in the preceding vision, we find here too an imagistic and dreamlike quality. Elements are connected in a manner that does not track ordinary "waking state" logic: the tree is felled, and the resulting stump lies bound with metal bands amid the wet grass. The **band of iron and bronze** ties the vision to the original vision of Dan. 2. The wet dew on the stump, however, provokes an association with an image of the king as an animal in the field eating grass like a beast.

1. This observation is found in Stanley Walters's lecture notes entitled "The Structure of the Book of Daniel."

2. The popularity of apocalyptic themes in contemporary novels and movies bespeaks the mood of our time and so the relevance of Daniel. Mysterious watchers appear at the end of Cormac McCarthy's otherwise grim *The Road* (New York: Vintage, 2006).

The merged vision of tree, stump, and beast offers another example of a multiplicity of biblical allusions. The most common of these is the prophetic trope of the proud king as a tall tree that must be "cut down to size" by God. Isaiah 2 is the best known example: "For the LORD of hosts has a day / against all that is proud and lofty, / . . . against all the cedars of Lebanon, / lofty and lifted high" (2:12–13). Nebuchadnezzar is an example of such pride and must be brought down.[3] The allusion's moral lesson is equally clear. This reference is conjoined midrashically to Ezek. 31, where the Assyrian Empire is likened to a great tree providing shelter to the birds of the air. When in its pride it is toppled by ruthless foreign kings, the remaining trunk[4] is all the beasts of the field have (31:13). This second passage deliberately relates the pagan rise and fall to the story of salvation: the great tree is the envy of the Edenic garden (31:8–9), and the kingdom, when it is felled, tumbles all the way to Sheol (31:15–17). There is found the inevitable destination of Pharaoh, the type of despotic Gentiles, and all the uncircumcised (31:18). The implication of the fall of the Gentile king from his heights ramifies outward to the status (or lack thereof) of the Gentiles in general in the story of salvation.

As is often true in Daniel, this passage implies a contrast between the false universal rule—the tree of Nebuchadnezzar that would offer shade but is cut down in its pride—and the true universal rule and care of God. This contrast will be played out in more detail later in the canon. The false tree is chopped down so as to leave but a stump of a kingdom. This is in contrast to the stump, the remnant according to Isaiah, out of which will come Jesus (11:1). In one of his parables Jesus likens the kingdom of God to a small seed (namely, the ragtag band gathered around himself)[5] that will grow into a great tree that provides shelter for all the birds of the air and the beasts of the field (in deliberate allusion to both Ezekiel and Daniel). From Christ the holy seed miraculously springs the treelike church, his body, gathering from all the nations, in anticipation of the universal reign of God. The salvation-historical overtones we found in Ezekiel, of Eden lost and Sheol undergone, find their completion as well.

Let us return for a moment to the pagan allusion, so as to see better the way that pagan and scriptural associations are played off one another. Phenomenologists of religion point out that the *arbor mundi*, the tree that brings life, is found in the mythology of many cultures of the world.[6] (The early church capitalizes on this association in its references to the cross as the *arbor vitae*.) Daniel deploys

3. Jerome 1958: 49 adds the useful allusion to Ps. 37:35, where the impious person is compared to a sprawling tree.

4. Other possible allusions bear with them greater complexity. The stump that remains makes the reader versed in scripture think naturally of the stump in Isa. 6, which is the exilic seed and for which restoration will eventually come. Again, while the association of this stump with the king of Babylon may not make sense, at the level of the logic of images its association with exilic political travail does.

5. Joachim Jeremias, *Rediscovering the Parables* (New York: Scribner, 1968), 118.

6. E.g., Mircea Eliade, *The Sacred and the Profane: The Nature of Religion* (San Diego: Harvest, 1959), chap. 1.

these pagan associations to expand the power and reach of his message (cf. the emergence of the beasts from the sea in Dan. 7 and Dan. 9; Goldingay 1989: 87–88). The *arbor mundi* as the pagans understand it falls down and is reduced to a stump; a second tree, offering more life to the world, is yet to come.

4:25 you shall be made to eat grass like oxen—The modern psychopathological diagnosis is lycanthropy (so Pusey, as cited by Collins 1993: 228). More significant is the theological message. The heart that rebels against God is also corrupt beyond understanding; in it there is a deep vein of irrationality and even madness that manifests itself most dramatically in the king himself. One can think of the moments in mission history when witness has meant withstanding the onslaught of the mad king, from Nero to the Red Chinese Gang of Four. In this passage we are given the modest consolation that this madness eventually works to the destruction of the king himself. The story of the king driven to madness by his own hubris is a theme that seemed to strike a chord in the popular imagination of the Middle Ages. In an Anglo-Saxon poem, just before he descends to the eating of grass, the king declares, "You are mine, the great and famous city that I built to my honor, a broad empire. I repose in you, city and homeland I will possess."[7] All this belongs rightly to God. (Similarly in the medieval mystery play *Ludus Danielis* the focus is on the kingly hubris and madness, though with the focus on Belshazzar in Dan. 5 and the excess of the punishment of the lions' den in Dan. 6.)[8]

4:27 atone for your sins with righteousness—Anderson argues that, with the shift from Hebrew to Aramaic, there was a concomitant shift in the root metaphor from the bearing of a burden or disease to the carrying of a debt. The latter led naturally to the idea of almsgiving as a means to work down the deficit. Anderson finds the prime evidence for this change in this verse. He goes on to relate this new idea to the concept of righteousness as the redressing of a wrong, in this case of buying oneself out of debt slavery. This idea is taken up in Christian tradition, for example, in the following passage in the *Didache* 4.5–6: "Do not be one who stretches out his hands to receive, but shuts them when it comes to giving. Of whatever you have gained by your hands, you shall give the redemption price for your sins."[9]

4:34 when that period was over, I, Nebuchadnezzar, lifted my eyes to heaven, and my reason returned to me. I blessed the Most High—The first purpose of Nebuchadnezzar's healing is that he might praise God. In this it resembles the preceding chapter, whose goal is that the Gentiles might testify to God's deeds. So the king is not presented as an unmitigated epitome of evil. Rather he embodies that confused mixture of inchoate hope and longing with irrationality that is Daniel's view of the Gentile world.

7. Daniel Anlezark, ed., *Old Testament Narratives* (Cambridge, MA: Harvard University Press, 2011), 289.

8. E.g., Noah Greenberg, *The Play of Daniel: A Thirteenth-Century Musical Drama* (Oxford: Oxford University Press, 1971).

9. Gary Anderson, *Sin: A History* (New Haven: Yale University Press, 2009), 150.

In this, more positive vein, several traditional interpreters focus on the tropological sense. Jerome observes that God restores Nebuchadnezzar after he shows contrition, and he interprets this as God relenting from the judgment Nebuchadnezzar deserved (1958: 54). He notes others, especially the Ninevites of Jonah and Hezekiah, where God showed mercy and drew back from punishments they deserved. When we truly humble ourselves and lift our eyes to heaven, God in his mercy can even change the judgment set against us. Melanchthon predictably interprets the passage in relation to the Reformation polestar of justifying faith. Though Nebuchadnezzar was rebellious and evildoing, his faith is the occasion, then, for God's grace that justifies the godless pagan like Nebuchadnezzar. As a result he becomes an exemplar of the true nature of faith (1543: 72).

DANIEL 5

5:1 **King Belshazzar made a great festival for a thousand of his lords**—While Dan. 5 is another tale of divine judgment on kingly insolence and Gentile madness, we feel the jarring contrast with the note of contrition and faith on which Dan. 4 ended (Melanchthon 1543: 77). The chapters assume a chronological arrangement in which Belshazzar follows his father Nebuchadnezzar, and Darius, his successor by invasion and overthrow, follows in turn in Dan. 6. The historical-critical problem is that Belshazzar was not Nebuchadnezzar's son, and so the succession does not track the extant historical sources (Collins 1993: 29–33). Jerome's solution is as good as any—namely, that "father" is a general term for any progenitor (1958: 55). The imprecision reinforces the sense that the kings in their folly are interchangeable, though Belshazzar does seem to represent a nadir of debauchery, if not cruelty.

Both Xenophon and Herodotus confirm this picture of feasting on the eve of military destruction (Goldingay 1989: 107). As a concrete expression of Gentile kingly madness, the vessels deported from the temple in Jerusalem reappear. This is the fulfillment of the prophecy against Judah in Isa. 39:6, the culmination of the humiliation that was the exile. Their removal showed a lack of respect for the worship of the Lord. Now their use in this bacchanal is the utmost in blasphemy. There is also an allusion in this traditional story to Antiochus Epiphanes, also called "Epimanes," the crazed, who himself had a lurid sexual resume.[1]

There is a close connection between Gentiles turning away from God and turning toward moral turpitude (so the argument of Rom. 1). This connection seems most vivid in empires on the verge of disintegration, where decline of power is

---

1. 2 Maccabees 5; also Polybius, *Histories*, trans. Brian McGing (Oxford: Oxford University Press, 2010), 26.10.

accompanied by a decline in inhibition and morals.[2] Yet when the finger appears, the king is immediately thrown into perplexity and terror. Declining power, gold, sex, drugged inanity, blasphemy, edgy nerves—the opening tableau is an extraordinary telling account of the moral vacuity of pagan empire in its succinctness, as true now as then.

5:5 immediately the fingers of a human hand appeared and began writing—The image is a unique one, a finger suddenly appearing and writing. The point is that God will find his own ways of communicating; his word will have its say, even to a drunken and insolent pagan king.[3] Throughout the book God turns up in every place that seems most unlikely and forbidding: the barracks of the exiles, the furnace, now the wall facing the debauchery, soon the beastly pit. God's presence is uncanny, irrepressible, open to Gentile and Jew alike, as free to come in judgment as in mercy.

I have noted long-standing christological interpretations in each of the preceding chapters, as well as the ones to follow. Daniel 5 is no exception. Hippolytus reflects on the finger and wonders at the miracle of the Word coming in physical form so as to speak plainly to the Gentiles: is that not a figure of the incarnation (2000: 162)? The case for this type might seem the most far-fetched, but if one considers the chapters as a series, one can find an ongoing theology of the divine presence through his word in the middle of suffering, within which plan this reference finds its place.

5:17 let your gifts be for yourself, or give your rewards to someone else— This verse may be compared to Daniel's refusal to eat at the king's table in Dan. 1. He will not be drawn into the matrix of rewards and threats that are the royal court. He must maintain his independence in order to fulfill his prophetic ministry vis-à-vis the king. Daniel has served Nebuchadnezzar and already received various emoluments—what is the difference? The question is one of discernment, for here he perceives that this reward compromises his freedom as a minister of God's word.

5:21 the Most High God—This term is used consistently in this section. It is appropriate to conversation with, and the confessions of, Gentile kings. At the same time we should not overlook the gospel claim implied herein: the God who reigns from eternity is not above the concerns of this world, but intimately involved in them. He addresses particular sins in remarkable and immediate ways as he exercises a universal involvement and control over human history. This close involvement in human affairs of the Most High God is the heart of the scandal of the incarnation of Jesus Christ.

An example from the Christian mission to the nations is apropos. We are accustomed to references to the Father in relation to the incarnation. But to the pagan

2. On the contemporary moral debates of the mainline churches N. T. Wright comments, with the *Pax Americana* in mind, that declining empires are characterized by moral confusion in their cities and by wars at their borders (in a talk at the conference on international Anglicanism at Wycliffe Hall, Oxford, in 2002).

3. Lacocque 1976: 108.

Bugandans, for example, who first hear the gospel in the 1870s, the wonderful shock of the message is not that the Son was born among us, but rather that the Father should care enough to send him. They believed in a Most High God, but involved was precisely what he was not, and in the intervening void between us and him a host of lesser entities had to be appealed to and dealt with.[4] We need to borrow some of this surprise at the scripture's message about the worldly involvement of the Most High.

5:22 and you . . . have not humbled your heart, even though you knew all this—One stream of traditional interpretation of this passage had to do with the duties of the Christian prince and the judgment attendant on his failure to perform them (Melanchthon 1543: 78–85). This might seem a strange passage for this theme, since Belshazzar is most decidedly not a Christian prince. This tradition saw the worldly duties of the prince to include the protection of the faithful and the provision for the teaching of the gospel. The worldly exercise of power was to be informed by the gospel, and so it was to be the "left hand of God" (Luther). In his lawlessness Belshazzar exemplifies judgment on the prince who fails to accomplish these duties.

It was a commonplace of Reformation-era commentators to see the depredations of the Turk as the consequences of failure to "humble the heart" of the Christian leadership and to heed the written warnings of God's law. The Turks, then, filled the role played here by the Medes. In the tradition of the Christian prince this stands in contrast to the humility and repentance of the sort Nebuchadnezzar showed in the preceding chapter.

5:25 MENE, MENE, TEKEL, and PARSIN—The words are hidden yet made plain. They are unusual and yet allude to prophecies known to the hearers. In accordance with the prophecies of both Isaiah and Jeremiah, the Medes come to wreak rightful vengeance on the Babylonians.[5] Melanchthon emphasizes the words as an expression of divine consolation typical of this genre: the evil you encounter around you is numbered in its days, so that a clear limit is fixed (1543: 88). In fact, the idea of the numbering of the days of the evil kingdom until it is divided and comes to an end anticipates the visions of the later chapters of the book.

4. John V. Taylor, *The Growth of the Church in Uganda: An Attempt at Understanding* (London: SCM, 1958), 252–53.

5. The fulfillment of these passages may help to explain the reference in light of Darius's not being a Mede.

DANIEL 6

This chapter concludes by extolling God's everlasting reign: "His kingdom shall never be destroyed, / and his dominion has no end" (6:26). Similar doxological conclusions to the preceding stories also extol God's endless reign: 4:3 (at the end of the furnace story) and 4:34 (at the end of the tree story). There are additional verses with similar import, though they do not fit the pattern perfectly: in 2:21 God owns the times, and in 2:44 his kingdom stands forever. The coming chapter will also conclude with this doxological note: "Their kingdom shall be an everlasting kingdom" (7:27). We might guess some kind of liturgical function or liturgical antiphonal genre for 2:20; 4:3, 34; 6:26; and 7:27. It would seem more than coincidence that the stories end in this formulaic manner, though it could simply be a rhetorical device to bind them together. If these conclusions had a hymnic feature, this has implications for how the preceding stories themselves functioned in the postexilic community. In this case, it may well be that evidence of the liturgical use of the text is actually in the text itself.

6:3 soon Daniel distinguished himself above all the other presidents and satraps because an excellent spirit was in him—The Joseph-like echoes of these chapters continue (see Gen. 41:37–40).

6:4 so the presidents and the satraps tried to find grounds for complaint against Daniel in connection with the kingdom—Envy is obviously at work here, but other echoes and allusions are also to be found, including the leitmotif of the rage of the Gentiles. Consider Ps. 2:1–2: "Why do the nations conspire, / and the peoples plot in vain? / . . . The rulers take counsel together, / against the LORD and against his anointed." Here too we find the plotting of a ruler. The references to the establishment of Zion, Yahweh's claim on the ends of the earth, and the warning that kings must show wisdom are all themes picked up in the story as well.

6:7 whoever prays to anyone, divine or human, for thirty days, except to you, O king, shall be thrown into a den of lions—As in Dan. 3, a collision between idolatry and faith in the one God is contrived, in this case with specific malice of forethought toward Daniel. Now the oppression stretches even as far as private observance. The worship of other gods is not outlawed, but a period is contrived wherein the superiority of the king over all other objects of obedience is established. Of course the satraps realize that this is precisely what a pious Jew cannot do. There is, as always, a pseudoreligious dimension here, since the edict designates only Darius to be the object of petition. Keep your gods, says the edict, so long as first and last your requests come to the king, and so undercut those deities.

6:10 although Daniel knew that the document had been signed, he continued to go to his house, which had windows in its upper room open toward Jerusalem, and to get down on his knees three times a day to pray—The private act is performed so that it becomes a public confession. The point is not that Daniel is looking to be punished, though the text is careful to point out that he knew exactly what would follow. He is doing what he has always done, performing his orisons to his God. That it becomes a matter of civil disobedience is the satraps' issue, not his. The political nature of prayer emerges most naturally in this way.

On the details of Daniel's prayer we find an interesting and early example of orientation of the exilic Jew's prayer toward Jerusalem. It may be noted that in the early stage of his career in the seventh century AD, Mohamed began with this orientation, and only in the Medinan period did he change to the *qiblah*, the orientation toward Mecca.[1]

Christian commentators find additional spiritual senses in the details of Daniel's prayer. Jerome notes that he prays in the upper room, a prefiguration of Christ's prayer on Maundy Thursday prior to his suffering (1958: 65). The plausibility of this particular reading is enhanced as we consider the series of christological references in Dan. 1–7 and the consistent theme of faithful Israel suffering at the hands of the Gentiles to the end that "thy kingdom come." We also find a persistent anagogical reading, expressed by commentators in varied but similar ways. Chrysostom finds in Daniel a type of the believer who is looking for the "glory of God" that is the real end of all Christian praying (1856: 270). Finally, tropological readings are appropriate to the different circumstances of the commentators themselves. Focusing on the deadly test itself, Hippolytus reads the passage as an allegory in which Babylon is the world, Darius the devil, the satraps those who oppress Christians, and so on (2000: 178). In a less harsh vein, Melanchthon notes that Darius is actually sympathetic to Daniel and seeks a way out of the corner his edict forced him into; he is an example of the Christian ruler with *fides infirma* who needs to be shored up and to recall his obligation to support the faithful. In the face of such a king the Christian must offer a loyal, nonviolent, but firm witness (1543: 96).

1. This has never been a feature of the Christian tradition, whose eschatological orientation from the start has excluded a primary geographic feature of this sort. See, e.g., Gregory Dix, *The Shape of the Liturgy* (Westminster: Dacre, 1945), chap. 9.

6:12 the thing stands fast, according to the law of the Medes and Persians—The law binds Darius as much as it does Daniel. Even here we may find theological undertones. The claim of the law's immutability infringes on the divine prerogative; nothing is really immutable but God and his faithfulness. As we shall see as the book progresses, immutability is precisely what the Gentile kingdom in its pride cannot claim.

6:16–17 Daniel was . . . thrown into the den of lions. . . . A stone was . . . laid on the mouth of the den, and the king sealed it with his own signet—The midrashic echo of Ps. 22 is heard again: "O LORD, do not be far away! . . . / Save me from the mouth of the lion!" (22:19–21). Daniel's tribulation exemplifies the suffering of Israel at the "beastly" hands of the Gentiles. The prominence of that psalm in typological and christological readings of the passion of Christ makes such a reading unavoidable for Christian readers. The popularity of this scene in early Christian catacomb art offers an example of how this had been so throughout the church's history.[2] In Mark we see the lions celebrating in their own docile way the New Adam who now rules a restored and gardenlike creation.[3]

The heart of this christological reading is to be found in the reference to the pit into which Daniel is thrown. The pit suggests the depth of hell, where Jesus descends. In Daniel this descent forms the backdrop to the theme of ascent that is coming in Dan. 7. This contrast anticipates that of Jesus: "When it says, 'He ascended,' what does it mean but that he had also descended into the lower parts of the earth?" (Eph. 4:9).

6:24 the king gave a command, and those who had accused Daniel were brought and thrown into the den of lions—The genre of the stories in Dan. 3 and Dan. 6 is the courtly tale of reversal,[4] from being downcast to being restored. The reversal is completed as, once again, those who were complicit in the persecution are themselves killed.

This story is best read in comparison with Esther, for both require of their exilic Jewish heroes "the wisdom of serpents and the innocence of doves." In both cases they navigated the risky shoals of court life (even in its relatively more benign Persian form). Of both *hochmah* and courage are required. We find a number of common themes: the wine-soaked royal party, royal rage, the twist in the plot whereby the evildoer falls in his own snare, though in the case of Esther the villainy

2. A good example is St. Aphrahat, *Demonstrations II*, "On Persecution" (Baker Hill Kottayam: St. Ephrem, 2005), 221. On the catacomb art of martyrdom in North Africa, with its special interest in the iconography of Daniel in the lions' den, see Juliane Ohm, *Daniel und die Löwen* (Paderborn: Schoenigh, 2008).

3. Compare a similarly eschatological reading of trial in Mark 1:13: "He was with the wild beasts; and the angels waited on him."

4. For the role of reversal in the genre see, e.g., Z. Stefanovic, "Daniel: A Book of Significant Reversals," *Andrews University Seminary Studies* 30 (1992): 139–50, cited in a helpful bibliography of genre and social-scientific studies of Dan. 1–6 by David Valeta, "The Book of Daniel in Recent Research I," *Biblical Research* 13 (2008): 330–54.

is displaced onto Haman (as an interesting aside, in the case of Esth. 8:8 a royal decree is reversed, while in Dan. 6:12 this is impossible).

6:28 so this Daniel prospered during the reign of Darius and the reign of Cyrus the Persian—Several concluding words are in order. First of all, critical commentators note how Dan. 6 shows evidence of contributions and redactions from all the eras in question—Babylonian, Median, Persian, early Greek, Antiochian. Criticism itself reinforces here the sense of an ongoing tradition, which conduces to a more complex perspective on the *vaticinium ex eventu* question.

DANIEL 7

As I indicated in the introduction, Dan. 7 occupies a unique and pivotal position, since on the one hand it is part of the Aramaic block of chapters, and yet it inaugurates the night visions (Dan. 7–12).

The four beasts of Dan. 7 are reminiscent of the four sections of the statue in Dan. 2, both referring as they do to successive kingdoms. Furthermore, Dan. 6 has seen the man of God seemingly abandoned all night to the wild beasts, and now in the nighttime beasts crawl forth to attack the people of God. This hinge is rendered stronger by both Dan. 6 and Dan. 7 resulting in a decree to all the "peoples, nations, and languages" of the earth in praise of God's eternal kingdom (6:25–26 and 7:14). The action is linked, though the potential victim has changed from the individual to the corporate. The work as a whole shows more cohesion than modern critics sometimes credit it with.

The issue of coherence between the major blocks of material in the book is not merely one of genre, but also of mood and accompanying attitude toward the Gentiles. The wise, resourceful, yet principled, pragmatism of the first chapters does give way to a night of pessimism from which only the apocalyptic arrival of God himself can free the children of Israel, and yet the contrast should not be overdrawn. We can acknowledge the shift, but need to ask what that contrast really tells us. Rather than assuming ill-sutured sources, we would find a writer/redactor who can use chiaroscuro to a purpose. We have in the two sections a narrow perspective, followed by a wider-angle lens perspective. Questions of personal ethics, of fidelity and survival, find a pause as God lifts the believer up for a moment to see the panorama, both gruesome and hopeful, of what he is really doing, a wider vista the viator can readily lose. (Cf. the similar shift from admonition about faithfulness in Dan. 1–3 to the divine throne scene in Rev. 4.)

We find here an initial suggestion that, in addition to the historical/personal level of the struggle of faith, there is, in parallel and con-consubstantially, a struggle in which "we do not have to do only with flesh and blood." There is a drama in the heavenly realms themselves. This theme will emerge more powerfully in Dan. 10. This perspectival contrast is a dimension of the witness of this chapter, and the critical tension becomes an occasion of interpretive insight.

On the issue of its visions cohering with the later chapters, the best question may be the simplest. Why does the visions section of Daniel offer us four accounts of the events that led up to the affront of the "little horn" Antiochus, each in veiled or symbolic language of some kind (Dan. 7, 8, 9, 10–11)? The obvious fact is that the accounts cannot be harmonized or reconciled; each tells its tale in a distinct way. One could argue happenstance; the redactor has them and lays them out end to end. Still, it is a better assumption that he has given thought to the structure of the whole and how the four contribute to a single message.

One answer is that the four accounts offer insight into Antiochus through different themes and styles. The first presents a larger framework of history, the second picks up Dan. 7's animal symbolism in a narrower account, the third retells the tragedy from the vantage point of personal confession, and the fourth conveys a detailed historical-military account in thinly veiled language. The redactor offers us four vectors on the same reality. All four lead to Antiochus, who is presented in all cases as a picture of hubris, as the king who does as he pleases (in contrast to obedience). In each case we are reminded that the end awaits, at which point these offenses shall cease.

The four accounts have a connected or interlocking structure. The account in Dan. 7 reminds us of Dan. 2 and so serves to stitch the story and vision sections of the book together. Daniel 8 resembles in its style what preceded. Then the reference to the abomination in Dan. 8 is picked up in Dan. 9 and Dan. 11 and becomes the prominent theological fact amid all the historical accounts.

Daniel 12 includes allusions to all the preceding vision chapters and so seems to be a kind of reprise or conclusion for the whole.[1] Elements from what has preceded are recapitulated: the man in linen at the river, the times, the shattering of the people, the abomination. It is the end to which reference was made at each step along the way. What all the accounts share are the crisis toward which they narrate and the end that is its real resolution, the climax of the book as a whole. Kratz puts the relation of the chapters this way: "Chapters 9 to 11 fill out the description of the vision's reception [i.e., of Dan. 7–8], carry back into the visions themselves the historical details of the last decisive phase of history before the expected end, transport the events on earth to heaven, and count the days until the end. Why almost the same thing is said successively in four ways is explained by the redaction of the narratives and the gradual increase of the visions."[2]

In support of the coherence of these chapters of the book, though from a different angle in each chapter, we may observe a series of elements that recur

---

1. Lacocque 1976: 248–49 calls it an "epilogue" and cites its allusions to passages in Dan. 7–11.
2. Reinhard Kratz, "The Visions of Daniel," in *The Book of Daniel: Composition and Reception*, ed. John Collins and Peter Flint (Leiden: Brill, 2001), 91–113.

throughout the chapters. Taking Dan. 9 as a kind of devotional interlude, thus allowing for the continuity of Dan. 8 and Dan. 10–11, we can find the following elements: Daniel's incapacity before the divine revelation (8:27; 10:15), including a sleeplike trance (8:18; 10:15), the interpretive (and in Dan. 10 the polemical) intervention of the angels (8:16; 9:21; 10:16; 12:1), especially in the face of the kings of the Persians and Greeks (8:20; 10:20; 11:2), themes of assurance about the final outcome through numbers (8:14; 9:25), and writing and sealing a book (8:26; 10:21; 12:1).

Another way to think of the matter may be spatial. Where the action takes place in the whole of Daniel is exile, the connection of whose settings is reinforced, for example, through interpretation of prior prophecy (Dan. 9). The last form of this exile is the crisis of desecration itself, and Dan. 7 serves to place this scene as the final tableau for the book as a whole.[3] The following chapters retreat and return to this same place from different angles, but each arrives at the place it is bound for. Of course these chapters—and all that has preceded, the exile itself, Israel's and so humanity's—find their culmination in the restoration of life and the kingdom of God, first spoken of in Dan. 7 and lastly in Dan. 12. The resolution that is the kingdom of God bounds the crisis that is the kingdoms of this world. The court of Nebuchadnezzar has passed onto the court of the Lord, where angelic vision is granted; the kingdoms of this world have passed finally into the kingdom of the Ancient and the Son. Though the book unfolds across time, it has only two places, and one passes into the other (cf. Rev. 11:15: "The kingdom of the world has become the kingdom of our Lord / and of his Messiah"). Insofar as the transition is found in Dan. 7, we may again argue for its centrality to the book as a whole. The first place moves through time, though all its iterations are Babylon. Each place has an above and below, in the sense that there is a second struggle in heavenly places mirroring the one we see. The second place, the *Malkut*, abides but also arrives. Here again we may note how accurate to the spirit of Daniel Augustine was with his two cities, whose intermingling and clash make up all of human history. History is of the greatest interest—and yet of little interest to Daniel; the details of corrupt Gentile machination can be conveyed with great detail, as in Dan. 11, and yet their point remains an irrelevance.

7:1 **he wrote down the dream**—Previously, in the prophets, writing has been associated with sealing a work until such time as it can rightly be heard (Isa. 8:16), and we find this theme here as well (Dan. 12:9). Daniel writes the vision down for his own hearer/reader himself or herself. (Related to this is the rabbinic view that Daniel writes what is to be scripture, for he must recite it as well; Malbim in Goldwurm 1972: 192.) Transmission now is entailed in the very receiving of the revelation.

3. Bullinger compared Dan. 7 to a cartographer offering the wide vista of a whole land; see Willet 1610: Dan. 7, Q. 2.1.

7:2 the four winds of heaven stirring up the great sea—The verse conveys great perturbation (Calvin 1993: 10–11) and a sense of fear in the face of the destructive and uncontrollable. As with Satan himself, we are dealing here with a bounded terror, since even the four beasts emerge in ordained sequence. Similarly, the sea is stirred up by the **winds of heaven** themselves. So Jerome hears an echo of Deut. 32:8, where God gives to the nations set bounds—here they pertain even to mysterious evil from those nations (1958: 72; Calvin 1853: 11–12).

four great beasts came out of the sea—The beasts emerging from the turbulent sea bespeak the mystery of evil in God's world and its history. They remind us of the beasts with whom the children of Israel must contend in their exodus, as the psalmist tells us, even as they allude to the cosmogonic monsters told of by Israel's neighbors. The beasts are not simply a literary device to adorn a historical passage, but rather serve to deepen the mystery. Their beastliness continues as a theme in Daniel, in which evil entails the subhuman, the animal, in human, even articulate form—here we may compare Nebuchadnezzar's descent into animality in Dan. 4. One might also compare this to the manner in which Israelites thought of the sea itself, which evinced the same uncontrollable turbulence, danger, that God in his mercy had bounded.[4]

Like the Balrog arising from the depths in J. R. R. Tolkien's *Lord of the Rings*, the beasts offer us no explanation of their origin, but point us back to a disaster at the very outset of the world. Here, as so often in Daniel, the image is taken up directly in Revelation, where the "beast from the sea" emerges in Rev. 13, and the struggle that ensues essentially recapitulates its exemplar.

As to the passage's antecedents and influences, a great deal of historical-critical energy has been devoted to finding the antecedents of the beasts and the Son of Man in surrounding Near Eastern cultures,[5] and the parallels are indeed interesting. One can, for example, note the similarity to the battle of the divine Baal and the sea monster Yam in Canaanite myth, or the vision of the Netherworld in Akkadian, where one also finds a monster emerging in a night vision only to be defeated by the divine conqueror. However, the closest parallels to the scene in Dan. 7 are in fact found in the Old Testament. The genre of the night vision is found in Zech. 1–6. In the central action in Ps. 68, the Lord brings the Israelites back "from the depth of the sea" (68:22), and "rebuke[s] the wild animals that live among the reeds" (68:30) as he comes "rid[ing] in the heavens" (68:33). The writer here may have been influenced by mythic traditions of neighbors and may even be appropriating them in conscious opposition (in a manner similar to Hosea's use of *heiros gamos* material in order to challenge it; Collins 1993: 292). We may readily imagine that the external influences worked through the Old Testament material itself.

4. Ludwig Koehler, *Hebrew Man*, trans. Peter R. Ackroyd (New York: Abingdon, 1954), 109.
5. Jürg Eggler, *Influences and Traditions Underlying the Vision of Daniel 7:2–14* (Fribourg: University Press, 2000), lists them exhaustively.

These scriptural allusions serve to expand the reach of the passage to all of humankind, as well as to the limits of our experience of evil. By this subterranean means Israel's specific witness moves outward to find points of connection with the widest range of human reality. Furthermore the beasts in their symmetry and sequence tell us something about the nature of evil itself—namely, that it has a false structure and solidity that mimic those of God's creation. Philosopher of hermeneutics Paul Ricoeur spoke famously of the manner in which symbols "give rise to thought"; these features of the symbol offer insight even before it comes to be explicated.[6]

In the history of interpretation in the Christian tradition the great interest is of course in the identification of the four kingdoms and the ten kings of the "little horn" in turn: is it the Caesars? Russia? the caliphs? The further trajectory in the history of effects of this passage has been through a figure like Joachim of Fiore, who influenced a number of subsequent exegetes in finding in the fourfold pattern the key to the final, culminating phases of human history. We may, in the most expansive sense, find a trajectory from Joachim to a figure like Hegel and on to varied secularized versions of the schema of history in progressivism, Marxism, clash of civilizations, and so on.

The beasts in their antiorder are a schema of destruction in both Dan. 2 and Dan. 7; in response, the denouement is a divine arrival from straight overhead. Each passage first presents a pattern to history and then calls it sharply into question. So it is a caveat for all such schemes, even as it borrows from them, and as such it offers a caveat to Christian exegetical efforts at decipherment as well, lest we have our own historical scheme, overt or covert, at work.

Daniel 7 echoes Dan. 2 (and so Dan. 3), but the more limited menace of the latter has now become cosmic and pervasive. It is in the shadow of this menace that we find the seeds of the idea of a pattern to world history (though we find something of the Greek idea of the decline of the ages as well), for Dan. 7 presents a picture of four successive claimants to world empire. To be sure, the Greeks (and their successors the Romans) were not the first imperialists, but they were the first actually to conquer most of the known world and the first to develop the notion of universal history in their imperial wake.[7] The passage is of course not extolling the glories of the *imperium*, but mimics its presumptuous claim to universality and perfection so as to overcome it. There is a fourfold pattern, culminating with the Western ruler (Greece or Rome), the Persians' oppressor.[8] Daniel is capitalizing on prior universal historical/political schemes to undercut their pretensions and claims.

---

6. His hermeneutic, however, lists overly toward the horizon of the performative.

7. Arnaldo Momigliano, who cites Herodotus and Polybius, in *On Pagans, Christians, and Jews* (Middleton, CT: Wesleyan University Press, 1987), 46–52.

8. For the theory of a Persian anti-Roman source behind the structure of the vision in Dan. 7, see David Flusser, "The Four Empires in the Fourth Sibyl and in the Book of Daniel," *Israel Oriental Society* 2 (1972): 148–75.

Whom should we understand the beasts to be, and in particular, who is the fourth beast? I have already pointed out the parallel between the fourfold pattern of Dan. 2 and Dan. 7, a structural cord binding the earlier chapters to the later. Christian interpreters have not been of one mind as to which chapter is clearer, and so which should be interpreted in relation to the other.[9] The answer lies not in the beasts per se, but rather in the fuller account of the decisive divine intervention.

Where is this sequence of events understood to fit into the salvation history? The answers can coexist with the judgment that the "little horn" refers to Antiochus, since the question of the typological meaning remains open. For a number of interpreters, the identification of the Son of Man with Jesus requires that the fourth kingdom be Rome. Likewise Jewish interpreters find the fourth kingdom to be the Romans who in AD 70 defile the temple again. Furthermore the elastic meaning of "Rome" enables the passage to address various situations in which the interpreters find themselves. These extended senses of the *Pax Romana* include the divided medieval empire,[10] the pope in Rome, even the Turks who came to control Constantinople.

Threaded through the question of the identity of the fourth kingdom is a second: when is the text referring to the first coming of Christ, and when to the second? For example, for Nicholas of Lyra and Burgensis Dan. 2 refers to the first coming of Christ, but Dan. 7 to his second; while, for Calvin, Dan. 7 refers only to his first coming (1993: 46). In this thicket of interpretation, the best answer is that of Willet, that we find in Dan. 7 a type of the coming of Christ, begun in the first and finished in the second (1610: Dan. 7, QQ. 41, 43–44). According to the realized dimension of Christian eschatology, the beasts are already vanquished and the Son at the right hand of his Father, though we who live between the coming await the revelation of that reality openly and in glory.

7:4 the first was like a lion and had eagle's wings—Andrew of St. Victor's comments on these verses imply an echo of the oracle about the fall of Babylon and the return of the exiles in Isa. 13–14. There one may find the following themes: the tumult of the nations, the taking captive of the captors, the falling of those who would have ascended thrones in heaven.[11] This last image, of the casting down of those who would ascend in hubris as the humble one(s) ascend, is a close echo of Dan. 7.

and a human mind was given to it—Traditional commentators who find here a reference to Nebuchadnezzar (such as Saadia Gaon 2006: 526 on the Jewish

9. So Willet 1610: Dan. 7, Q. 5.1, 4, cites Calvin that greater clarity was needed since the testing would be greater as well.

10. One finds this interpretation in the eccentric commentary of Isaac Newton, *Isaac Newton's observations of the Prophecies of Daniel and the Apocalypse of John* (Lewiston, NY: Mellen, 1999).

11. Andrew of St. Victor, *Expositio super Danielem* (Turnhout: Brepols, 1990), 54–55. One should note here the darkening of the sun and moon and the travail of mothers. I argue below that Mark 13 is a Danielic discourse by Jesus through and through, and this shared allusion serves to affirm this.

side and Theodoret 2006: 177 on the Christian) may well be right; if so the allusion to his restoration to a right mind in Dan. 4 is another link back to the
preceding chapters.

7:5 another beast appeared . . . that looked like a leopard—The four heads
of the leopard could be the Persian kings or the generals who succeeded Alexander the Greek. That they refer to successive empires notable for their ferocity
and swiftness is clear. Of more interest to the Christian reader is Hos. 13:4–8,
with its reference to a ravening lion, bear, and leopard, which would seem to have
influenced the vision (Collins 1993: 295). There it is the Lord who "will become
like a lion to them" as punishment for their betrayal. For Daniel as for Hosea,
even bestial evil is under the watchful divine providential eye.

7:7 a fourth beast, terrifying and dreadful—Some commentators note the
"abominable," hybrid nature of some of these creatures, worse than the beasts of
nature. We can combine this with the observation in 7:8 that the "little horn" has
eyes like human eyes. We are dealing with a human bestiality that retains only
the appearance of its humanity.

This raises several important theological issues. Solzhenitsyn provides a modern literary midrash on the theme of human bestiality in *The Gulag Archipelago*:

> Evildoing . . . has a threshold magnitude. Yes, a human being hesitates and bobs
> back and forth between good and evil all his life. He slips, falls back, clambers
> up, repents, things begin to darken again. But just so long as the threshold of evil
> is not crossed, the possibility of returning remains, and he himself is still within
> reach of our hope. But when, through the density of evil actions, the result either
> of their own extreme degree or the absoluteness of his power, he suddenly crosses
> the threshold, he has left humanity behind, and without perhaps the possibility
> of return.[12]

The human being is a creature who has in himself or herself the possibility of
descent to the bestial, indeed it is possible for the human to become more bestial
than beasts, because we should have moral conscience. This possibility is most
visible and the risk greatest as we act in herds. It is no accident that human bestiality is associated with the power and pretension of empire. Where one so declines
as to be incapable of restoration, only the form of the *imago Dei* remains. Even
so, such a person, in his or her damned rebellion, remains a human being. While
this risk of sin is especially great in the structures that we project from ourselves,
the externalized humanity of a system, it is found not only there. Individuals too
have a struggle between the bestial and the child of the holy ones of heaven in
them. Hence there is a place for reading Dan. 7, as the medievals did, in a more
moral and personal way.[13]

12. Cited in Edward Ericson, *Solzhenitsyn: The Moral Vision* (Grand Rapids: Eerdmans, 1980), 167–68.
13. E.g., Gilbert, in Mark Zier, *Expositio Super Danielem: Critical Edition and Study I* (diss., University
of Toronto, 1983), 42–43, on the beast and the fire of love in the heart of the individual monk.

7:9 thrones were set in place, / and an Ancient One took his throne—The expression **Ancient of Days** (= NRSV's **Ancient One**) is found only here; the parallels to similar divine titles may be readily acknowledged (Collins 1993: 190), though it is harder to say how their influence was brought to bear on this use. It could be that we have an implied polemic: in contrast to the beasts in their limited times (and their gods as well), now comes the one who truly surpasses all times. He is at work in time, but as the Ancient of Days has "prevailed over days and times."[14] This is in implied contrast to the insolent ruler who would change times (7:25), for all times are already in the hands of the Ancient of Days. The central role of the times is underscored. They are meted out and known by God, even when their reckoning is hard for us. The Ancient of Days not only imperturbably reigns over, but also permeates a scene that seems to humans both urgent and foreclosed.

But who exactly is the Ancient of Days? Some commentators point to God himself in his eternity (Iunius in Willet 1610: Dan. 7, Q. 39.5), but the preponderance of Christian commentators identify him with the person of the Father,[15] since they understand the scene as a whole to be the ascension of Jesus.

Not one, but an unspecified number of thrones are set up. It is not clear for whom they are intended: angels? saints? One rabbi even suggests kings over whom God presides in council. Rashi offers the theologically suggestive, though speculative, opinion that the thrones are for judgment and for mercy (in Goldwurm 1972: 203). We cannot tell, but what we do know is that all these parties are focused on the central action taking place between the Son of Man and the Ancient of Days.

Christians note Jesus's words in Luke 22:28–30, which bear directly on our passage. There Jesus tells the disciples that because they have suffered with him in his *peirasmoi*, his eschatological trials, he,[16] who has been given dominion (*basileia*) by his father, will give them thrones to share in "judging the twelve tribes of Israel" (which means taking a share in the kingship over the people of God).

Excursus: The Relationship of the Throne Scenes in Dan. 7 and Rev. 4–22

In the introduction I noted the close relationship between Dan. 7 and Revelation. The book as a whole is an extended, almost collagelike, visionary reflection on the tableau of the throne in Dan. 7. The scene itself begins in Rev. 4,[17] though with more detail about the glorious appearance of the Ancient of Days and his throne and with elaboration of the Son of Man as the wounded Lamb now added. The thrones, the thousand thousands, and their songs of praise in Rev. 5 are drawn directly from

14. Andrew of St. Victor, *Expositio super Danielem*, 161.
15. In the Middle Ages, e.g., the *Glossa ordinaria* (see Willet 1610: Dan. 7, Q. 32.1); in the Reformation, Calvin 1853: 33.
16. The parallel in Matt. 19:28 actually uses the expression "Son of Man."
17. Even the opening chapters are a kind of echo, insofar as each is a section of exilic wisdom for survival with faithfulness.

Dan. 7 and recur in Rev. 7. The opening of the sealed book is elaborated throughout Rev. 6. The theme of the scroll is developed in Rev. 10. In Rev. 11, we are told in a song of praise that the raging of the nations has ended and that "the kingdom of the world has become the kingdom of our Lord / and of his Messiah, / and he will reign forever and ever." The latter constitutes an apt summary of the transition that lies at the heart of Dan. 7 itself. The book then proceeds with a battle of Michael and his angels with the dragon (Rev. 12; cf. Dan. 10), a scene with a ten-horned beast with a composite form of leopard, bear, and lion (Rev. 13; cf. Dan. 7), and a proclamation that the hour of judgment had come (Rev. 14; cf. Dan. 7).

The next three chapters offer in succession prophetic songs about the fall of Babylon, the praise songs of the nations, a reprise of the struggle of the angels and Satan, and the opening of the books. It is as if the author circles around and intersplices all these Danielic themes. The book ends with a vision of the city whose streams flow from "the throne of God and of the Lamb," a final vision of beatitude recapitulating one last time the Danielic throne scene from and around which all the action in Revelation has moved. In sum, Revelation is a kind of fugue on Daniel, rearranging, reflecting further, adding detail, revealing more about the central characters, but all the while keeping the original setting, dramatis personae, and leitmotifs.

With so close a relationship, what enduring witness does Dan. 7 have about this scene, in contradistinction to its fuller and more vivid successor? What is the "surplus of meaning" provided by this prior witness to the ascension? Of the four horizons of interpretation I discussed in the introduction, the original Danielic scene preserves the plain sense related to the exile. This in turn guards against interpretations that are overly spiritualized, speculative, or mystical (as interpretation of Revelation may readily tend to be). Daniel 7 also helps as the reader grapples with the practical perplexities of exilic life. Furthermore, Dan. 7 is a prospective account of the ascension that as yet knows nothing of the "how" of the atonement. Though the battle rages, matters are already resolved, the beast burned, the Son presented, the nations drawn. We hear nothing of the battle between good and evil (here in Dan. 7, at least), and so the passage has a certain effortlessly and decisively indicative quality that is consistent with God's word that is spoken and comes to pass.

and the hair of his head like pure wool—How can God the Father in his holiness and unutterable mystery be described in this vision as an old and white-haired man on a throne? Commentators have several strategies to answer this question. Saadia Gaon mentions that he has heard this complaint from the Islamic Mu'talizite school and counters that the symbol of the old man stands not for God himself, but rather for his glory (2006: 536). Calvin says that God offers "varied forms according to human capacities," in keeping with his doctrine of accommodation (1853: 31). According to each suggestion God takes the initiative in offering a picture appropriate to his nature. We may also note the typically biblical restraint of depiction, according to which we can see "around" him, but cannot behold his face or self. Finally we may as Christians see the whole scene as an extension of the revelation of the incarnate Second Person of the Trinity, who, ascended, comes to the enthroned Father; his incarnation is the divine act that puts anthropomorphism on a new footing.[18]

7:9–10 his throne was fiery flames, / and its wheels were burning fire. A stream of fire issued / and flowed forth from his presence—In form our present passage is a throne theophany, and so its closest relative is the vision of the chariot of fire with its wheels within wheels in Ezek. 1:4–28, revealing as it does the glory of the Lord (replete with winds, fire, creatures, and a humanlike creature). The fire expresses the terrible holiness, the wheels his instantaneous swiftness. Toward such a God we cannot work our way. The fire flames forth when and as it will (Exod. 3:2, 14). So it was at midnight for Pascal, who did not find an approach through the philosophers, but could only cry out secretly "Fire!" The nature of this fire was well captured by the scholar of religious experience when he called it "shaking and inviting,"[19] for it is experience of that which surpasses and undoes human experience, which could destroy us but grants that we should live. This consuming fire (Heb. 12:29) is not to be taken lightly, nor can it be brought under our purview, construction, or use. The commentators rightly perceive in the fire of the throne a glint of the fire of purgation and judgment.[20] The first use to which this fire is put in the passage is the immolation of the beast (Dan. 7:11).

This passage is one of the sources of the extravagant Merkabah mysticism of Jewish interpretation, and Christianity has its own analogues. The prevenience and holy otherness of God set the necessary prerequisites for all mystical readings and practices of the church. One might think as well of the myriad forms of charismatic worship that set their attention on the glory of the Lord and the experience of its effects. The breathtaking advance of Pentecostalism in global Christianity receives both warrant and corrective in a passage such as this one.

If the form of the passage is prophetic throne theophany,[21] we may note that other parallel theophanies consist of the *visio Dei*, followed by the calling of the prophet. In our passage, however, we look in vain for the latter. Are we to understand Daniel's writing and sealing of the vision to be his call? Or may we as Christians take the call to be missing and read, in our own canonical way, the unsealing and the suffering mission of the church of Revelation to be the calling deferred and finally realized?

The action in this scene takes place in its own realm, and yet it is human history that God is taking control of. It comes as the cessation of history and is also given as a vision of a reality in the center of history in all its painfulness. This

---

18. Such was the conclusion of the iconoclastic controversy in the seventh century.

19. Pascal, *Pensees*, trans. John Warrington (London: Dent, 1960), 203, frag. 737; and Rudolf Otto's famous "*mysterium tremendum et fascinans*" in *The Idea of the Holy* (Oxford: Oxford University Press, 1968).

20. Andrew of St. Victor, *Expositio super Danielem*, 62–63.

21. Matthew Black, "Throne Theophany, Prophetic Commission, and the 'Son of Man,'" in *Jews, Greeks, and Christians: Religious Cultures in Late Antiquity: Essays in Honor of William David Davies*, ed. Robert Hamerton-Kelly and Robin Scroggs (Leiden: Brill, 1976), 57–73.

bifocal nature of the scene reminds us of Hebrews, where we also find the rest as a state within, above, and ahead of the pilgrims. The ascension is an event in the life of Jesus that draws the nations to himself and into the church, which cannot be seen as simply separate from the history of the world, nor as reducible to it. The two planes are distinguishable but not to be separated; both must be kept continually in view. God's drawing of the Gentiles is of prime significance to this other plane, and yet this action is inseparable from the horror and fragility of the world history of empires.

7:10 and the books were opened—I have already mentioned the reference to the sealing of the words in 12:9. Another reference to a book is found in 10:21, where inscribed in "the book of truth" are the deeds thereafter shown in the vision to happen. We can well imagine that the book opened here tells of the events of which the ensuing verses describe. Are we to understand the opening to set these events in motion? The idea of their being written assures us that they are bound to take place and reminds us that what will occur conforms to what God wills and says. We naturally turn next to 12:1, where the book seems to contain the names of those bound for eternal life. It would be consistent with the first use to see this as the inscription of God's saving future acts applied to individuals.[22]

7:13 one like a human being—The qualification **like** parallels that of the beasts who have preceded the **Son of Man** (= NRSV's **human being**) in the action. It may also indicate an altered quality of a vision and again adds the element of reticence appropriate to descriptions of the divine in the Old Testament.

It is natural, next, to wonder to whom does this **Son of Man** refer? While there is a relation to the beasts, a key as it were, matters are much less clear here. The range of possibilities and the difficulty in adjudicating which is correct remind us of the debate over the identity of the Suffering Servant passages of Isa. 40–55. The minimalist position holds that the phrase refers simply to a human being, perhaps with special emphasis on his fragility and humility. As such he is presented as a stark contrast to the ferocity and power of the beasts he will overcome (Goldingay 1989: 149–53 lays out the range of options well). At the maximalist pole is the **coming with the clouds** in the Old Testament being what the Lord does when he comes in power and vindication. A divine epithet is clearly attributed to the Son of Man. Somewhere in the middle might be found an interpretation such as that of Collins, who points out that the expression elsewhere in the later chapters is used of angels in general and Michael in particular. So Collins identifies the **Son of Man** as an angel (1993: 304–10). Or,

22. There are, however, many other interpretations of these books. Here is a smorgasbord of possibilities: all the evil done by Gentiles to Jews (Saadia Gaon 2006: 545; Ibn Ali Jephet, *A Commentary on the Book of Daniel*, trans. D. S. Margliouth [Oxford: Clarendon, 1889], 35), the preaching of the gospel (Calvin 1853: 36), and the scriptures (Bede) (in Willet 1610: Dan. 7, Q. 37.1–6). These may be understood as more specific or particular ways of speaking of the books of the coming deeds of God, i.e., parts of the "plot" revealed in Dan. 7. Other readings, e.g., that the books tell of our conscience (Jerome 1958: 79) or of our sins (Rashi in Goldwurm 1972: 204), point us toward more tropological readings.

alternately, is this symbolic figure a stand-in for the whole nation, since the Son of Man receives **dominion** in 7:14 only to have it given to **the people of the holy ones of the Most High** in 7:27?[23]

Interpretation, however, is more complicated than determining an original referent. While acknowledging that such a referent is ambiguous, the later Christian tradition is unanimous in finding here a typological reference to Jesus Christ. Ascended, he comes to the throne of his Father, and as a result of the ensuing Gentile mission, the nations follow in his train. Our question could equally well be this: what does this subsequent interpretation, based on the employment of the Danielic reference in the New Testament, do to our initial question? Here the ambiguity of interpretation becomes fecund. In its range it suggests a trajectory. The Son of Man is a fragile human being; the Son of Man is the Lord of hosts—resolving the tension is the history of the first half millennium of the early church as it reflected on the New Testament's witness about Jesus Christ. Even in the period of the apostolic fathers,[24] the category of the angelic could be fluidly in play for the interpretation both of the nature of Jesus and that of the Holy Spirit. We see with the hindsight of the tradition of canonical interpretation that the range for the Son of Man forms the field in which christological and Trinitarian interpretation will eventually take place.

and was presented before him—The presentation is imagined to be part of some kind of investiture, since it involves the handing over of authority. It could well be that the royal liturgy behind Ps. 2 pertains here. The reference to the raging of the nations may have corresponded to some kind of enacted liturgical battle or opposition.[25] An investiture or coronation scene comports well symbolically with the ascension of Jesus to his Father. It provides the template for our own worship: the defeat of our own resistance at the declaration of Christ as king and our resultant praise.

7:14 to him was given dominion—The nations' service, including the giving of honor, is the form by which the authority of God may be duly recognized. In the performative reading, the due service of the nations is worked out in history even as it finds historical expression in worship in the congregations of the faithful. Such is the "liturgy" due God from the nations "from the rising of the sun to its setting" (Mal. 1:11). Our worship is to be missional, our mission doxological.

---

23. Lacocque 1976: 146 is an example of this view. Since I have mentioned the ways in which the schema of the four kingdoms was related to visions of empire, I should mention how Daniel's saints were also seen to prefigure later kingdoms and empires. The Daniel tradition spawned a postliterature—and pseudoliterature—in the next millennium that provided warrants for kingdoms Byzantine and Muslim. See Lorenzo DiTomaso, *The Book of Daniel and the Apocryphal Daniel Literature*, Studia in Veteris Testamenti Pseudepigrapha 20 (Leiden: Brill, 2005).

24. *Shepherd of Hermas* Sim. 5–6, in *Apostolic Fathers*, trans. Kirsopp Lake (London: Heinemann, 1913), 2.164–83.

25. On this score Sigmund Mowinkel's imagination is suggestive in *The Psalms in Israel's Worship* (Grand Rapids: Eerdmans, 2004), 106–92, where the celebration of the king in Zion at the New Year overcoming his Gentile/beastly adversaries is often the backdrop for the worship we read of in the Psalms.

Theologizing itself is doxological, since we are talking of what we cannot yet see face to face (1 Cor. 13:12), and worship shares this quality of being revelationally guided talk about what is shown but has not yet been fulfilled.[26] The experiential dimension of worship, including the ecstatic and charismatic, takes its bearings from the stage on which the action is set.

kingship—Given the prominence of the concept of the "kingdom of God" in the New Testament, it is surprising to realize that this is the only place in the Old where an approximation to the phrase is found.[27] To be sure, the Psalms declare that Yahweh reigns (e.g., the royal psalms, Pss. 95–99), and this tradition surely lies behind the present use. But the kingship or dominion as something to be handed off or praised may be traced back to this passage. So one can read the proclamation of the nearness of the kingdom by Jesus himself in Mark 1, in the context of John's announcement of the end of the kingdom before and the victory over Satan after. This proclamation, understood to declare the coming of a king (*euangelion*), has a distinctly Danielic background.[28]

For theological purposes, it is important to notice again how the passage places this phrase into relation with a web of other terms that affect how it may legitimately be used. One ought not to invoke the kingdom of God as something wider than traditional Christology allows, as nineteenth-century liberalism tried to do. Nor should it be understood as something that leaves behind consideration of the church: the coming of the nations to worship with Israel is the main action of the *Malkut*. But it is surely wider than the parochial concerns of any particular denomination, locale, or era—it is the whole movement of the Gentiles, and from the perspective of the whole of completed history, that is offered here.[29]

that all peoples, nations, and languages—There is a complex pattern of gathering and scattering both in the background and the action of the book. The nations are threateningly gathered into a unity at Babel (read Babylon), in the hubristic manner characteristic of empire, and must be scattered by God in Gen. 11. Now the action is in a sense reversed. The people of God are scattered in exile, so that by God's providence those nations might be gathered in to God. The multiple languages consequent on Babel remain, but they are offering a single glory. The

---

26. Wolfhart Pannenberg's "Analogy as Doxology," in *Basic Questions in Theology* (Philadelphia: Fortress, 1970), 1.212–38.

27. David Wenham, "The Kingdom of God and Daniel," *Expository Times* 98 (1987): 132–34, points out that the readiness to trace kingdom talk, but not Son of Man talk, to the *ipsissima verba* comes from a failure to see the common Danielic reference.

28. O'Donovan, *Desire of the Nations*, 88–90.

29. In Christopher Morse's *The Difference Heaven Makes: Rehearsing the Gospel as News* (London: T&T Clark, 2010), the language of heaven is rehabilitated helpfully in terms that we would call existential/performative. "Heaven" (or "kingdom") has meaning as the whence of God's coming to us, as the person of the saga narrated to us, and as the promise proclaimed to us. The book both highlights the existential dimension and preserves his mysterious transcendence. But the mode of encounter Morse does not mention is mission, the global gathering of Gentiles, and this commentary would offer to his argument this augmentation.

Pentecost story in Acts 2 is the bookend for the Genesis passage, its outworking this verse in Daniel.

should serve him—We are meant to hear an echo of the words of Nebuchadnezzar in 4:1: "To all peoples, nations, and languages that live throughout the earth: May you have abundant prosperity!" The false claimant is contrasted with the true, even as the raging of the former is overcome by the heavenly victory of the latter. Here we may compare the mimicry that is often pointed out in the Christmas story, where the true universal good news of a *sōtēr* ("savior"), weak though it seems, is contrasted with a false one.

In this verse, and elsewhere in this chapter, the key Old Testament text providing background is Ps. 68. The echoes are remarkably extensive: an exultant song is lifted up to Yahweh, victorious, who is described as the one "who rides upon the clouds" (68:4) and "ride[s] in the heavens, the ancient heavens" (68:31). He gives "the desolate [exiles?] a home again" (68:6). He scatters kings; he comes with "thousands upon thousands" (68:17) to Zion. To that place of worship he leads the defeated nations as "captives in [his] train" (68:18). He defeats "the wild animals that live among the reeds" (68:30), a phrase evoking both creation and exodus. Now all the kingdoms of the earth are required to sing to the Lord (68:32). What does this strong thematic precedent tell us? While the form of the prophetic night vision may be newer, and some themes introduced (the angelic role, the Son of Man coming on the clouds, the historical scheme, etc.), the discontinuity associated with the apocalyptic genre should not be overemphasized. The centerpiece of Daniel develops a *Gestalt* of themes already found in the tradition.

The idea of the nations as the prizes, offerings for God in the victor's train, reappears in the New Testament, and as such it is important for Christians. Their role, as we hear here in Dan. 7, is to praise God, their creator, the one who providentially willed their restoration. This same image of the Gentiles in the train of the triumphant, resurrected, ascended Christ is found in 2 Cor. 2:14: "Thanks be to God, who in Christ always leads us in triumphal procession." That it is the Gentiles' time to be summoned is a sign of the impending end. That summons, what Christians call mission, is inseparable from the identity of the ascended Christ toward which they are drawn. This same connection is confirmed in the second application of the image of the captive train, in Ephesians, where the main point is the "mystery" of the inclusion of the Gentiles (3:3, 5). The verse in question is Eph. 4:8, a quotation from Ps. 68:18: "When he ascended on high he made captivity itself a captive." It is found there in a passage about unity, perseverance in suffering, and diversity of gifts in the one body, the church, for its mission to and by the Gentiles. This allows us to think of the church, in Danielic style, as a single, comprehensive, embodied reality as it is drawn in praise to the Father by the Son. This is the real heart of the history of humankind in the *kairos* of the ascension, though the raging of nations continues for a time and has its own passing reality.

We find repeated appropriations of the phrase **peoples, nations, and languages** in Revelation. There the three are sometimes complemented by a fourth, which would convey the perfection of the time of fulfillment: sometimes "nation" is added, and sometimes "kings,"[30] to indicate that transition of authority from the nations to Christ—the emendation is more Danielic than Daniel. The nature of the victory through the shattering of God's people and the wounding of the Lamb himself is developed through the connection between the two. Powerlessness as the context of the transfer of power is underlined.

Finally we may point to a tropological reading, against the performative horizon. The Christian is called to humility, as we hear the rabbinic reading, which speaks of the giving of honor, praise, and power as the restoration of all that the persecution by the Gentiles has stolen from Israel (Mayenei haYeshuah in Goldwurm 1972: 207).

7:15–18 Calvin offers the best application of the verses to address the condition of the ordinary Christian, for we, like Daniel, become anxious at the commotion around us, in answer to which we are reminded that our real citizenship is in heaven. But, lacking a handy angel, of whom are we to ask for such a reminder? Our own pastor is to be as an angel who serves as a messenger and interpreter of the same word from God Daniel hears (1853: 47–48).

7:22, 27 the holy ones of the Most High ... the people of the holy ones of the Most High—We have, with this phrase, the same allusive ambiguity we found with "Son of Man" (which Goldingay 1989: 148 aptly categories as "tensive symbols," following Wheelwright). One can more readily list these ambiguities than solve them: Are the saints in question earthly or heavenly beings? Is the Son of Man to be understood in some sense as the corporate representation of them as a people? A good place to begin is with some Old Testament themes that are the verse's background and so inform its interpretation: the heavenly council, with the Lord enthroned before the angelic beings (as well as the subordinated "gods of the nations"), the fluidity of people and personality in Isaiah's Servant Songs, and finally the royal psalms, (perhaps) with the newly crowned king before the Lord, (presumably) at a liturgical gathering of the people in the temple.

Though identification may be exegetically difficult, the location is clearer and of equal importance. We should think of all these actors together in a single dramatic scene. In all three background traditions, that scene is courtly and/or liturgical: the Lord victoriously enthroned, the representative one ascended to him, the people gathered around, along with the heavenly ones, before whom the nations and their gods are subservient (or judged or amazed, etc.). It is the tableau that is ultimately most telling, as we can see from its appropriation in Revelation (and that we continue to recall in the eucharistic liturgy as we pray "with angels and archangels," before we are spiritually taken into the holy of holies by Jesus's sacrifice, once offered).

7:25 he shall attempt to change the sacred seasons and the law—The immediate reference is to Antiochus's suspension of the calendar of temple worship

30. Bauckham, *Climax of Prophecy*, 263–65.

and his blasphemous insertion of the Saturnalia (Lacocque 1976: 153). But the deeper sense, which we find throughout Daniel, is that times belong to God. Plans to control or change them are an affront to him, who alone in his sovereignty "changes times and seasons, / deposes kings and sets up kings" (2:21). Homiletically we can see modern claims to control history and schemata toward that end (e.g., workers' paradise, global Sharia, "end of history," even a rigid and detailed Christian dispensationalism) as attempts to change the times.

and they shall be given into his power / for a time, two times, and half a time—If we take 12:5–13 to be a kind of reprise of the apocalyptic chapters that have preceded, then the most obvious interpretation of **a time, two times, and half a time** is (more or less) the 1,290 days of 12:11, which is roughly the span of Antiochus's terrorization of Jerusalem. This does not, however, exhaust the expressive power of this compressed phrase. The symbolic designation shows us that it is a time period set within God's plan and control. It has a relation to the biblical and perfect number seven. For God to come in half the allotted time is to say that he will come "with all deliberate speed." His coming may seem to tarry (a time and then times), but its final arrival will be sudden (a time cut off). Like the seventy years multiplied in Dan. 9, this half-seven may be subject to reinterpretation. Its coming may be elongated or hastened according to his will (see comments on calculation in Dan. 8). God's time can arrive only on time.

7:28 here the account ends—The explanation of the preceding vision may seem almost as encrypted as the vision itself. Why are matters not made clearer to us? Saadia says that we have reached the "limit and ends of prophecy"—namely, the "final resting place" (2006: 560)—and we must await the time of salvation to learn more. We have, in other words, heard what we are able, in our present state as *viatores*, to hear. There is a kind of doctrine of accommodation here as well, for which the symbolic and open-ended nature of the communication is suited (cf. 1 Cor. 13:12; 1 John 3:2). This in effect responds to an implicit sense we may have at times that a work like Daniel is too malleable and underdetermined. We are reassured that what can and should be said under our conditions has been said, though we may be no more settled in our spirits than Daniel himself.

DANIEL 8

The vision of the animals in Dan. 8 obviously follows on that of the preceding chapter, though the symbols here are less mysterious and allusive. The form of the vision is most reminiscent of Ezek. 8 (as Goldingay 1989: 200, among others, points out). There an angelic figure transports the prophet in a vision to the temple, where he beholds the "abominating" defilement of the temple, which results in the wrath of God. Of course, in Ezekiel's case the idolatrous abomination was Israel's own doing and caused them to be sent into exile. Now the very height of abomination is the Gentile king's doing, and it "fills up" sin so as to lead to the "appointed time," at the end of the time of wrath, when the extended exile may itself end.

8:7, 22 two horns . . . four [horns]—Here again we find the human who has descended to the subhuman, not in some romanticist notion of the primitive, but rather in the power and complexity of empire. The beasts can be summed up as horns, as destructive things. We may compare this descent of the creature to a thing to that of the *machine*, the mechanism. This may be one reason it is hard to get a metaphysical fix on Satan and the evil powers—are they personal or structural? (One may compare the debate about the biological status of viruses as living creatures.) This is exactly the point, since the descent has, at its heart, the depersonalized. By contrast, relation to God always calls the creature into conversation with another person: "Adam where are you?" For this insight modern theology was helped most by the personalism of the great Hasidically informed Jewish philosopher, Martin Buber.

Here we may acknowledge the witness of those who emphasize the clash of empires, God's and this world's, which is key to understanding the New Testament (as well as a book like Daniel) and lies behind the life of the church today.[1] We

---

1. One can think, e.g., of a magazine such as *Sojourners* or a New Testament scholar like Ched Myers in his *Binding the Strongman* (Maryknoll: Orbis, 1990).

need to bear in mind how pervasive the empire of this world is, encompassing as it does Marxist, socialist, Islamist, and capitalist versions. In some of the reactions against empire may also be found the pedigree of romanticism, which also pioneered in the modern reaction to machine. There is a connection between the critique of empire and opposition to the tyranny of the machine. The voices of cultural pessimism are well known—for example, that of Jacques Ellul—who prophetically warned two generations ago about the technologization of social relations that thinks of the human in terms of a machine.[2] The consequences of this are not hard to find: the utilitarian in ethics, the grasping of the power of life and death, the absorption of all human activity into the arithmetic of market relations through sensation and propaganda, science that is reductionist, the humanities that are ultimately nihilistic, and so on. It may be that science fiction writers, with their interest in robots and humanoids, grasp the possibilities better. Already Western governments see no problem with genetic hybrids (if only for brief incubation and study!) of human or fish or frog. Already scientists wonder if one binary carbon system called the computer and the other called the brain could be fused, lacking as they do a significant qualitative distinction.

The point here may be drawn directly from a witness like Daniel against the adversary who is a horn: the church of God, in its witness to God, will soon be the only witness on behalf of the human as well. To be sure, the structures of the machine are inevitably found inside the church as well, for we are also citizens of the city of this world. This does not mean that only believers are really human. But it does mean that there will come a time when only believers can remind the city of this world what the human is. This is the real issue that peeks out from the culture wars, confused though those clashes be, and it abides as the reason seemingly secondary debates matter.[3]

8:9–12 With the appearance of the little horn, Antiochus, we arrive at the destination of the vision, where the symbolic language becomes harder to decipher. The best insight into Daniel's meaning is again found in hearing the echoes of other prophetic passages. Collins points our attention to Isa. 14, a dirge and taunt against the Babylonians of Nebuchadnezzar—and so the passage's most appropriate background (1993: 332). The Babylonian king falsely claims to ascend the heavenly throne, above the stars themselves (14:12–14). The presumption against God found in the little horn is the same seen in Isaiah's "Day Star." The reference to the stars has several additional resonances in Dan. 7–12. We have heard at the end of the previous chapter about the "holy ones," who are in close fellowship with people of God. We will see again in Dan. 10 that affront against the God of Israel entails a wider spiritual warfare. Finally, in 12:3, the resurrection destiny of the saints will be compared, as with the angels, "like the stars."

2. Jacques Ellul, *The Technological Society* (New York: Knopf, 1967).

3. Gershom Scholem connects the beasts of Daniel with the figure of the *golem* in kabbalistic writings, for this humanlike creature wrecked havoc upon the earth "by the power of the tellurian element," but at the leave of "the name of God"; *On the Kabbalah and Its Symbolism* (New York: Schocken, 1996), 182.

8:13 how long?—The oft-repeated lament and cry for divine help in the Old Testament is found, for example, in Ps. 74, where the heathen have desecrated the sanctuary in Jerusalem. The psalmist is then reminded that the God of Israel, who "broke the heads of the dragons in the water" and protects the soul of the innocent from "wild animals" (74:13, 19), still saves, for he establishes the times of day, the stars, the bounds of earth of the seasons (74:16–17). But in our chapter these words come from a holy one, and the question is asked in order that the answer might be given. The limit of the quantum of the sins of the Gentiles is set (Dan. 8:23), and the time of deliverance sealed. In this way the use of **how long?** resembles a passage such as Num. 14:11: "And the LORD said to Moses, 'How long will this people despise me?'"—a rhetorical question that declares the time of the setting right to be on the way.

the transgression that makes desolate—See comments at 9:27.

8:14 for two thousand three hundred evenings and mornings; then the sanctuary shall be restored—No question is more perplexing than that of the detailed, seemingly conflicting sets of numbers to predict coming events, especially in Dan. 8, 10, and 12. The easiest ways to dismiss the problem are closed to us. On the one hand one could take the historical-critical situation of Antiochus's reign as sufficient explanation for the numbers, perhaps turning to a psychological (neurotic need for control), political (need for courage of an oppressed minority), or sociological (cognitive dissonance) explanation. On the other hand one could set out to do the sums, find a correlation, and so await one's addition to the cemetery of failed arithmetic schemes. In this faddish era, with kabbalah in vogue, one could try some numerology of one's own, though 1,335 does not offer ready symbolic sense. On this score, we part company with many of our forebears, not least Luther, who valued Daniel precisely because of the reliability of his calculations to predict historical events.[4] At least we may offer, in keeping with a moral reading, that the numbers say God is in charge, and their imperviousness to interpretation says that we are not to know how. This is true enough, but still we wonder about the numbers' detail and their seeming conflict one with another.

On the topic of calculation the opinion of the rabbis is informative. Up until the medieval period there was greater reticence about predicting through the use of numbers. The rabbis cited, from Daniel itself,[5] Belshazzar's mistaken interpretation of Jeremiah's foretold seventy weeks as an example of the risk, and even the sin, of calculation. Though the medieval rabbis were more willing to give specific interpretations of the numbers, in large measure because the arrival of the Messiah seemed more imminent, they retained some qualms. Rashi said that calculations were not misguided unless their proving wrong led to the weakening of believers'

---

4. Martin Luther's preface to Daniel in *Works* (Philadelphia: Muhlenberg, 1939), 4.420.

5. Guenther Stemberger, "Die Jüdische Danielrezeption seit der Zerstörung des zweiten Tempels am Beispiel der Endzeitberechnung," in *Europa, Tausandjähriges Reich und Neue Welt: Zwei Jahrtausande Geschichte und Utopie in der Rezeption des Danielsbuches*, ed. Mariano Delgado, Klaus Koch, and Edgar Marsch (Freiburg: Universität Verlag, 2003), 139–58.

faith, a guideline that implies that counting should have an edifying intent (in Goldwurm 1972: 212–13). So numbers can be accounted for, albeit cautiously, but their moral and spiritual effect is never out of view.

This leads us to the most important interpretative guideline on the subject, from no less an authority than Jesus himself. Mark 13:32—"but about that day or hour no one knows, neither the angels in heaven, nor the Son, but only the Father"[6]— addresses the abiding question "how long?" but also alludes to numerological speculation in the Danielic lineage. Could the angels here mentioned be those who bring the numbers to a bewildered Daniel and who figure so prominently in the related apocryphal literature? Jesus does not say that there is not a day and hour to be known, only that we are not to attempt to know it. Numbers should encourage us in the proper spiritual posture: "Watch!" At the same time, Jesus insists that signs derived from Daniel can be observed and that his own words, infused with its words, will not fade with time into insignificance (Mark 13:31). The advice derives from the Son of Man himself, whose "coming on the clouds" remains imminent, though we still await it. The day and hour are hard to reckon, not least because Christian time itself must be reckoned in a new way. Not only Daniel has mysterious, overlapping time schemes: so does postresurrection history.

Surely the hardest part of Mark 13:32 is that even the Son does not know the times. Omniscience is a divine attribute. It is in his kenotic reality as incarnate that the Son does not know the times. In short, that which we try to calculate is divine knowledge, though stated in human terms. In heaven, according to the *scientia Dei* that the saints and angels have, we will understand their calculations. We can understand divine knowledge only analogically. That there will be an end is understandable on our own terms, but the doing of the sum is not. Here we might offer as an example the fig tree, whose leaves provide the parabolic sign of the coming fulfillment. Jesus's curse of the fig tree earlier (Mark 11:12–14, 20–24) was a sign of the coming of the foretold judgment, in which the disciples must have faith. But in a related parable in Luke 13:6–9, the deserved judgment is delayed by the patient owner, for an extra season, in case there be repentance. For us numbers and their alignment, historical prediction and its fulfillment, may seem a fixed business. Either God wills what the scheme calls for, or else he is patient, blessed be his name; in the latter case he has chosen to abrogate the predicted events. But surely God's relationship to events, to their willing and knowing, is not like ours, nor is his relationship to their representation in numerical schemes, even of his own revealing, transparent to us. To think these numbers to be in our ken to reckon is akin to thinking of God's willing as on a par with our own. Likewise apocalyptic predictions do not impose a rigid, fatalistic set of iron bars on history. Our God can bring the kingdom in power in the resurrection of his Son, for which event we still wait! These are numbers, susceptible of counting, and they

6. If we consider the other closely related passage, Acts 1:7, we hear a debate involving Christ's disappearance in a cloud and when he should be expected to return. All this has a Danielic ring as well!

will be counted, but for now only by God. For us they remain an "open secret,"[7] luminous and encouraging mysteries, which may be understood, and trusted, as signs of his coming, but for now without benefit of arithmetic.

8:16 Gabriel, help this man understand the vision—The angelic milieu in which the struggle and victory may be found for the people of God is an idea foreign to most Western perspectives, be they liberal or conservative.[8] This has been to the detriment of the cause of Christian mission, since tribal cultures in Africa and elsewhere have recognized the gap between these Western accounts of the world and that of the New Testament. This has been a major factor, for example, in the success of African independent churches. This is also related to what missiologist Paul Hiebert calls the "excluded middle,"[9] the evacuation of the intervening space between God and humans in cosmology, where the divine can be active in the concreta of people's lives. Reading Dan. 8–11 in conjunction with the missionary mandate of Dan. 7 and in light of the sense of "the times" in Dan. 12 helps to give the angels serious metaphysical and theological consideration, without giving them too much of a role, on the salvation-historical stage. How do these controls exerted by the larger framework work?

The New Testament worldview assumes, throughout, a creaturely order that included "powers and principalities," which is to say, orders of angels, good and evil. Christian worship entails being taken up into heavenly realities in the company of angels.[10] At the same time, New Testament belief in angels is controlled and directed wholly by Christology. The battle in the heavenly realms, as well as on earth, has been resolved in the victory of Christ, even as it continues for a time (Eph. 6). The mediatorial role of the angelic has been superceded by the accomplishment of the Son of God (Heb. 1–2). This subordination should not, however, be confused with disenchantment or demythologization per se. The latter project erased not only supernatural entities, but orthodox Christology as well. A robust and orthodox claim about the divinity of Christ is abetted by a thicker metaphysic.

At the same time, modernity's extensive cultural fascination with the angelic and demonic is a reaction to the aridity of our own worldview. It finds its roots in the romanticist interest in the macabre and creepy. This contemporary cultural attraction is reminiscent of the later Roman Empire, an age of excessive rationalism that could flip easily into an undiscriminating spiritualism, like the seven demons slipping in the backdoor.[11] Our own age's interest in the experience of spirituality

7. This is the title of a book by Lesslie Newbigin (Grand Rapids: Eerdmans, 1995).

8. An exception is the school of power evangelism, associated with a figure such as John Wimber, which emphasizes the territorial in a fashion reminiscent of Dan. 10:13–14. Such an approach seems to give too much credence to the powers in lieu of the accomplished victory foretold in Dan. 7.

9. Paul Hiebert, "The Flaw of Excluded Middle," *Missiology* 10.1 (1982): 35–47.

10. Susan Garrett, *No Ordinary Angel: Celestial Spirits and the Christian Claims about Jesus* (New Haven: Yale University Press, 2008), chap. 2 (entitled "Angels to the Throne").

11. Such is the argument in E. R. Dodds's *The Greeks and the Irrational* (Berkeley: University of California Press, 1951).

is not an interest in God, but rather in the creaturely (hence experience-able) that exceeds our usual experience of created things. In other words, our age is after the angelic, which is suggestive of the divine, but readily and disastrously mistaken for it. It is at just this point that the mission of the church to the modern (and postmodern) world needs to pay attention to the remarkable upsurge of charismatic and Pentecostal expressions of the faith. For all their excesses and divergences, they help to overcome our truncation of cosmology and so help us hear significant parts of the New Testament. So long as the christological control is firmly in place, a Christian reading of Daniel contributes to this end.

A profound and deeply Danielic account of the angels' place, borrowing from but also expanding on Barth's view, may be found in Robert Jenson's *Systematic Theology*. In this period "between the times," angels are to be understood as intrusions of that future eschatological, creaturely, obedient reality into the present, opening wormholes back where things look blocked. Jenson draws this conclusion from angels seeming to show up in both the Old and New Testament at key junctures, such as exile, incarnation, and the approaching eschaton. They are retrojections of heaven into the earthly scene. So Jenson can systematically tie together the *Gestalt* of themes in the latter chapters of Daniel and offer an ontological account of angels consistent with them.[12]

8:17 The introductory comments on Dan. 7 emphasized the thematic complementarity of the visions in Dan. 7–12. Another view, which focuses keenly on the redactional seams, is found in Louis Ginsberg's analysis.[13] The work is particularly relevant to Dan. 8, since Ginsberg points out a number of tensions with the text: "holy ones" seem to be angels (8:24) or people (8:13); in 8:17 Daniel falls to the floor, but touches the floor again in the next verse; in 8:15 he seeks to understand the vision, though words of angelic explanation have intervened; in 8:19–26 the explanation is as difficult as the vision it explains; and in 8:17 Gabriel speaks about a vision of which he was presumably a part. (In fairness, commentators dispute most of the seams.) One can appreciate Ginsberg's insight into multiple redactional interventions, even if his reconstruction itself is debatable. Of more interest for our purposes is the way in which he relates the redactional history to

12. Jenson connects this eschatological understanding of angels to sacramentology; *Systematic Theology*, vol. 2: *The Works of God* (New York: Oxford University Press, 1999), 117–27. When the Eucharist is celebrated or the gospel preached, there too the word is efficaciously at work, coming from the future owned by God, to transform the present precisely by anticipating for his creatures their *telos*. This too is a creaturely work of retrojection. It is after all "with angels and archangels and all the company of heaven" that the eucharistic offering of praise and thanksgiving is offered. Here we may cite the strong stream of eucharistic theology that emphasizes this eschatological dimension (e.g., Geoffrey Wainwright, *Eucharist and Eschatology* [London: Epworth, 1971], as well as the orthodox tradition, e.g., Alexander Schmemann, *For the Life of the World: Sacraments and Orthodoxy* [Crestwood, NY: St. Vladimir's Seminary Press, 1973]), a dimension of which is angelology. Thus eucharistic theology cannot be reduced to symbol and ritual, education or social improvement, or, even, for that matter, mission; the dimension of awe is recalled, and in this dimension too mission is to take place.

13. Louis Ginsberg, *Studies in Daniel* (New York: Jewish Theological Seminary, 1948), 4.5–23.

intertextual midrash. Successive reinterpretations of Hab. 2:3 ("a vision for the appointed time")[14] bind the redactions of Dan. 8 (and beyond) together. We have already seen that Dan. 8 grows out of an Ezekielic vision. Here we find reflection upon a preceding layer of reflection on a word of preexilic prophecy. In Dan. 8:17b, 26b, the message is that the vision of Habakkuk "is for the time of the end."[15] Once we reach Dan. 10:14b and 11:27b, 35b, the vision conveys new information about the period prior to the end, "the wrath." We learn in 12:4 that the sealing of the scroll until the "end" that the prophet spoke of is not only because it is far off, but also so that "many shall be running back and forth, and knowledge shall increase" (NRSV margin). But once we reach 12:8–13 the sealing until the end is because the vision itself remains "secret and sealed" until its time. Seeing how different voices on a single prophecy are part of an intra-Danielic midrashic debate helps us to find a subtle coherence-in-tension in the text. It also opens fruitful ground for the Christian theologian: the end spoken of is final, yet it provides its own scenario, and the crucial central actor in the throne scene remains "secret and sealed" to Daniel.

8:25 but he shall be broken, and not by human hands—It is worth noting that Daniel gives support to postmillenialist and premillenialist alike. This alone should suggest to us that these categories for our eschatology do not suffice. At the least Daniel performs a negative function, as a check on too much emphasis on either outlook. It is the disruption of both pictures, as of the apocalyptic scenario as a whole, that is distinctive of the gospel. Either scenario can be an affirmation of the utter possession of human history by God who does reign and will reign as Ancient of Days and the coming Son of Man. In this way the parts of Daniel that lead to either eschatological conclusion—"four kingdoms" (postmillenialist) or "the end is not yet" (premillenialist)—are both governed by the christological content.

---

14. Given the connection between the two prophets in Bel and the Dragon one wonders if the two traditions touched somehow.

15. Ginsberg, *Studies in Daniel*, 4.35.

DANIEL 9

9:2 I, Daniel, perceived in the books the number of years that, according to the word of the LORD to the prophet Jeremiah, must be fulfilled for the devastation of Jerusalem, namely, seventy years—There is a growing literature about and increased interest in references between books of the Old Testament—that is, allusions and interpretations of texts in other canonical books. This feature of the scriptures is theologically important for several reasons. First, it means that the delivery of prophecy and the subsequent assembly of books into a canon cannot be bifurcated so easily. Already the meaning of texts is happening "between" texts. By this internal dynamic, not only do books need to be read whole, but the Old Testament (and for Christians, the entire Bible) should be read whole as well. Second, in the case of Daniel, we should think of the author as a scribal prophet. This in turns helps us to overcome any sharp distinction between apocalyptic as a child of wisdom and as an outgrowth of prophecy. Third, intertextuality as a tradition of interpretation internal to the canon encourages us to think of an ongoing postcanonical tradition of midrash on the already-midrashic authoritative books.

This growing school of thought can guide us in our interpretation of Dan. 9, for the chapter is an extraordinary case in point of intertextuality. While most examples of intertextuality in the Old Testament involve allusion, ours is a case of direct citation. How is the prophecy in Jer. 25:11 about the exile lasting seventy years to be understood? How can it make sense of a longer interval of exilic life for the people of God? The most important assumption is the most obvious: the prophecy from Jeremiah is not exhausted by the most obvious interpretation of the number seventy, but is more elastic in its capacity to explain human history. We might say that the hermeneutical concept of an interpretive tradition is implicitly accompanied by a theological assumption about providence and divine freedom:

the word is able to provide a series of true interpretations as human history moves ahead. History conforms to the divine template in new configurations.[1]

The explicit midrash on Jer. 25 is in fact only the beginning of the matter, and the intertextual readers help us to see the further interpretive overlays. Daniel offers a prayer. This alone might be readily understandable if it asked for illumination, but in fact it is a prayer of contrition, rich with Deuteronomic language. The other key passage, however, is Lev. 25–26,[2] which also gives insight into the question of numbers and prophetic fulfillment. There we read about the obligation of the sabbatical year, as well as the jubilee after the seventh seven. In Lev. 26:32–39 we hear that, when the people are not obedient, the land will become desolate and they will be taken into exile. The land will then, by a harsher means, have its sabbatical.[3] (Here we see one context in which to understand the coming reference to the "abomination of desolation," though here, surprisingly, the desolation is brought by the people of God upon themselves.) Then we hear this: "But if they confess their iniquity and the iniquity of their ancestors, in that they committed treachery, . . . then I will remember my covenant with Jacob" (26:40, 42). (A second and similar background passage is Ezek. 7, where the prophet hears of an end to come from the "four corners" as a result of Israel's "abominations.") So the intercessory prayer of Daniel has the interpretation of Jer. 25 as its text and the call to contrition of Leviticus as its mandate, with the coming desolation of the present moment as its occasion.

The mention of an end leads us to the second passage on which the intertextual school has focused: Dan. 9:27, and in particular the prophecy of a "decreed end."[4] The background passages that refer to a decreed end are Isa. 10:23 ("for the Lord GOD of hosts will make a full end, as decreed, in all the earth") and 28:22 ("now therefore do not scoff, / . . . for I have heard a decree of destruction / from the Lord GOD of hosts upon the whole land"). In both cases the promised end will come upon Israel as well as the rest of the whole earth. Behind each case is the idea of a remnant that will survive (in Isa. 10 the echo of the prophecy about Isaiah's child is clear). It is as part of that remnant that Daniel hears this word of hope and judgment, and it is as part of that implied remnant that he offers the prayer of contrition in the preceding lines.

How does this chapter shed light on intertextuality and vice versa? Fishbane summarizes the interpretive approach in the following way: "By strategically and cumulatively assembling numerous prophetic pronouncements the author leads us into the mental world of wise believers . . . and the tangle of authoritative traditions which encoded their universe and provided an atmosphere of confidence in

1. E.g., Ephraim Radner, "Doctrine, Destiny, and the Figure of History," in *Reclaiming Faith*, ed. Ephraim Radner and George Sumner (Grand Rapids: Eerdmans, 1993), 46–84.

2. Michael Fishbane, *Biblical Interpretation in Ancient Israel* (Oxford: Clarendon, 1988), 447–57.

3. Anderson, *Sin*, chap. 5.

4. R. E. Clements, "The Interpretation of Prophecy and the Origin of Apocalyptic," in *Old Testament Prophecy* (Louisville: Westminster John Knox, 1986), 187.

the inevitability of the apocalyptic forecast."[5] Another way to say "tangle" might be "web": it is in this layered field or context that the Danielic reinterpretation must be heard and, more generally, the canon as a whole.

Such an intertextual web bears for contemporary Christian exegetes more than historical or theoretically hermeneutical interest. It suggests a way of working with the canon and understanding the theological task. One Old Testament scholar of this school, Odil Steck, articulates some of these Christian theological interests by connecting it to the idea of "reception history," according to which the meaning of the text continues in a tradition that assures both the historical nature of individual texts and their interpretations as well as the wider meaning of its movement (i.e., trajectory).[6] The usual questions about historicity on the one hand and the imposition of a creedal interpretive guide on the other come into play. The discerning of a movement requires having a discriminating principle by which to recognize outliers and to avoid the devolution of texts and readings into historicized beads on a postmodern string of arbitrary signs.

It is not only the citation of Jeremiah and its web of allusions that is intertextually significant in Dan. 9. There is also the intervention and validation provided by the appearance and interpretation of no less than the archangel Gabriel (9:21–27). This raises a new set of hermeneutical problems. Fishbane says that here the interpretation of Jer. 25 moves from a prophetic midrash on an earlier prophecy to direct and supernatural pronouncement. One might argue that appeal to an angel amounts to a kind of circumlocution for God, as we find the more circumspect "kingdom of heaven" in Matthew in place of "kingdom of God." But in this case it conveys to us something more: the interpretation is not only to be taken as another midrash, but should convey the same authority as the text itself. The *angelus interpres* presents us with this claim, even though his new word is itself an interpretation.

The inherent tension here is easy to grasp if we consider what Fishbane calls interpretation among the scribal apocalypticists such as Daniel: "mantological exegesis."[7] The arrival of an angel or the gift of the Holy Spirit in the "word of the Lord" is in a sense trump; it is more than another interpretation vying among midrashic claimants. It asserts that it "speaks with authority and not as the scribes." And yet it takes its place among various authoritative words, and it does so by interpreting another word. We as Christians note that just as Dan. 9 reopens the question of Jer. 25's seventy years, so the question of the true jubilee, the "year of favor," is re-reopened with Jesus (Luke 4:19). The angel gives the imprimatur,

5. Fishbane, *Biblical Interpretation in Ancient Israel*, 493–94.

6. Odil Steck prefers the term "reception history" but is certainly influenced by the hermeneutical concept of the history of effects; see *Prophetic Books and Their Theological Witness* (St. Louis: Chalice, 2000), 158. In relation to this hermeneutical school, one may note a similar borrowing in Pannenberg, whom I will discuss in the excursus in Dan. 12. Steck places this influence against the horizon of the eschaton as the totality of meaning, a Danielic twist in itself.

7. Fishbane, *Biblical Interpretation in Ancient Israel*, 479–95.

and yet the interpretation of the vision itself awaits its time, beyond Habakkuk's time, beyond the Maccabean time, to Jesus and so on to us.

We have as a result two themes for Christian interpretation demonstrated in Dan. 9, the intertextual web and the shift to pronouncement, and we wonder how exactly they fit together. The angelic attestation, intertextually, now is Gabriel at the annunciation, the angelic host at the incarnation, the angel sitting in the empty tomb, the angels escorting the ascended Son, the heavenly host around the wounded Lamb before the throne. Old Testament texts suggest a trajectory fulfilled in the revelation about Jesus and thereby defining the new, pneumatic criterion and starting point for interpretation. Christian interpretation as such is both continuous and new in relation to that prior web. It turns out that the seventy years of exile end only at the resurrection-ascension and on the last day and that the interpretation of the texts in the canon has to be held open yet wider in hope of these events.

I might offer here one last connotation that the presence of Gabriel suggests. Poor Daniel is throughout these latter chapters sickened, exhausted, at a loss, confused. A weight of interpretation and a foreboding of the fearful coming end incapacitate him. The angels are his protectors (Dan. 6) and his defenders (Dan. 11), and these roles should be held in concert with the role of these divine messengers to convey understanding of the scriptures. They function in the later chapters of Daniel as divinely provided guarantors of the encouragement needed for Daniel to hang on and have hope. With the word we are assured that we will be given the power to hear what we must hear. In short, we may connect angelic ministry in Dan. 7–12 with important Reformation themes such as the perspicuity of scripture (that they are clear on what is needed for salvation) and the inner testimony of the Spirit. God may be trusted to work through the scriptures to make himself known and to preserve those to whom he speaks. Without this, in the face of hermeneutical ambiguity and quandary, our heads too will ache like his!

9:4–19 Daniel is seen as an exemplar of Christian prayer here,[8] particularly under duress. But how do we fit this intercessory role with the rest of the work? One of our guiding principles has been the aim of finding in seams and tensions insights into the book's message, and nowhere is this clearer than in Dan. 9, where Daniel confesses his people's sin and prays for mercy in a work that emphasizes the divine control of a history whose contours are already decreed. Historical critics conclude that this chapter does not fit with the usual profile of apocalyptic literature, but from the perspective of Christian doctrine the tension is fruitful. It has been normative for Christians both (1) to believe in God's providential care of history and in his gracious and sovereign electing will and (2) to exhort its members to pray for forgiveness and to intercede for their needs. In other words, the supposed tension of Dan. 9, amid the latter chapters, parallels the theological question of the relationship between divine and human agency in theology, and

---

8. Aphrahat, *Demonstration I*, 72.

between submission and intercession in the Christian life. Jerome makes the point by saying that God appoints both the deliverance and its human means, which in this case is the prayer for mercy (1958: 90–91). Likewise Calvin points out that this chapter was a favorite of St. Augustine in his battle with Pelagius (1853: 189).

There has also been considerable critical debate about the source and date of the prayer itself. Contemporary commentators agree that the Hebrew of the prayer is superior. Its theology is consonant with Deuteronomic themes, and its assumption that the seventy-year period has passed could be consistent with an earlier dating. The chapter reads smoothly without these verses, though it also seems to be well integrated with what precedes and follows. It finds a context in similar communal prayers in Ezra/Nehemiah, but also has a parallel in works of the second century BC such as the Letter of Baruch (Collins 1993: 359). Perhaps the best we can do is to say that the prayer may be a preexisting public liturgy of contrition, perhaps from an earlier point in the Persian era, and that it may well have been integrated into the chapter as a whole by the second-century author (Goldingay 1989: 232–38). It is theologically significant to note that the passage came to be incorporated into the Yom Kippur liturgy, with 9:19 assuming as it did the status of "the Kyrie eleison of the Jewish Scriptures" (Lacocque 1976: 182, 187). Daniel's repentance and his questioning of the times have been evocative for later Judaism, and this has made the passage key to their ongoing searching out of God's purpose and plan.

Another way to get at the seeming incongruity of the passage in these latter chapters is to ask this question: Whose are the sins that require contrition, which will need to come to a conclusion (9:24)? We have seen in the preceding chapter that the sins of the Gentile oppressors must reach their limit in a period called "wrath" (8:19, 23). But now in Dan. 9, the "transgression" to be "finished" (9:24) would appear to be Israel's. Whose sin is it anyway? On this very question Anderson sheds new light. He finds the roots of Jeremiah's prophecy of the seventy years of exile in the ten "weeks" of years required to "repay" the Sabbaths that were not kept before the exile (according to the logic of Lev. 26).[9] But was the guilt yet deeper, requiring a yet longer repayment? Anderson sees this as the question behind the midrashic reopening of the meaning of Jeremiah's seventy years. All of this, of course, works from a logic related to the depth of Israel's sin. What, then, are we to do with the measure of Gentile oppressors' sin? It is at this point that Anderson makes an original contribution. Repossession of the land is dependent on Israel's sin, but the return, brought about in the defeat of the Gentiles can take place when *their* sin has reached the requisite measure to merit dispossession. Anderson cites Gen. 15:16, in which the suffering of Abraham must continue yet awhile, since "the iniquity of the Amorites is not yet complete." The debt and its repayment have several parties, and so several divine computations.[10]

---

9. Anderson, *Sin*, 79.
10. Ibid., 88.

We may extrapolate from this argument one step further. The emphasis on guilt, contrition, and prayer in Dan. 9 is neither an intrusion nor a hiatus in the larger Danielic plan. Rather, the differing emphases on the question of guilt, the full measure, and payment conspire together to make just the nuanced point that Anderson describes.

9:10 have not obeyed the voice of the LORD our God by following his laws—Reformation authors hear in this passage a reinforcement of their Pauline teaching on the necessity, use, and impotence of the law. Calvin emphasizes the "second use," the law showing the children of Israel their sin and their need of the mercy of God. It is only as criminals that they can come before him (1853: 157, 161). Melanchthon finds here an illustration of the inability of the law to save (1543: 149–51). Both authors predictably find in the papacy of their time the prime counterexample. Calvin balances this stress on an awareness of human sinfulness and repentance with the prevenience of God's grace: while Daniel is yet speaking, the answer is already swiftly on the way (9:21).

9:22 Daniel, I have now come out to give you wisdom and understanding—Among medieval interpreters, none was more interesting than Rupert of Deutz, who offers what might be called a spiritual-symbolic kind of anagogical reading. First, in the book as a whole he discerns seven sacraments or mysteries of the Christ's life, presented typologically. Rupert also imagines that the book as a whole describes a great duel between Christ and the antichrist across human history. This duel is presented through seven symbols (found in Dan. 2–7 and also in the rereading of Jeremiah in Dan. 9). In other words the book is historical in the general and sweepingly Augustinian sense of the two cities contending across human history. Rupert says that Dan. 9 "is an image of another greater captivity, a captivity which in the one son Adam befell the entire human race. . . . These 70 years of captivity signified all time, in which the people of God make pilgrimage in this age."[11]

9:24 to finish transgression, to put an end to sin—Wright addresses the question of the messianic assumptions of the time of Jesus; his answer places Daniel at its very center, and, given the importance of and interest in his project, his argument merits summarization.[12] He begins with Josephus's careful and veiled statement that, in the period of the Jewish War, "in that time," there was an "ambiguous oracle" of a "coming king." Given the reference to chronology, Wright guesses that Josephus is referring to Dan. 8 and Dan. 9, the latter having an explicit mention of "anointing." But Wright understands that a more generalized kind of reference is at work, one in which the cumulative witness of Daniel is brought to bear. So Josephus also has in mind the reference to the stone that destroys the fourth kingdom in Dan. 2, a verse to which he is demure in his reference, due to

---

11. Zier, *Expositio Super Danielem*, 49.
12. N. T. Wright, *The New Testament and the People of God* (Minneapolis: Fortress, 1992), 289–99, 313–20.

the danger of the idea of the destruction of the Roman (as the fourth) Empire. These two in turn strengthen the messianic sense of Dan. 7, with its reference to a coming divine kingdom. All three in concert have a messianic import. This in turn is reinforced by intertestamental writing such as 4 Ezra and 1 Enoch, which show an explicit dependence on Dan. 7 in their messianic descriptions (e.g., the Son of Man like a Davidic lion in the former). Wright shows well how a web of references conspires to lend a messianic sense.

As to Wright's approach to eschatology more generally, we can certainly sympathize with Wright's rejection of crudely dualistic readings of apocalyptic and of his criticism of a concept such as heaven when it seems to involve rejecting or abandoning the created order. However, in the service of this point Wright sometimes leaves the impression that the choice is between maintenance of the space-time continuum, within which apocalyptic references are metaphorical, and dissolution of that order. Surely he himself would agree that the kind of transformation described in apocalyptic literature could involve a vast, metaphysical change—"we will not all die, but we will all be changed, in a moment, in the twinkling of an eye, at the last trumpet" (1 Cor. 15:51–52). As Torrance eloquently shows us, resurrection requires rethinking what we thought we knew of space and time.[13] The end of death also means the transformation of time itself; Barth speaks of an eschatological time, since we will remain creatures, but what does that mean? And then there are the angels, so prominent in Daniel; they are creatures without extension, and yet they are certainly not metaphors in Daniel. We, who live in the era of wormholes, quarks, and dark matter, are reminded that there are stranger things afoot here than are dreamed of in the simpler contrast between time-space maintained or erased.

9:24–27 after the sixty-two weeks—The passage is notoriously difficult. It seems compressed, with a number of expressions used only here and of ambiguous meaning: Is it referring to a holy one or a holy place? to an anointing or anointed? Some suggest that these verses might be a separate unit sown into the vision.[14] As a result, the verses' meaning may be inherently underdetermined. Farris, in his work on the history of their interpretation, finds two axes along which both Jewish and Christian interpretations of the terminus of the seventy years tended to fall: (1) Jerusalemic (stressing the fall of the anointed place) versus christological (stressing the loss of the Messiah) and (2) preterist (the prophecy of a present reality) versus futurist (the prophecy of something not yet come to pass).[15]

---

13. Thomas Torrance, *Space, Time, and Resurrection* (Grand Rapids: Eerdmans, 1976), makes creative use of the theory of relativity on this point.

14. M. H. Farris, *The Formative Interpretations of the Seventy Years of Daniel* (diss., University of Toronto, 1990). I am indebted to his thorough work throughout this section.

15. On the axes, see ibid., chaps. 5–6. Zier, *Expositio Super Danielem*, 202–3, offers a concise chart of all the possibilities as they have occurred in the history of interpretation, with the following as termini ad quem: (1) invasion by Romans: Africanus (from Artaxerxes to Tiberius), Clement (Cyrus to Vespasian), Tertullian (Darius I to Vespasian); (2) incarnation: Eusebius (Cyrus I to Maccabees, with the last week

The salient features of the history of its interpretation are the following. The Septuagint translation tended to occlude the christological possibilities of the passage. This was a factor in interpretation, both Jewish and Christian, which listed toward the Jerusalemic side. In fact the possible reference to a Messiah was sometimes rediscovered when contact was made with the Hebrew text or a cognate (e.g., the Syriac translation and its rediscovery in the scholarly work of Jerome).[16] Christians understood the terminus of the seventy years to be the death and resurrection of Jesus, and Jerome's rediscovery made their task easier.

As to the second axis, for historical reasons both Jews and Christians were, for the most part, stout preterists. Jews found the "cutting off" in the tragic events of AD 70 or 135. Christians pointed to Jesus's death or the fall of Jerusalem as judgment upon that event (and in fulfillment of the Gospels' prediction). Futurist interpretations were outliers: for example, on the Christian side when the Severan persecution inspired imminent expectations of the end (which needed to be dampened by Hippolytus), and on the Jewish side when Sabbatai Sevi made his failed messianic claims in the Middle Ages.[17]

This, however, is not the end of the matter, any more than the sixth-century BC setting of the Servant Songs in Isa. 40–55 is the end of the matter. We are, after all, dealing with an expanded prophetic interpretation of a prophecy; there is a surplus of meaning in the original passage itself, predicting events that in turn open on to further events. We can also see a kind of fit between this passage in Daniel and the story of the events leading to the death of Jesus, where a mysterious messianic claim is conjoined to a symbolic end to sacrifice and a prediction of a coming disaster. (I summarize an intriguing recent construal of this New Testament evidence in the comments at 9:26.) We may discern in these verses a kind of layered historical reference, first in Jeremiah, then in Daniel itself, and again when the passage is read in light of the passion narratives. The last, understood in relation to the messianic woes, implies a future event as well. The passage, with Jeremiah behind it and the Gospels (with their own expectation) before, extends itself like a telescope. We can find in the prophecy received and reinterpreted literal, typological, and anagogical senses knit together and leading on to one another. The passage itself moves us beyond the preterist/futurist distinction.

9:24 seventy weeks—I have already mentioned the morass of competing computations that takes up a considerable amount of the traditional Christian exegetical energy. Both the starting and ending points are disputed; if the **anointed prince** of 9:25 is to be Christ, then the references to the seven and the sixty-two weeks are in the wrong order; solar and lunar calendars have to be deployed to make things work, and even so troubles remain. It is helpful to think about the way that numbers are used in the periodization of history in biblical and intertestamental

leading to Christ; or Darius VI to Augustus); or (3) end of the world: Hippolytus (beginning of exile to end of the world—the last week is extended), Apollinarius (incarnation to end of the world).

16. Farris, *Formative Interpretations*, 280, 317–29.

17. Ibid., 143–57, 354–55.

literature (e.g., the forty years of disobedience in the desert or in Judges; Gold-ingay 1989: 258, who also points out the use of 490 years of punishment in the book *Jubilees*, using the idea of a sevenfold punishment from Leviticus). We have already seen that Jeremiah's seventy years is expanded into 490 with the help of the Levitical jubilee idea (of which the period to the return from Babylon is one of the seven cycles).[18] Such expansions of symbolic interpretation serve to remind us that God's sabbatical is not as we count and that the flexibility of his ordering reveals his patience as well as his power (2 Pet. 3:8–9).

to seal both vision and prophet—This may be understood to offer assurance that the vision will be fulfilled (see Collins 1993: 352–53 for the Old Testament parallels). But we must also note 8:26, where the sealing has to do with the vision awaiting its time, which remains far off. The two senses are not necessarily in conflict, but could coincide. It is worth noting that Hippolytus (2000: 274) finds here an anticipation of the breaking of the seals in Rev. 5, of which I spoke in the introduction.

9:25 the anointed prince—One may note the drumbeat of references to anointing and princes: the anointing of the holy place (9:24), the coming of the anointed (9:25), and the anointed one and the prince of the people (9:26). The anointed ones, anticipatory, false and true, and the relation of these figures to the holy place, for good and ill, are the interest of the passage. For the Christian exegete, the passage moves inexorably in the direction of Christ and his relation to the temple.

9:26 its end shall come with a flood—There is also an interest throughout the passage in the "cutting off" ("finishing" in 9:24) of the prince and of the "end" (9:24, 26, 27). The end will be of the temple, but then of the time decreed, so as to bring the end of iniquity. The Danielic theme of finality and abruptness is found here too. The time frame of the prophecy may have been extended, but only the fool would suppose this means an indefinite prolongation.

While the focus in this passage is on Israel and its enemies, the cosmic scope is not lost. The reference to the flood, which must have some echo of Gen. 6–8, and the echo of the final battle of Gog and Magog (already noted by Rabbi Salomon in Goldwurm 1972: 264) assume this wider frame, though it here may remain implied.

9:27 an abomination that desolates—To what does this expression refer? We need to start from these premises: (1) the two accounts, in Dan. 9 and Dan. 11, are referred to as a single event in Dan. 12, which may be taken as a redactional summation. In other words, we should not try to fit two abominations into some kind of story line, but should take the two earlier accounts as different angles on the same event. (2) The preponderance of historical views pointed to the

18. Gillian Evans in *Language and Logic of the Bible: The Earlier Middle Ages* (Oxford: Oxford University Press, 1984) rehearses the main medieval numerological assumptions: three for the Trinity, ten as the perfect limit, seven for purity, as it neither begets or is begotten.

deliberate desecration of the temple under Titus in AD 70, and the preponderance of historical critics to the prior desecration by Antiochus in 123 BC. The precursor of both was the destruction of the first temple prior to the exile, which provides the background for the whole book. (3) This chapter is a classic source of the concept that the exile does not end with the return under Cyrus, but is an ongoing historical and also spiritual condition. In this light the series of desecrations can be seen as the same polluting boar breaking into and defiling God's vineyard. All of these instances of that one paradigmatic exilic outrage share the abuse being directed deliberately to the most sacred place and act imaginable for an Israelite. (4) That original exilic defilement by an arrogant Gentile is related, as I have pointed out, to the defilement and desolation of their own faith by the idolatry of Israel itself in the prophets.

Where do these observations take us as Christian interpreters? I have already talked about the arterial relationship between Daniel and Mark 13, and this pertains to no passage more than Dan. 9. Pitre argues persuasively that the phrase "let the reader understand" (Mark 9:14) should be taken as part of Jesus's discourse and not as an aside of the evangelist, and he bases this on the similarity to other imperatives spoken by Jesus in Mark, some of them exhorting the hearer to attend to what is written in scripture.[19] Since so much of Mark 13 bears directly on Daniel in general and on Dan. 9 in particular, Jesus would have us hear his own prophecy as a fulfillment of the earlier word of Daniel itself.

Let us consider the other main points of Pitre's compelling reading. (1) The key aspect of the **abomination that desolates** is that it ends the temple sacrifice and entails the very destruction of the holy city itself. He substantiates these claims with interpretations of the references to unprecedented suffering, the suffering of women and children, fleeing to the hills, and the falling of sun and moon. (2) Pitre finds in Mark 13 the central theme of the protection of the remnant people of God. So Jesus enables his followers to understand what will happen, warns them against false messiahs, and discourages them from Danielic interpretation too fixated on numerological reckoning. Throughout all this, Pitre underlines Mark 13's expectation that Dan. 9 will be fulfilled in real events to take place at the end of time.[20] (3) In this context we may understand Jesus's cleansing of the temple as a prophetic enactment of the coming destruction of the temple as part of the scenario of eschatological tribulation. With that destruction would be triggered the coming of the Son of Man, the ingathering of the nations, and true worship in the cleansed temple. To this we may add the verse in which he cryptically refers to the rebuilding of the temple/his body in three days (Mark 13:58).

At the very least we may say that Jesus in Mark 13 interprets his own ministry in relation to the remnant of Israel in the coming eschatological tribulation, and

19. Brant Pitre, *Jesus, the Tribulation, and the End of the Exile: Restoration Eschatology and the Origin of the Atonement* (Tübingen: Mohr Siebeck, 2005), 309–13.

20. And so Pitre takes issue with N. T. Wright's reading of Dan. 9.

he does so in direct exegetical reference to Dan. 9 (among other passages). What may we then make of this as Christian exegetes? Let me return to my fourfold interpretation to supplement this account of the historical sense (but leaving aside for the moment the existential reading). We need to interpret these readings with the stereoscopic vision that sees their eschatological fulfillment both in the events of the end of Jesus's life and also in their universal revelation at the end of time. (In just this way the predictions of Mark 13 are promptly fulfilled in the events of Gethsemane in Mark 14.)[21] The blasphemous abomination is humankind's killing of God's Son; the woes are his pains on the cross; the desolation is the temple rent from top to bottom; the ingathering is the mission to the Gentiles by the new Israel in the wake of the resurrection; the new temple is the Spirit-filled worship of the church in anticipation of the new Jerusalem; the remnant to be warned and protected is likewise the church of Christ.

But in this case what can the abomination of desolation in its futurist sense mean? This leads on naturally to the next main topic, the question of the antichrist. Amid all the latter's interpretive confusions, the bass note is its witness to a profoundly corrupting reality within the household of God itself, one that mimics the true nature of Christ and the church. "Sacrifice" for Christians is Christ's atoning death and life-giving resurrection as the cornerstone of true worship as a responding "sacrifice of praise and thanksgiving" within the people of God. Now if the abomination is the desolate end of that sacrifice, the resulting bereftness of the Spirit of God's presence, and the continued exile (see Ezek. 2–4), to what, then, do these correspond for the *ekklēsia*? Here we may hear the Reformation indictment of Christian worship that amounted to works. Where it comes to accept, even revel in this fact,[22] it approaches the antichristic. Tendencies in Christian thought and worship that dispense with Christ's centrality or with the cogency of his atoning work or with the very hope of that new Jerusalem are also desolating. To be sure, the passage claims more than this, for it suggests that at the culmination of history these deficits will take on a blatancy, urgency, and destructiveness theretofore unseen. Not every bit of run-of-the-mill ecclesial stupidity is antichristic. But we cannot avoid the conclusion that the gutting of the faith from within is understood to have its own eschatological place, in addition to that shattering from without of which Dan. 7 and Dan. 12 tell us.

To be sure, Daniel contains no reference to the figure called "the antichrist" in Christian history.[23] But the destructive figure in Dan. 9 as well as Dan. 11 comes to

---

21. Craig Evans, *Mark 8:27–16:20* (Nashville: Nelson, 2001), 410, cites the use of "watch" in both Mark 13 and the Gethsemane scene; similarly Adela Collins, *Mark* (Philadelphia: Fortress, 2007), cites the use of "trial" (*peirasmos*) in both.

22. Taking this to an extreme, William Blake associated the abomination with reason, state religion, and codified morality in *Milton* 41.1.25; see Richard Schell, "Abomination of Desolation," in *A Dictionary of Biblical Tradition in English Literature*, ed. David Lyle Jeffery (Grand Rapids: Eerdmans, 1992), 9.

23. Bernard McGinn, *The Antichrist: Two Thousand Years of the Human Fascination with Evil* (New York: Columbia University Press, 2000).

be blended with the lawless one in 2 Thess. 2 and the Satan in Revelation. Insofar as all three imagine a climatically evil figure at the end of time, this seems fair enough, so long as we bear in mind that its relevance to Daniel is at one remove.

Amid a vast profusion of interpretations, one stream appealed to 1 John 1:18's mention of "antichrists" in the plural, and another thought about the figure in the corporate sense as the sum of our vices and infidelities, by analogy with the church as the body of Christ. Both these tacks can serve to make thinking about the figure more rational and balanced. At the same time we should be careful not to rationalize away the scandal of the passages themselves.

But what are we to do with the more wacky or dangerous interpretations of the figure? It has served at times to be the warrant for pogroms or to describe a political enemy. To what extent is a symbol responsible for the outer fringe of its readings? Can one make such a claim about the composite figure of the antichrist? This is a legitimate worry about a text like Daniel,[24] but, as an antidote, we do well to recall all its countervailing themes, including the mysterious control of history by God and the willingness of God's people to suffer patiently.

---

24. Rowan Williams, *On Christian Theology* (Oxford: Blackwell, 2000), 75.

DANIEL 10

The main import of the chapter is clear: the word afforded Daniel is confirmed by a vision conveyed by angels, at first overwhelming and eventually reassuring. The vision reveals a cosmic conflict parallel to the historical one. This cosmic dimension renders events that Daniel foresees as at once more dire and yet held more securely in the divine hand. While there is agreement on these general points, there remains debate over how to understand a number of the specifics of the chapter: times, identities, and so on. To these perplexities I now turn.

10:1 in the third year—Daniel 7–12 is to be read as a unit, with each section referring to what precedes and follows. We find here a recapitulation of the theophany/call in Dan. 7, reminiscent of the theophany in Ezek. 1, after which we find "a laying on of hands, an anointing, a credential conferred" (Berrigan finds also a "sending forth," though not of the sort we are accustomed to in prophetic calls).[1] Daniel's mission remains to receive and hand on the vision of "the end of days . . . those days" (10:14), revealed with each chapter in greater detail.

We have seen how Dan. 9 was itself a reinterpretation of Jer. 25. Similarly Lacocque finds in Dan. 10–12 midrashic prophecy with a series of Isaianic allusions. The "true word" is the proclamation of the end of the exile in Isa. 40:1, though of a more radical kind than there foreseen. Daniel's responding weakness has an Isaianic echo, to Isa. 6:5: "Woe is me! I am lost." As we shall see, Lacocque's reading (1976: 204) dovetails with Ginzburg's, who finds similar allusions in the coming chapters.

of King Cyrus of Persia—Collins points out that this was not how the king referred to himself; the wording looks back to the Persians in Dan. 8 and anticipates the appearance of Persia's angel later in the chapter (1993: 372).

who was named Belteshazzar—We are reminded, though the genre may have changed, this is the same Daniel about whom we read in the opening chapters.

10:2 at that time I, Daniel, had been mourning for three weeks—Commentators, both Jewish (Rashi in Goldwurm 1972: 269) and Christian (Calvin 1853:

---

1. Daniel Berrigan, *Daniel: Under Siege of the Divine* (Farmington: Plough, 1998), 79.

234; Willet 1610: Dan. 10, QQ. 5–6), have found here a reference to the failure of the Jews promptly to rebuild the temple, after they had been permitted to return under Cyrus (so the opening chapters of Ezra). Mourning over the temple still desolate has a thematic continuity with the vision of the desolation yet to come.

10:3 I had eaten no rich food—In the previous chapter Aphrahat saw in Daniel an exemplar of the efficacy of fasting, and here Calvin sees his fasting as a sign of obedience and sorrow, but not as a religious work of any sort (1853: 236)!

10:4 on the twenty-fourth day of the first month—Is Daniel deliberately fasting through the Passover, turning it into a Yom Kippur as a result of the exilic humiliation of his people (Lacocque 1976: 205)? Among the rabbis Abarbanel thinks this may have been so, because the delay of the rebuilding of the temple would justify such special penitence. The specific imperative from God could trump even the abiding commandment, a "teleological suspension of the ethical" that reminds us whose commandments they are.[2]

I was standing on the bank of the great river (that is, the Tigris)—The geographic reference provides a parallel with 8:15–16, with which our passage should be read in tandem, Dan. 9 presenting a kind of penitential interlude. We are also reminded of Ezek. 1:1, though the river mentioned there is a tributary of the Euphrates. The allusion is significant as one tries to decipher who is appearing in Daniel's vision.

10:5 a man clothed in linen—Who is this figure? The parallel with Dan. 8 suggests Gabriel (and so the rabbis read the verse; Goldwurm 1972: 272). The parallel with Isaiah suggests the Lord himself (so Lacocque 1976: 206, who points out that Gabriel then appears in 10:16). It is interesting that in Ezek. 1 the theophany includes the brilliant swirling of the "living creatures." It may be seen as a description of God himself, surrounded as he is by his attendant angels. As if this were not complex enough, Collins points out aptly that the description reminds us of the vision of the primal man in Ezek. 28:13–15. Christian exegetes have sometimes hedged their bets (1993: 375). The matter is made more complicated for Christian exegetes who find Christ appearing later in the chapter (e.g., Dan. 10:18–21, where Melanchthon [1543: 203–4] stresses that only Christ, and no angel, can save us from death and hell). The appearances have a kaleidoscopic quality, with a powerful suggestiveness that does not yet come into clarity with respect to the *dramatis personae*.

10:10 then a hand touched me and . . . he said to me, "Daniel, greatly beloved"—We may have several Isaianic allusions here. The angelic hand, in touching his lips, strengthens Daniel rather than purifying him, but in both cases the prophet is empowered for what follows (so Isa. 6:7). Daniel is addressed as **greatly beloved**, which may echo Isa. 42:1, where the Suffering Servant is the "chosen, in whom [the LORD] delights." In Isa. 49:7 that same servant causes "kings [to] see and stand up, / princes . . . [to] prostrate themselves." The theme of the Gentiles,

---

2. The phrase comes from Søren Kierkegaard's *Fear and Trembling*, trans. Walter Lowrie (London: Evergreen, 1994), 43–57.

at once punishers and due for punishment themselves, and yet at the same time due to receive the light of salvation (49:6), is shared by both contexts. In both Isaiah and here we also find the theme of understanding granted, which cannot be heard now but will be understood after the time of sealing.

Hippolytus offers a beautiful anagogical reading of this verse. It refers to the hand of Christ that will, at the end, reach out to us in death and call us to the tremendous vision of which we are here afforded a glimpse (2000: 284, 286).

10:14–17 **to help you understand what is to happen to your people at the end of days**—The implication of these particular phrases becomes broader and clearer over time and in light of the whole canon. The Greek translation's word for "end" in Daniel is usually some form of *telos*, but here the final times are called the *eschatai hēmerai* ("the last days"), a phrase open to the full weight of eschatological content and expectation in the New Testament. Such a translation, read in light of the leitmotif of the end and the hope of the rising of the dead, surely contributes to the eschatological trajectory of which this book is a crucial canonical part.

10:20 **the prince of Persia**—The references in 10:13 and here constitute the *loci classici* for the patristic doctrine (borrowed in large measure from Judaism) of the angelic patronage of the nations. "While each of the angels is entrusted with the care of each of us for guarding and protecting and ridding us of the wicked demon's wiles, the archangels are entrusted with the patronage of the nations, as blessed Moses informs us," says Theodoret (2006: 273; the passage in mind is Deut. 32:8). Within this metaphysically fuller picture of reality is found the notion that each nation has its own angel. The fathers went on to add that "the role of angels in the Old Testament is bound up with the Old Testament's preparatory mission, and ceases with the coming of Christ."[3] According to the fathers, then, at the point in the economy of salvation represented by Daniel, allotment of nations such as Persia and Greece to angels was in effect, though already one could find conflict of the sort seen in Dan. 10–11, since corruption and idolatry have already come into the world. This angelic guardianship of the nations prior to the incarnation allows us to imagine, to a limited extent, the special provision and allowance made by God for the nations prior to the advent of Christ. For the Alexandrians and Cappadocians it was also a way to find a limited use for other religious practices prior to the coming of Christ. This protocol ceased to pertain after the incarnation. In particular the fathers note the surprise and wonder of the angels at the ascension of Christ, as he takes captivity captive.[4] Within these parameters this understanding of the angels and the nations offers an opening to understand the religions to have a time-limited and time-bounded role in the economy of salvation.[5]

---

3. Jean Danielou, *Angels and Their Mission according to the Fathers of the Church* (Westminster, MD: Newman, 1957), 9.

4. Ibid., 43, 102.

5. For a creative contemporary use of this theme in a Christian theology of religions, see Gerald McDermott, *God's Rivals: Why Has God Allowed Different Religions? Insights from the Bible and the Early Church* (Downers Grove, IL: IVP, 2007).

If we look more carefully at the verses in question, it is hard to be sure what the struggle between the national angels amounts to. Are they representing competing interests on behalf of the exiles? Or are they good and evil angels in conflict? It is difficult to tell, since the realm of angels is both ordained by God and subject to corruption, as are the states to which they are assigned (so we may compare, for example, the account of the state in Rom. 13 to that in Revelation).

The verses also mention kings, in which Daniel has a persistent interest. There would seem to be a correlation between the heavenly angel and the earthly king. This nexus of political and spiritual power is found not only in the patron angels, but more widely in the New Testament understanding of the "powers and princi- palities." That it is hard to know at what level to take references to the *archontes* is the point. One may compare the ambiguity in Paul's use of "the elementary spirits of the universe" (*stoicheia tou kosmou*), which can refer to the physical elements, idolatry, metaphysical principles, and spiritual entities entailed in astrology.[6] Be- cause the creation is for a time in rebellion against its rightful order, we see this conflation of domains, this blurring of entities.

It is just this ambiguous, mutually entailed feature that has made contemporary theological reflection on the powers and principalities so fruitful. For example, anthropologist Rene Girard saw the drive toward violence permeating human societies as amounting to "powers and principalities."[7] They should not be fac- ilely demythologized, since the primal murder at the heart of every myth (and so every society) was real. Girard affords an interesting view of the latter chapters of Daniel; he sees the violent mythic history of the beasts propping up the rule of the rebellious princes/angels of the nations. Borrowing as he is from Durkheim, Girard sees a close connection between transcendent and social accounts. He is successful in showing how the powers make sense of power and corruption in the mysterious and corporate dimensions of reality. Still we may wonder to what extent they remain for Girard truly spiritual creatures waging war in spiritual places.

A number of recent authors emphasize the powers as metaphors for empire; one example is Brian Walsh, whose *Colossians Remixed* follows, with respect to the powers, a line of argument similar to that of Walter Wink.[8] Both authors see the powers as the inner spirit displayed by earthly powers. Such readings have a certain affinity to the witness of Daniel, since they take the phenomenon of empire itself seriously in its subtlety and pervasiveness. They are well aware that the powers extend their sway into the culture and mentality of the subjugated.

It is worth noting the homiletical power of this kind of political-systemic read- ing in our contemporary situation. The horrors of the modern twentieth century and the insidious invasiveness of the postmodern twenty-first have lent credibility

6. Louis Martyn, *Theological Issues in the Letters of Paul* (Nashville: Abingdon, 1997), 126–28.

7. Rene Girard, *Things Hidden since the Foundation of the World* (Stanford, CA: Stanford University Press, 1987).

8. Brian Walsh, *Colossians Remixed* (Downers Grove, IL: InterVarsity, 2004); and Walter Wink, *Naming the Powers, Unmasking the Powers,* and *Engaging the Powers* (Philadelphia: Fortress, 1984–92).

to such a line of thought. Authors such as Walsh and Wink, seeing the powers as the inner meaning of pervasive systems of control, understand how they operate within us and without us to convey a sense of grandeur, inevitability, and plausibility and to conceal their own dehumanizing selfishness. How can a culture of freedom and autonomy be in such bondage to addiction? How can the internet, promising universal access and intimacy, become such a purveyor of degradation? How can a sophisticated financial system, selling futures by algorithm, spawn such mountains of destruction and greed? The problems are beyond us, and yet they are ours, and the concept of the powers serves pellucidly to describe our situation. The immediate relevance of the witness of Daniel is obvious.

There, however, lies the challenge, for we need to avoid a straightforward correlation with political or social conditions. This would shortchange the metaphysical dimension, for it also involves a historicizing reading of the biblical texts. Here too Daniel has a contribution to make, especially if we read Dan. 10 in the larger context of Dan. 7–12. In addition to the passage about the angelic powers, we find his vision of the coming of the nations in Dan. 7, the moral exhortation of Dan. 9, and the vision of the end of all things in Dan. 12. No single hermeneutical strategy of correlation can comprise all the dimensions that the chapters together offer us.

Let me offer one final, corrective note on the destructive angelic powers. I have emphasized, as Dan. 10 does, the way in which they operate in the widest framework of nations and of movements of history. But is that the only place they reside? C. S. Lewis's Screwtape knows that we are deceived by discounting or overestimating his existence. Though in the thick of the evil of World War II, Screwtape was most effective in insinuating himself into run-of-the-mill daily venality.[9] Similarly in Sergei Bulgakov's *The Master and Margarita*, set in the center of the colossal evil of Stalinist Russia, the infernal one pops up at a casual "Go to Hell" or "The Devil take him."[10] In a more mission-oriented vein, John Taylor remembers talking to West African Christians about the difference between believing in spiritual creatures attacking or possessing a person from without, and neuroses working within one's psyche; to the listeners the difference paled.[11] They were readier to hear of a layer of created reality distinct from, but insinuated into, the one we are daily accustomed to, as witnessed to in the matter-of-fact account of Dan. 10, mixing as it does spiritual and historical-political-military realities. Third World churches may be better positioned, as in the case described by Taylor, to show us (with our own assumed dichotomies) what this intricate, insinuated, encompassing yet personal, nature of such powers is really like.

9. C. S. Lewis, *Screwtape Letters* (New York: Macmillan, 1961).

10. Sergei Bulgakov, *The Master and Margarita* (New York: Vintage, 1996).

11. John V. Taylor, *The Primal Vision: The Christian Presence among African Religion* (London: SCM, 2001), 43–44.

DANIEL 11

This chapter is a detailed and highly accurate account of Judean history from the Persian period on to the time of Antiochus (so Collins 1993: 377). Themes such as the abomination, persecution, and the awaited end now recur in this new genre—as I have suggested above, the same story is told once more, and from a different vector. But to what purpose? Goldingay proposes insightfully that the point is that all this detail, ambition, machination, and destruction, this "pointless sequence of invasions, battles, schemes, and frustrations," amounts to "sound and fury" (1989: 315–16). It amounts to the "running back and forth" we hear of in 12:4.[1] Humans will behave so, as if running about in an enclosed space, until the final bell rings. The part of Dan. 11 that finds its way into the summary in Dan. 12, it may be noted, is only the purifying, cleansing, and refining of 11:35 (quoted in 12:10)—the rest is dross. There is a sense of the evacuation we might associate with secular history, space cleared for meaninglessness, but only for a season. As with Ecclesiastes, the vacuous too has its place, as a foil, albeit a limited one.

While the substance of the chapter is historical narrative, the style has a formalized quality, whose closest echo may be a passage like Ezek. 38–39. Willet points out the parallel between Ezekiel's Gog and Daniel's "kingdom of the north" (1610: Dan. 11, Q. 19). This allusion is suggestive in several ways. The passage in Ezekiel looks back to the conquest of the Babylonians, itself a precursor of a coming, final conflict. Furthermore one should recall that the Gog-Magog passage follows immediately on the valley of the dry bones in Ezekiel; the nexus of themes offers a strong similarity to that in Dan. 11 leading into Dan. 12.

11:6 the daughter of the king of the south shall come to the king of the north—As I have said, the chapter expresses the *futility* and vanity of worldly kings and powers, their stratagems and violence, but that does not exhaust what the chapter has to tell us. Calvin underlines the theme of human *pride* behind

---

1. It may be what Mark 13:7 refers to as "wars and rumors of war."

their "perfidy" running throughout (1853: 279–81). The regal desire for power wreaks havoc around itself and eventually comes, by God's will, to destroy itself. If one supplements the chapter's account with a historical commentary on the sordid venality of the lives of the kings and queens in question, the similarity of this chapter to the *hubris* and *atē* ("madness") of Greek tragedy is reinforced. In more biblical terms, in keeping with a persistent Danielic theme, the rage of the Gentile kings is spent, and then God's appointed end comes.

Yet another way to think about the formalized manner of speech in Dan. 11 is to see these particular tyrants and battles as types found previously in scripture. The army from the north reminds us of the Assyrians, the rod of Yahweh's wrath on the tribes of Israel, and the kingdom of the south reminds us of Egypt and the witness of liberation in the exodus, or again of the conquerors from Babylon.

Finally we may see the formalized account highlighting an element of universality. To be sure, the actual scope of the account geographically and chronologically is, from a contemporary perspective of world history, limited. But in the way the account is told, even in its detailed specificity, it could be anywhere and anytime. The wars, intrigues, and disasters it narrates could as well be of the Saxons or Aztecs or Qin Dynasty.

11:14 in order to fulfill the vision, but they shall fail—Goldingay points out the echoes of Ezek. 7: the vision sought (7:26), disaster upon the "four corners of the land" (7:2), the repetition of the coming end, the abomination of the temple (which Ezekiel attributes to the faithlessness of the people of God themselves, a theme in the background for Daniel), and the judgment coming on those who violently enter there (1989: 298). The vindication of God's righteousness and the display of his glory (Ezek. 7:27: "And they shall know that I am the LORD") is the point of both passages and the baseline for any theology of history.

11:30 The willfulness of the string of tyrants is a major theme of the chapter. This goes to the heart of the idea of empire, the imposition of a will upon the whole world. Lacocque points out that Alexander, following his teacher Aristotle, intended to clear the world of the local gods so as to prepare it for the enlightenment of Greek rule (1976: 217). In other words, even the gods must be swept away so that the will of the maximum leader, readily equated with the spirit or will of the people, may prevail. I have already pointed out how this element of sheer self-assertion has come to be laid bare in the modern era and may be taken to be the age's most salient feature.[2] Antiochus sweeps away the pagan gods of ancestors and fertility—it is an odd moment to hear the writer criticizing the disregard of pagan worship. But a more virulent kind of idolatry, the worship of the ego of the tyrant, symbol for human *amor sui* in all its forms, has presented itself.

11:32–35 Calvin offers an eloquent reading of the passage according to the moral sense (1853: 322–37). God permits the true faith to be desecrated, not

2. Charles Taylor, *The Sources of the Self: The Making of the Modern Identity* (Cambridge: Cambridge University Press, 1989).

only in the world, but even in the church itself. But for the faithful this should not compromise their sense of the strength of God, "who foresees and decrees all things." In the face of those within the church itself who succumb to "blandishments" and "flatteries," the faithful are to hold fast. With Isa. 10:22 in view, the verse reminds us that Israel is still to be found in the remnant who continue to know God. In such circumstances real spiritual leadership will be found among those who teach, rather than in official positions, in "bishops and cardinals, abbots and pretenders, [who] strut about and stupefy" (Calvin 1853: 327) the masses. God will sustain them, though the help he sends be "small," just enough that they not be crushed (compare 1 Cor. 10:13). Nor is the solution of the Maccabees, to fight and overcome opponents militarily for the sake of God, available to us. "He does not thunder in the heavens and overthrow our enemies by the first stroke of lightning, but he enables us to contend successfully with our cross" (Calvin 1853: 331). While the faithful may seek a pure church, it is a stained and admixed one in which they stand.

11:33 the wise . . . shall give understanding to many—Collins understands the group referred to here as the party responsible for the book as a whole (1993: 385). Lacocque understands the verse to be a kind of midrash on the Suffering Servant in Isa. 52:13 (1976: 230). The usage is found at Qumran in a similar context. A remnant sees its role to provide insight into what God is up to in the threatening coming events on behalf of the people of Israel. The understanding that Daniel fosters is that insight works patience under suffering and hope in light of the appointed end (12:3).

11:35 refined, purified, and cleaned—This verse is picked up in Rev. 7:14, where the martyrs "have washed their robes and made them white in the blood of the Lamb."

11:36 the king shall act as he pleases. He shall exalt himself and consider himself greater than any god, and shall speak horrendous things—Christians find a typological reference to opposition to Jesus as the Messiah, as well as a reference to false Christs (Mark 13:22), even to the figure of the antichrist, and look to the end and the resurrection to resolve the sufferings of this age described in Dan. 11. It is humbling to remember that the rabbis too look to the end and the Messiah, though they identify the associated sufferings and corruptions with oppression from those who claim that Yeshua is Messiah. Ramban sees the one who does as he pleases in 11:16 to be Jesus. A number of rabbinic readers find in 11:36 a reference to the establishment of Christianity as a state religion and to the promulgation of **horrendous things** like the Trinity and the incarnation (Goldwurm 1972: 311). At the very least, this minority reading, which is the antithetical mirror image of the church's, ought to be a cause for humility. Goldwurm goes on to point out how the rabbis took conflicting views of this Gentile mimicry of the faith in the one God. Rambam called it idolatry, but Ramban saw it as a roundabout strategy of the God of Israel in preparation for the coming of the Messiah, one suited to the Gentiles: "All these doings of Yeshu . . . are only to pave the way for the messianic king and to prepare the world to serve Hashem together" (Goldwurm 1972: 313).

This is a classic case of a religious doctrine about an "alien claim."[3] The most creative and influential development of the latter rabbinic tack is surely Rosenzweig's *Star of Redemption*.[4] It is worth noting that here we find one of the ironies of a Christian theology of other religions. Melanchthon, for example, finds these new and distorting teachings by a pretender to refer to Islam; the pattern of thought mirrors that of the rabbis (1543: 326). Christian theologians throughout the tradition have offered the same twofold estimation found in Ramban and Rambam when they have sought to make sense of the Gentiles and their religions.[5] Christians, waiting for the eschatological resolution, find themselves in a contestation in which they construe, and are construed, in parallel ways. Meanwhile all three competing monotheisms find themselves at present in debate against a horizon of aggressive pluralism much like the second-century Jerusalem of Antiochus.

11:37–39 he shall pay no respect to the gods of his ancestors—These verses are particularly unclear and so have been open to numerous interpretations. In Rorschach-like fashion, Reformation-era interpreters found in the reference to **fortresses** allusions to the Turk and the pope! Some see the one referred to as overly drawn to women, others as cold to them altogether. Willet finds this ambiguity helpful, since the former favored a reference to Antiochus, the latter to the antichrist, so that taken together the readings pointed toward both (1610: Dan. 11, Q. 45)! The historical information derived from outside the text about Antiochus takes us a certain distance—namely, that he promoted the worship of Jupiter Olympius and holed his supporters up in the fortress called the Akra ("height") (Collins 1993: 387). His own moral turpitude and desire to cause affront to the traditional worshipers of the God of Israel is clear (even if in his eyes the worship of Zeus amounted to the same thing as the worship of the Lord).

11:41–45 he shall come into the beautiful land—These verses presented Joachim of Fiore and his influential historical schema with a problem! They seemed to describe events of the second century BC and yet are immediately followed by the events of the end time. One common solution was to imagine that the account skipped over intervening events (which were many). Joachim chose to see the verses themselves as referring to the battle between Christ and antichrist in the last days (which for him was the late twelfth century). This allowed him to interpret the earlier sections of Dan. 11 to refer to the events of the second century BC.

Joachim himself is of course remembered for his heterodox views on the Third Age of the Spirit, though to what extent this actually reflects the views of his followers is an open question. (Joachim's thought was revived by Hegel in his time,

3. William Christian, *Doctrines of Religious Communities: A Philosophical Study* (New Haven: Yale University Press, 1987).

4. Franz Rosenzweig, *Star of Redemption* (Madison: University of Wisconsin Press, 2005).

5. George Sumner, *The First and the Last: The Claim of Jesus Christ and the Claims of Other Religious Traditions* (Grand Rapids: Eerdmans, 2004).

and Jürgen Moltmann in ours, which fact alone assures its relevance to contemporary reflection.) Joachim also had views about what he called *Concordia*, the correspondence between events in different epochs of creation and salvation history. For example, the seven days of creation correspond to the seven eras of Old Testament history and the seven phases of church history. Hence second-century tumult around Antiochus corresponds to the deadly threat of the Muslims under Saladin in the twelfth century AD (whom he understood to be the "little horn" of Dan. 12).[6] As threatening as the outward assault of the Saracen was the corruption of the church from within, due to *cupiditas*. Joachim's view on *Concordia* lent credibility to the interpretation of the end of Dan. 11.[7] The Sabbath of creation, the resurrection of Jesus as the fulfillment of Israelite history, and the coming age of peace for the church all corresponded to the seventh phase.

Joachim's interpretation with its urgently eschatological emphasis influenced high medieval Franciscan concepts of interpretation, Christian life, and mission. The theology and spirituality of Bonaventure and others maintained the Joachite sense of correspondences, incorporating as it did the sevenfold schema of church history going back to Augustine's *City of God*.[8] They also borrowed from the *doctor gratiae* his reticence about precisely how much one could know about the plan of the end. They added to these theological themes a Franciscan spiritual emphasis on conformity to the cross. From all this grew a missionary zeal, along with a martyr's hope, so that the "fullness of the Gentiles," and finally Israel as well, could be gathered in ahead of the resurrection and the final coming of the kingdom. Nowhere is the connection between a Danielic reading, a universal historical framework, and missionary urgency more clearly bound together.

11:43 the Libyans and the Ethiopians—The issue in the history of interpretation of Dan. 11 has been this: to whom does this verse refer—Antiochus or antichrist? Jerome notes that Antiochus never conquered either country, and so opts for the latter (1958: 140). On this score Nicholas of Lyra creatively offers his "double literal senses" solution.[9] Daniel 11's historical details abut the sudden arrival of the end, "like a thief in the night." Not least for this reason, some reference beyond Antiochus seemed necessary. The antichrist is an actor in the larger, encompassing biblical scenario whose conclusion is here imagined. Both may be said to be "referred to"—though in a complicated, perhaps oblique way.

6. E. Randolph Daniel, *The Franciscan Concept of Mission in the High Middle Ages* (Lexington: University of Kentucky Press, 1976), chaps. 1, 5.

7. Zier, *Expositio Super Danielem*, 117.

8. Daniel, *Franciscan Concept of Mission*, chaps. 2–3.

9. Zier, *Expositio Super Danielem*, 190. John of Murro spoke of a "historical sense" and of a "principal signification of history," terms that bind the references together helpfully.

DANIEL 12

12:1 a time of anguish—The term used in the Septuagint, *thlipsis*, refers in the New Testament to the great final trial, and is applied both to the end of the world and to the suffering and death of Jesus. Together they make up the Christian understanding of the messianic woes, for which idea, in the period prior to Christ, this passage is a *locus classicus* within the scriptures. We may also note that in Dan. 12:10 the righteous will undergo testing, *peirasmos*.

The Danielic vision comprises an important part of the background for the Lord's Prayer: "your kingdom come" (as we see it arrive in the passing of the beastly kingdoms of this world in Dan. 7), "on earth as it is in heaven" (as we see in our glimpse of the relation of the earthly and heavenly battle in Dan. 10), "forgive us our debts, as we also have forgiven our debtors" (for confession and forgiveness accompany the great return from exile in Dan. 9), "do not bring us to the time of *peirasmos*, but rescue us from the evil one" (as we see in Dan. 7–12), "for the kingdom and the power and the glory are yours" (so Dan. 7 and here in Dan. 12), "forever" (as in the decisive Dan. 12). In light of the deeply Danielic nature of Jesus's prayer, we may ask ourselves what is added, and what abiding witness does the book of Daniel retain? As if an Old Testament in miniature, Dan. 7–12 offers the elements to understand Jesus's ministry: the Father and Son, the unleashing of the rage of history and its end, the simultaneous heavenly scene and the timeline, and so on. But the jigsaw pieces are only pulled into a coherent picture with Jesus himself.

In Dan. 12:2–3 we find the clearest reference to a resurrection of the dead at the end of time. (Ezek. 37 may also be cited, though the vision seems to pertain, on its own account, to the restoration of the people of Israel in exile, an issue hardly absent from our passage as well.) The best precedent in the preceding scriptures would be Isa. 24–27, where the prophet describes the condition of exile at one point as desolation (24:12) and terror in a pit (24:17). In the great feast in Jerusalem, death, "the veil spread over the nations," will be removed. Both death and the enmity of the Gentiles are marks of the primordial alienation from God. The day of deliverance from both is likened to victory over the sea monster Leviathan and is celebrated thus: "Your dead shall live, their corpses shall rise. / O dwellers in the dust, awake and sing for joy! / For your dew is a radiant dew" (26:19).

How are we to factor in the context in which the Danielic verses were written? The relationship to the passage that has preceded, describing in detail the cruel machinations of the Antiochean era, leads many modern interpreters to find here a social-psychological explanation for the roots of the idea of the resurrection of the dead in Israel's literature. The nation's martyrs have been unjustly struck down, and the idea serves to resolve the fairness issue and to maintain hope under duress. The wrong the believers see is not the last word. Sometimes the argument is augmented by reference to Middle Eastern neighbors, though the Persians not burying their dead proves awkward.

A particularly insightful perspective is offered by Levenson.[1] He agrees that Dan. 12 does have in view the restoration of the nation, but that this concern, coupled with the God of Israel's conflict with death and the scope of his promises as the God of creation itself, moves inexorably in the direction of the resurrection of the dead. Though it is not found explicitly earlier, it is already spiritually and theologically entailed. More specifically, the rabbis insist that resurrection must precede healing, so that the identity of the people of Israel as the elect may be preserved. In other words, the doctrine is the outworking of the deep logic of the Old Testament, especially in relation to God's calling of Israel.

From a canonical perspective, this passage (along with its penumbra of in-tertestamental "children") has been utterly formative for the understanding of resurrection in the New Testament. A salient example should suffice. In 1 Cor. 15, the New Testament's most extended discourse on the topic, one finds a highly Danielic scenario of the preceding victory of Christ: the defeat of the powers (15:24) leads to the delivery of the kingdom by the Son to the Father. As to the question of the nature of these resurrected bodies, the analogy of the celestial body (15:40) is reminiscent of Dan. 12:3. Similarly, the white-robed young man in Mark 16:5 resembles the man in linen (Dan. 10:5; 12:6). The Daniel passage is the *locus classicus* for the doctrine of the resurrection of the dead, against which New Testament passages borrow, resonate, and inquire.

Beyond a genetic relationship, the effect this passage had historically on the New Testament, what witness does it continue to have vis-à-vis the interpretation of those later passages and to our understanding of the resurrection of the dead? First, the Danielic event takes place at the conclusion of the contention with the beasts, which is to say, the claimants to empire. They form, as we have seen, a foil to the work of God, since empire epitomizes the pursuit of a center for all human beings and all authority in themselves rather than in God. They are now

1. Jon Levenson, *Resurrection and the Restoration of Israel: The Ultimate Victory of the God of Life* (New Haven: Yale University Press, 1985), 181–91.

decisively and finally defeated. This is what theologian Robert Jenson calls the political meaning of resurrection—the only real solution to "the problem of a center" is found at the end of history.[2] Thus the passage has a valid sense in which it unmasks the inherent pretensions of empire. Second, we may recall the profusion of historic detail, "sound and fury signifying nothing," that has proceeded. In those seemingly interminable struggles the end comes. It does so because God in his providence and mercy brings history abruptly to its end. In other words, the summative Dan. 12 protects against all kinds of spiritualizing of the eschaton, to which other passages may be open. God will indeed bring the end "when we least expect it, as a thief in the night." Third, the definitive quality of the passage is balanced by its mystery—these truths are sealed until the time, not only from us, but from Daniel, whose head hurt at each revelation! Even their unsealing was in mysterious symbolic form, which remains not only in Revelation but in 1 Cor. 15:51 as well: "I will tell you a mystery! We shall not all die." Fourth, as we shall see, since the doctrine of the resurrection grows organically from the most basic theological commitments of Israel, we ought not to think about resurrection, even as Christians, without some consideration of "Israel after the flesh." Paul's scenario for the ingathering of Israel, after that of the Gentiles, in Rom. 11, is in a sense a reflection on this piece of unfinished business. Daniel is to go his way in peace, his lot on the final day assured, not only because he is part of the church-in-waiting, but also as a son of Israel. The resurrection bespeaks the physicality of final salvation and so its connection to creation; the status of Israel is inseparable from these themes as well.

Excursus: In Conversation with Contemporary Systematic Theology

Before we look at the specifics of the chapter itself, we benefit from considering its themes in relationship to contemporary systematic theological reflection on the resurrection of the dead. We might summarize the major deployments of eschatology in general and the resurrection in particular in the following way. Insofar as the liberal tradition understands resurrection as a symbolic evocation of a vindicated human state, it finds in it an assurance of the ultimacy and the justice of God, though we may doubt these here (so, e.g., Tillich). As Abraham Heschel famously said, there is "meaning beyond the mystery." Similarly Rahner understands the last things as a symbol for the courage of deciding in faith in the face of our own death.[3] We may assign these readings to what we have tagged "the performative" and so acknowledge their legitimacy and pertinence in Christian living. (Here we may classify as well liberationist voices who find in the resurrection a symbolic

2. In Carl Braaten and Robert Jenson, *The Last Things: Biblical and Theological Perspectives on Eschatology* (Grand Rapids: Eerdmans, 2002), 33–42.
3. Karl Rahner, "The Hermeneutics of Eschatological Assertions," in *Theological Investigations*, vol. 4 (London: Darton, Longman & Todd, 1966).

affirmation of hope for their cause, though it would be harder to find a warrant for their vision of political activism in the text before us.) Still, the temporal frame and the physical resurrection in its abruptness in Dan. 12 remind us that these sorts of readings alone do not suffice.

The next generation of eschatological theologians, without jettisoning these concerns, emphasized, in reaction, the futurity of the resurrection. For Moltmann the "not yet-ness" of hope is itself the engine of the energy of transformation.[4] Pannenberg offered a complex theology in which the unfinishedness and future orientation of all human searching for meaning make humans predisposed to hear a message of final salvation. His theology is a correlation of human question and revelatory answer, but in a futurist key. He understands the end as a purifying fire for the whole world's adoration of the triune Life.[5] Both theologians offer accounts consonant with the final chapter of Daniel, though futurity per se as a structure of human thinking and acting,[6] and so as a point of contact for the Christian proclamation, goes beyond the witness of our book, where the Gentiles show no such potentiality.[7] Pannenberg also had an interest in theology and cosmology, the latter having its own sense of an end at a "time certain" (with their own kinds of abstruse numbers!), which also represents a fruitful encounter between apocalyptic themes and secular wisdom.

Each stream of contemporary systematic thinking on the end as witnessed to in Dan. 12 supports one horizon of its interpretation, the existentialists supporting the performative and the theologians of hope the futurist/eschatological. The chapter serves to remind those with one particular reading of the witness of the other horizons. In this spirit, we may point in modern theology to resolutely christological readings such as von Balthasar's, which rightly understand the end as the unveiling of the eschaton that has occurred for the whole world in his death

4. Jürgen Moltmann, *The Theology of Hope: On the Grounds and the Implications of a Christian Eschatology* (London: SCM, 1969).

5. On unfinishedness see Wolfhart Pannenberg's *Anthropology in Theological Perspective* (Philadelphia: Westminster, 1985); on purgation see his *Systematic Theology* (Grand Rapids: Eerdmans, 2004), 3.608–20.

6. C. K. Barrett (cited by Paul Bradshaw, *Pannenberg: A Guide for the Perplexed* [London: T&T Clark, 2009], 62) observes a natural affinity between apocalyptic and speculative idealism that is ultimately problematic to the former: futurity, conflict, the victory of the Son—these are all absorbed into a metaphysical system. In fairness, Pannenberg managed to rework the Hegelian philosophical inheritance so that the agency of the triune God coming into history was preserved. In this way he puts the apocalyptic vein in scripture in the service of an emphasis on the contestability and the questionability of God's reign until the day of the resurrection of the dead. This does capture a feature of the later chapters of Daniel. As such, his system, based on what one might call an *analogia futuri*, has taken real futurity seriously and so has sought to work out Danielic themes in a systematically thoroughgoing way. But is the articulate sense of victory over finitude matched by a consistent sense of the redemption from sin, as would be required by the biblical, including the Danielic, witness as a whole (see Dan. 9)?

7. The work of Teilhard de Chardin (e.g., *The Phenomenon of Man* [New York: Harper, 2008]) with his Omega point as hominization warns us of letting this point of contact come to dominate the content of the Christian affirmations themselves. If the witness of Daniel tells us anything, it is that the end foretold in Dan. 12 does not emerge in some immanent way, by some historical dynamic, from within.

and resurrection, but for which the witness of Daniel serves as a reminder of a real and distinct end.[8]

Perhaps of greatest interest, given this guarding and balancing role for Dan. 12 amid modern systematic construals, is the more recent narrativist stream. In line with such a view, the latter chapters of the book compose a kind of stage, entailing temporal extension from the exile and its recapitulation under Antiochus and the Romans, finding its center in the events of Jesus's life and extending on to some point of conclusion. One can plausibly claim that theological arguments make sense only when they assume such a framework.[9] At this point of course the standard queries for postliberal appeals to narrative are heard: What does it mean to explicate "historylike"[10] narratives? Is it just the idea of a narrative that is required? What, then, about reference to an actual history? If history itself is not so important, then are we not thrown back on a new kind of Kantianism, in which narrativity per se is the condition for the possibility of theological claims? At this point the usual questions about relativity and truth-claiming rush in. But what exactly does truth-claiming look like when eschatological statements, themselves enigmas wrapped in mysteries, are concerned? The critique is well founded, insofar as it insists that these, and all other doctrinal claims, must be taken in a realist sense, and we might say that the latter chapters of this book, for all their elaborate symbolism, support this insistence. But what does eschatological realism look like? Would it not be something like a reading that takes all of our four delineated horizons into account at one and the same time, the realism of the exilic context, of application to the person Jesus Christ, read in relation to the specifics of the readers' concrete lives, against the backdrop of a definite, though still shadowed, end?

at that time Michael, the great prince—As I have already suggested, Dan. 12 culls from the preceding five chapters and brings them (and human history) to a conclusion. Thus the chapter signals that we are to read this half of the book as a whole, so that it in turn can aid our interpretation of that whole. References to angels and the abomination allude to what has preceded; of equal interest is the reference to the times, which looks back to Dan. 7 and now offers an account of the culmination there foreseen (so Rashi in Goldwurm 1972: 318).

Once again, much of the debate among interpreters has been over the time to which the events of this chapter refer, and how to relate the different interpretive senses to one another. For example, Willet relates the events historically to the

8. Nicholas Healy, *The Eschatology of Hans Urs von Balthasar: Being as Communion* (Oxford: Oxford University Press, 2005), 214: "With regard to the tension between 'realized' and 'future' eschatology, Christ's return to the Father has in fact already occurred, and to that extent the realized eschatology of John is fundamentally correct."

9. I am here indebted to the late Robert Johnson of Yale Divinity School, who argued for two types of modern theology, one that assumed such a teleological framework and one that did not.

10. As Hans Frei called them in *The Eclipse of Biblical Narrative: A Study in Eighteenth and Nineteenth Century Hermeneutics* (New Haven: Yale University Press, 1974), 10.

time of Antiochus and analogically to Christ's return (1610: Dan. 12, Q. 9.3–5). To be sure, Dan. 12 takes place after that crisis, but how long after? We do best to take our lead from the passage itself: it tells of a time, then a prolongation of that time, and finally of an end coming suddenly and by surprise. The events under Antiochus are the template. But what is the dilation of time to which **that time** refers? The expression has a kind of elasticity within itself that "talks back" to its diverse interpreters.[11] Daniel 12 is really about the end itself in its abruptness that must be immediately after the historical crisis and its later replications. Whatever the time and times may be, the time of the "half a time" is the end time, and it is to that day that the opening **at that time** refers. So, interpret as you will, this chapter insists on a closing bracket not only to this series of chapters, but to human history and all its enumeration.[12]

Given the great interest in our time in interreligious relations in general and the sibling relations of the Abrahamic traditions in particular, it is worth noting how medieval and reformation interpreters often understood this final act of history to involve one of these interlocutors (we may compare contemporary evangelical premillennial interest in Israel). For Jephet the approaching end meant a struggle with Islam.[13] For reformers such as Melanchthon, it meant a struggle with the twin opponents the pope and the Muslim. Remarkably, one rabbinic reading understands the two angelic figures foretelling the meantime in 12:7 to be Christianity and Islam (Abarbanel in Goldwurm 1972: 323)! Another trajectory of interpretation read Dan. 12 through the lens of Rom. 11 and understood the passage to refer, not to the church, but to the restoration of Israel under the authority of Christ (in the patristic period, Theodoret 2006: 317; in the postreformation period, Thomas Brightman).[14] It turns out that each faith has its own expectation of the end, and for each the others figure as harbingers. Dialogue is always, then, in some way, eschatological debate, which for charity's sake requires eschatological restraint and patience: "But . . . go your way, and rest" (12:13).

As to **Michael**, I have already discussed the role of angels, but it should also be pointed out that the name literally means "one as God" (Willet 1610: Dan. 12, Q. 2), and so he is seen as pointing typologically to Christ, especially when read in conjunction with Rev. 12:7–12, where the victory of Michael is the victory by "the blood of the Lamb."

11. It is also worth noting that **as has never occurred** echoes prophetic references to the exile and to the exodus. As is usually true in the logic of the scriptures, the "new thing" God does follows the saving shape of what has gone before, even in the end time, which is its own kind of new creation, new return, new exodus. So events that fill the "dilated" time may predictably be seen to follow these patterns.

12. Nor should we too quickly dismiss the assumption of Christian interpreters such as Jerome and Theodoret that the passage cannot refer primarily to Antiochus since the end in fact did not follow. We would want to nuance the judgment, but their realist assumption concurs with a central Christian doctrinal commitment.

13. Jephet, *Commentary on the Book of Daniel*, 73–74.

14. Catherine Firth, *The Apocalyptic Tradition in Reformation Britain* (Oxford: Oxford University Press, 1979), 172.

everyone who is found written in the book—We find yet another reference to a book—is it the same one as before, or different? Goldingay thinks it is different, for here at the end of the work it refers to Daniel itself, which will be unsealed by the events of the Maccabean time, or better yet, their perception (1989: 309). Goldingay's interpretation may be right as far as it goes, but the events foretold are not then fulfilled in a historical sense, and so the reference remains open to further fulfillment. One concise summation might be that the three books of the latter chapters of Daniel represent judgment (God's acts), truth (as it describes itself), and election (the names of the saved). However God's act is to both judge and save, his truth is his faithfulness in action, and his word efficacious—the books are in each case understood from a different angle, but are also one. One traditional reading combining several elements is Nicholas of Lyra's *conscriptio electorum in divina mente* (as noted in Willet 1610: Dan. 12, Q. 6).

The recording of the names of the elect in the book was taken in the Reformation tradition to confirm the gratuitous nature of salvation by the predestining grace of God (Willet 1610: Dan. 12, Q. 6). Long before our births our names are already recorded. This of course raises other questions. The controversy over double predestination emerges with the question whether the names of the damned are also written down. And what of cases where the Bible speaks of names being blotted out? Are these cases of the elect failing to persevere? One solution was to argue that the erasing had to do with our coming to know God's electing will, while the writing in the book itself is set (Thomas Aquinas, *Summa theologia* 1 Q. 24.3). As I have already suggested and as we will see again, recourse to the Western tradition's grammar of divine election, grace, and human agency is the crucial matrix for making sense of the perplexity of numbers and predictions in the book that are foreordained.

12:2 many of those who sleep in the dust of the earth shall awake—This direct reference to restoration from the dust of the earth is a bulwark against substitutions of the hope of immortality for the bodily resurrection.[15] As such, it is also an account of a new creation tied closely to the first (Bullinger points out that the reference to **dust** underlines this point, in Willet 1610: Dan. 12, Q. 12). So, for Christians, creation, the resurrection of Jesus, and the eschaton make sense of one another; they are all the same sort of event, God bringing life out of nothing. At first, it would seem that Tanner proposes an eschatology without precisely this futurist dimension, based on contemporary science "without preoccupations concerning the world's future."[16] To be sure, as she works out the implications for the incarnation and crucifixion for eternal life with the triune God, one may worry

15. In his *Introduction to Medieval Islamic Philosophy* (Cambridge: Cambridge University Press, 1985), 19–20, Oliver Leaman mentions how, for Ghazali (as well as for Maimonides), the belief in the last day opposed all philosophical appropriations of the faith that tended toward divine necessity, emanationism, or an ontological monism.

16. Kathryn Tanner, *Jesus, Humanity, and the Trinity: A Brief Systematic Theology* (Edinburgh: T&T Clark, 2001), 102.

about an account that seems to emphasize what we mean to God and does not give much account of the resurrection of the dead, without which the resurrection of Christ itself cannot make sense (1 Cor. 15). But a closer reading reveals this to be unfair. What Tanner means by a "world without a future" is that death is as real and final for the world as it now is for us. Whatever a futurist resurrection of the dead may mean, it cannot have to do with anything immanent in the world, nor anything that does not assume the real and total death of the world. Then Tanner describes how God in his faithfulness will extend this life beyond death for his creatures, whose new life is in him, but remains creaturely nonetheless. Tanner calls this new kind of life "spatialized" instead of "temporalized" (it may be noticed that the tradition tried to make sense of the eternal creatureliness of angels in just the opposite way), but this is only to say that creaturely life in the kingdom is of a sort we cannot describe, since our bodies are now spiritual (1 Cor. 15:40). Even Tanner's account cannot get away from the "before" and "after" of our death and of the resurrection.[17] Her account is a profound one that ends up sounding very much like a traditional account of the mystery of life in the kingdom of God and its relation to time and eternity. In a grammar of eschatology, anyone who wants to affirm the reality of death, the hope of eternal life in the risen Christ, and our ongoing creatureliness is bound to have moments corresponding to Tanner's cosmic winter and her metaphysics of creaturely coinherence in the triune life, as well as her struggle with the language of time.

We may add to this string of requisite elements the event quality of the resurrection, though here too analogy is involved. Such an event is unthinkable, incalculable, indescribable, and yet we would err not to call it an "event." It takes place in history, it is part of a narrative, as we see here, but it is of its own kind.

A number of interpreters stress that this verse is addressed from a church crushed to a church similarly brokenhearted. They are trampled down, already on their way to being dust. Saadia Gaon speaks of a word to the people of God in "humiliation and disgrace" (2006: 655). Later, and on the Christian side of the aisle, the Puritan George Joye talks of consolation amid destruction.[18] We venture here into a more tropological or performative kind of reading. I have already raised the epistemological question about the extent to which being crushed is in fact a valuable lens through which to see the book—the oppressed or the martyr church can hear its witness better. Here we are reminded that the scriptures, because they are God's efficacious word, can do in us what they describe in history. Truly to hear the word about life from the dust enlivens the "pulverized." The typological/eschatological and the tropological readings are connected because the same God who creates *ex nihilo* is active through the word even as it attests to him.

17. Ibid., 118–19.
18. Richard Bauckham, *Tudor Apocalyptic: Sixteenth Century Apocalypticism, Millenarianism, and the English Reformation, from John Bale to John Foxe and Thomas Brightman* (Oxford: Sutton Courtenay, 1978), 279.

There is considerable interest in the commentaries about the verse's compressed statement that **some** receive **everlasting life, and some . . . shame and everlasting contempt**. The place to begin for us as Christians is with Matt. 25:31–46, which opens with the Danielic "when the Son of Man comes in his glory, and all the angels with him, then he will sit on the throne of his glory."[19] How the Gentiles have treated the new Israel ("the least of these") will tell the tale before the returning Christ. It is as if, in the Matthean scene, the terse statement in Dan. 12 is filled out in light of the tableau in Dan. 7. In the story of the sheep and goats the raising to life and to shame will not only be a division of faithful and unbeliever, but also will turn on the treatment of the people now shattered.

There is a resistance in some Jewish interpreters to understand all of the rejected to be raised, since the point of the event is the vindication of Israel—perhaps they are to see their shame and then return to the dust. So, Abarbanel understands all to be raised, but so that the unjust Gentiles might see the vindication of God's people whom they oppressed (this would be an example of the counterreading by Israel that we as Gentiles as well as Christians need continually to hear) (Goldwurm 1972: 320).

As a number of commentators point out, **many** in Hebrew can often be used for "all."[20] It is true that Dan. 12 is the culmination of Dan. 7–12, and so of the vindication of the people of God. And as I have already said, the people of Israel are to be raised, as opposed to simply the raising of individuals at the great Assize, as seems to be so in Islam. The scope of the last event must be as great as God's first act of creation. God is now known transparently to be the Lord of all the earth, of all history, the creator and judge of all human creatures.

The enduring theme of the vindication of Israel in the resurrection has something to say to our own understanding of ecclesiology and indeed of soteriology. Christians should note that the many raised are the people of God; after the "shattering" the salvation of the "holy people" is accomplished (12:7). While there will be no marrying in the resurrected life, and no temple, and no sea or sun, we would err to say there will be no church. We are not simply individuals strolling about the new Jerusalem. On the contrary we may point to a vision like that of Gregory of Nyssa, which imagines us more like a single body, connected to one another more intimately than we can experience here, and so all the more ourselves.[21] The bride who is the church inhabits the new Jerusalem in Revelation. This puts in question all ecclesiologies or missiologies that treat the church solely

19. It is interesting to muse about the whole of this chapter in the light of Daniel. Matt. 24 is the Matthean version of the Danielic midrash that is the "Little Apocalypse." In Matt. 25 itself the story of the bridesmaids is a story about dealing with the delay, and the story of the talents with a kind of hiding away of the news of the mystery so that the Gentiles can get no profit though it should now be their time; so Joachim Jeremias, *The Parables of Jesus*, trans. S. H. Hooke (New York: Scribner, 1963), 51–53, 58–60.
20. So, Jesus is a "ransom for many," itself an echo of Isaiah.
21. This was pointed out to me by Rowan Greer; see his *Christian Life and Christian Hope: Raids on the Inarticulate* (New York: Crossroad, 2001), chap. 2.

as a tool or function for the sake of something else—for example, saving souls, working justice, or some other activity.

The end comes suddenly, "in the twinkling of an eye," and it comes as something discontinuous with ordinary events, though not discontinuous with God's creative and redeeming purpose. In other words, it comes vertically, every bit as much as the stone who is Christ descending in Dan. 2. Here as there we find a direct implication for Christian mission, which witnesses to the gospel whose final culmination is to be brought about by this direct and sovereign act of God. As I have already stressed, the kingdom is in no sense built, nor does the end grow organically out of the expansion of the church, nor can it be provoked by any action on our part, be it progressivist or revolutionary. Again, the church as messenger of the gospel is itself one of the signs of the end, not its means.

12:3 lead many to righteousness—This reminder leads naturally to consideration of the following verse. I offer as a shining example Thomas Bray,[22] the founder of the Anglican Society for the Propagation of the Gospel and so one of the founding eighteenth-century figures in the establishment of Protestant global missions. He understood missionary work in direct relation to the imminent expectation of the end. Those who are bringing many to the righteousness given graciously by God are missionaries working in advance of the resurrection of the dead. We have already seen the connection in Franciscanism, for example, among the early Franciscan missionaries to the New World, who also had reflected on texts like Daniel.[23] This reinforces the inherent link between the idea of mission and Christian belief about the eschaton for which I have argued.

12:7 the man clothed in linen . . . when the shattering of the power of the holy people comes—Reformation exegetes found this verse to be consonant with their perspective and their circumstance. George Joye, a sixteenth-century English reformer, and Melanchthon (whom he cites) find consolation for the "little flock" assailed by tyrannical forces with only the word of God in the form of "our lips, our pens, and our papers" for their defense.[24] Both, in their own idiom, capture the verse's assurance to the church, though it seems imperiled, due to the provenience of God's grace and the triumph of his word; appearances notwithstanding, a greater power is on their side, with the final victory of the resurrection impending.

12:10 the wicked shall continue to act wickedly—In this and the following verse, we hear of the purification of the righteous through suffering, and the evildoing of the evil, until the time at which the outrage of blasphemy reaches its outer limit, providing a mysterious kind of boundary, moral and temporal. Then

22. Thomas Bray, *Apostolick Charity: Its Nature and Excellence, Considered in a Discourse upon Daniel 12:3* (London: Holt, 1700). I am indebted, here as elsewhere, to my editor, Ephraim Radner, for this highly apposite citation.

23. Note *Millennial Literatures of the Americas*, ed. Thomas Beebee (Oxford: Oxford University Press, 2009).

24. Joye, *Exposicion of Daniel*, 232–33.

the end will come. The righteous and discerning will be blessed if they can endure. How exactly are we to understand the verses in relationship to one another? Must the good and evil goals be accomplished for that end to come? What is the relationship, in other words, between God's hand directing and God's hand being withdrawn for a time from the human scene?

We can relate these verses, then, to the debate in both the philosophy of religion and in theology proper about theodicy. Why does God allow it? Can any consequent good overmatch the horror involved of even a small portion of the "evil doing evilly" (so the complaint of Ivan in *The Brothers Karamazov*)? How does the ordering of all history, which we see in this chapter, relate to the allowance of this evil? Which is to say, in classic theodicy terms, how do God's power and goodness relate in the face of such evil?

Most of the possible strategies for an answer to this question are present in our chapter: the "permissive will" (Thomas Aquinas, *Summa theologia* 1 Q. 23.3) that allows the evil to do evilly for a time, the moral effect of suffering for purification, contrast by which the righteous will shine, all for the sake of doxology to God (which would seem to have been the tradition's main answer when they turned to the question, which was not as often as we moderns). One answer not present in our passage, but added by a Christian reading, is that in which the crucified Son of Man bears the suffering that the righteous undergo on his way to victory.

How does the manner of setting forth the issue in Dan. 12 inform possible answers to the question of theodicy? All Christian answers to theodicy are best understood as eschatological. The moral, juridical, esthetic, and divine participatory moves all seem abstract and logically handicapped on their own; they all make most sense as anticipations of the perspective when the "circle is unbroken" on the last day. They all assume the eschatological scenario, and movement toward its conclusion, which lies at the heart of these chapters.

none of the wicked shall understand, but those who are wise shall understand—This echoes Isa. 56:9–12, especially as a precedent for the sealing of a prophecy until such time as it can be understood. Does this verse challenge the Reformation commitment to the perspicuity of scripture? In response Calvin emphasizes the prudence that holds to sound and basic teaching even in the face of affliction (1853: 377, 387–88).

those who are wise shall understand—If the exile was a dislocation and threat of an unprecedented kind, "such as had never been seen," then the crisis of the Maccabees and all the subsequent crises in their train felt this same shock to the core. The main point is to see the manner in which the traumas illumine one another, to see them as a kind of palimpsest. The book sets out exile as one of its hermeneutical keys, then relates subsequent crises to that one, relates them in turn back to the *Ur*-crises of exodus and creation, and invites future exiles to join the file. The book can be understood only as a series of responses to life-and-death identity crises, each disruptive at the profoundest level—the abomination is precisely the disruption so profound that it is hard to take it in. Sometimes when we say "tradition" we think of something stolid, but we see here how tradition has to do with adaptation to successive ruptures; it is a template for understanding what at first would seem to defy intelligibility within the tradition's own terms. As such it displays a particularly powerful range of explanatory potential, for it is a tradition based on its own series of "epistemological crises."[25] In this the book is a true heir of its prophetic forebears.

In light of this more rapturous and radical sense of tradition, what "cultural adaptation" might mean cannot be reduced to certain symbolic accommodations. It has also to do with the postexilic, with the proclamation of the resurrection, with life from the dead. It is hard to express life from the dead as a culture theory—if there is an inculturational model for Christianity it is nothing more or less than reading the struggles of Christians in a place through a book like Daniel.

12:11–12 one thousand two hundred ninety days . . . the thousand three hundred thirty-five days—The book presents a variety of numbers that appear to need reconciliation; here the divergent tallies are lodged next to one another. The search for a creative explanation for the gap is not new. Theodoret added a scene to the drama's final act, the coming of Elijah after the fatal blow to antichrist and before the arrival of Jesus (2006: 315–17). In the Middle Ages and beyond some claimed that the few days between were the "refreshment of the saints," a kind of respite from the torments of the antichrist, an eschatological timeout.[26]

In the modern era, the classic historical-critical explanation, going back to Hermann Gunkel, is that the failure of the end to arrive at the conclusion of the first total of days sent the Hasidim back to the drawing board. Collins appeals to more recent sociological theories of cognitive dissonance to explain why being wrong in such a matter doesn't silence the claimants in embarrassment, but on the contrary emboldens them. He also points out compellingly that both totals roughly approximate to the three and a half years of "a time, two times, and half a time" of 7:25. An equally creative historical-critical solution working from the same assumption is that the totals represent differences involved in intercalation (1993: 400–401). In each case the explanation for two numbers is that the author had to get his eraser out.

For argument's sake, let us grant Gunkel's thesis that the divergent numbers represent disappointed expectation, even error. The writer recalculates, perhaps by another calendar. In fact, that recalculation in the text is of a piece with the recalculation that ensued throughout much of the history of Christian interpretation: erasing and refiguring take place not once, but many times. Let us say that the erasure in the text becomes a kind of precedent. What then? Are we simply to see this as discrediting? And if not, how are we to read this verse?

---

25. The phrase is from Alasdair Macintyre, *Whose Justice? Which Rationality?* (South Bend, IN: University of Notre Dame Press, 1988).

26. E.g., Robert Lehrer's "The Refreshment of the Saints: The Time after Antichrist as a State of Earthly Progress in Medieval Thought," *Traditio* 32 (1976): 97–144.

I return to what I said in an earlier chapter about numbers. Our guide here is rabbinic; on one account the reference to the fire in 12:10 has to do with that purification that allows the interpreter to think on the numbers without losing hope if the calculations go wrong—for that despair would be the most mistaken reading (Rashi in Goldwurm 1972: 327). The times themselves, as set forth by God, and our reckoning of them, are distinguishable. In a similar vein Sanhedrin says that the coming of the Messiah can be sped up out of mercy, but it cannot be infinitely delayed, for there is a terminus ad quem fixed by God (in Goldwurm 1972: 324). Moving in the opposite direction, but to the same effect, Calvin (1853: 392) attributes the divergence of numbers to God's patient and merciful "prorogation" of the end time (citing Matt. 24). Whether speeding or delaying, the true time is firmly in the hand of God. There is a time appointed, to be sure, but flexibly so, for the appointment and its implementation belong equally to God. To say that the time predicted was wrong or that the numbers are hopelessly at odds is to disregard God's utter sovereignty over human and worldly contingency. The numbers will all work out, and they will be made to do so as he fulfills his plan that he is working out for salvation.

Here I may address the frequently heard claim that the long delay of the end, as found, for example, in the numbers of Daniel and the history of its interpretation, is a source of embarrassment and reconnoitering for Christians and skepticism for their critics. But we need to think differently, and more theologically, about this delay. First of all, the coming of the kingdom and the resurrection of the dead are anticipated in the resurrection and ascension of Jesus. The coming events, his return, and the general resurrection are in one sense subsequent events, but they are also completions and revelations of that accomplished event. The time of the eschaton has its own christological logic. John Henry Newman compares this to the discovery of a vast canyon, which one may spend more or less time subsequently running around the brim.[27]

12:13 but you, go your way, and rest; you shall rise for your reward at the end of the days—The book concludes with the promise, to Daniel, of rest, and in so doing it evokes the great theme with which the Old Testament opens, in the creation account in Gen. 1. All creation, all history, even in its most pessimistic and turbulent periods, is still oriented toward the eternal Sabbath that is God's purpose throughout. The theme of rest or a resting place also evokes, first, Israel's arrival in the promised land and, second, the arrival of the ark into the temple in Jerusalem. Our present chapter involves, insofar as the context is exilic, frustrations of both salvation-historical expressions of rest. As penultimate types of rest are removed, the hope of Israel expands to that *telos* when the rest at the last will match the hope

---

27. "For so it was, that up to Christ's coming in the flesh, the course of things ran straight toward that end, nearing it by every step; but now, under the Gospel, that course has (if I may so speak) altered its direction, as regards his second coming, and runs, not toward the end, but along it, and on the brink of it; and is at all times equally near the great event that, did it run toward, it would at once run into"; John Henry Newman, *Parochial and Plain Sermons* 6.17 (Ascension Day, on Rev. 22:20) (San Francisco: Ignatius, 1987), 1326.

at the outset. In this regard it is helpful to consider an exilic prophetic passage such as Isa. 66: no earthly rest suffices, given Israel's own sin (66:1, 3–6).[28] Israel is punished, but the recompense of its tormentors is not far away (66:6); in fact, it suffers birth pangs of the new thing God is doing (66:9), the metaphor that came to be common for the messianic woes. Then the nations will be drawn (66:12), and the Lord will come with a chariot of fire (66:15). In the meantime Israel is to be purified (66:17), using at last new and purified temple vessels (66:20). At last the moment of a new heaven and new earth will come (66:22). Once again we can hear the echoes of earlier prophecy in our present work and in so doing gain insight into the way that themes in Daniel cohere one with another.

That rest and our inheritance in it remind the Christian reader of Hebrews.[29] (The epistle is particularly illuminating for it understands the rest to be achieved as Jesus has already entered into the heavenly holy of holies, the equivalent in priestly terms of his kingly ascension.) We may understand Heb. 4 as a sermon on the theme of eschatological rest in a manner that may be assumed to have Dan. 12 in its background. The eschatological trial is compared to that testing in the wilderness that preceded entry into the promised land. But the kerygmatic is highlighted. Its hearing places a requirement on the hearer, to respond faithfully to the good news of the kingdom in Christ, to stand firm, to put his or her hope in the rest ahead. The performative horizon of the passage comes to the fore—the promise of rest is a word addressed to the listener, right now, as the author of Hebrews, quoting the psalmist, insists. This is so because prophetic words, in the epistle or in Daniel for that matter, are neither mere information nor speculation, but the word alive and acting on its hearer. The utterance of Dan. 12 places the hearer in a moment of eschatological urgency that demands acknowledgement and response. We hear the word, and through it God hears and sees us, as well as everything in creation (Heb. 4:13), as will be made translucent on the last day. Rest as promise, in its assurance, consolation, and demand, happens, not simply theoretically, but in the actual hearing of the passage—sitting back and musing about the word's possible application to us is disallowed. Hebrews helps us hear Daniel's rest in its existential immediacy, and so it helps to overcome the common prejudice that such apocalyptic literature promotes merely a resigned ethical distance.

The spirituality of this passage involves acceptance that we are servants assigned a time and task. We are called into and out of service; we as Daniel, must accept our "dimission"[30] even in the struggles that persist and remain urgent. The wisdom

28. Otto Bauernfeind, in *Theological Dictionary of the New Testament*, ed. Gerhard Kittel, trans. Geoffrey W. Bromiley (Grand Rapids: Eerdmans, 1965), 3.627.

29. On the subject of Hebrews and Daniel, we may note the former's interest in what sets Jesus apart from the angels (Heb. 1–2); here we find the New Testament working out the distinction that is crucial to its Christology but left as a piece of unfinished business in the latter.

30. E.g., John Owen, "'The Laboring Saints' Dimission to Rest': A Sermon Preached at the Funeral of the Right Honourable Henry Ireton, Lord Deputy of Ireland: In the Abbey Church of Westminster, the Sixth Day of February 1651" (London, 1652).

to accept the call to be withdrawn is one that every pastor, missionary, Christian at large, must learn, and in so doing comes to praise God's sovereignty over the yet perplexed historical scene.

A totalizing postmodern critique of discourse challenges all narratives that impose a meaning on all persons for its purported intellectual imperialism. Narratives that claim closure and so are not open to revision or critique are seen as hostile to the integrity of the other. This passage would seem particularly prone to this critique, offering as it does a vision of the final judgment on all humankind and sealing its word until that time. But it would be fairer to say that our passage answers, indeed challenges, just such critiques. History will go its way, and interpretations likewise, both in truth and in error. The resurrection of the dead and the resulting kingdom of God stand in contrast to the kingdoms of this world, which presume just such proud and totalizing claims, rightly characterized as imperialistic. The hoped-for resurrection alone can offer the most potent critique to human pretensions to transcendence and finality, for it is not a human claim on others but rather the Creator's reclamation of all his creatures; Matt. 25 suggests to us that, while the ensuing judgment will have closure, our comprehension of its shape should not claim it prematurely. Furthermore the passage offers hope to a very particular and hard-pressed people of Israel and so serves a purpose that is the very opposite of ideological power gathering.[31] As to its closure, the conclusion of human history is indeed determined, but by the transcendent God alone. The word to be fulfilled is already spoken, but as that word Jesus opens this and all the scriptures to a new light, even as he opens human history in this "in-between" time to witness and the inclusion of the Gentile world. By contrast the nihilism of postmodernism, like all the ideologies of the kingdoms of this world, represents its own kind of totalizing discourse.

31. A response to works like Jean Francois Lyotard's *The Postmodern Condition: A Report on Knowledge* (Minneapolis: University of Minnesota Press, 1984) can be found in Richard Bauckham's *Bible and Mission: Christian Witness in a Postmodern World* (Grand Rapids: Baker Academic, 2003).

DE SPE—A CONCLUDING
TROPOLOGICAL POSTSCRIPT

At the end of the matter, how might we summarize the contribution of Daniel for the Christian in our moment, and church, and world scene? It describes and encourages the virtue of hope.[1] We may read the earlier chapters of the book as illustrations of that virtue, showing courage, spiritual constancy, steadfastness in suffering. And we may read the later chapters as an unveiling of hope's *telos*. (We have come to see in our time how virtues can be understood only in the fuller context of the community practicing them, its narrative, and especially the end to which that narrative points—in just this sense the explication of hope can be seen to bind the book together.)[2] This must be, for us who are creatures in time, a historical end, which is, as Daniel's own use of *telos* reminds us, both a termination and a goal.

We who struggle to be hopeful live in a time and world in which Daniel is readily compelling. Auschwitz, Mao, MAD, Pol Pot, Iran with warheads, greed and collapse, the great flu, the coming thaw, humanoid clones, postmodern nihilism—apocalypse as cosmic disaster is disturbingly easy to assimilate. The one who hopes begins with a realistic view of history, which is to say the concentric circles of exile in which we live.

A real philosophy of history unveils destinies of salvation and disaster.[3] But the book has nothing to do with a cultural penchant for disaster; it is firmly fixed

---

1. Throughout this postscript I have been aided by a reading of the existentialist Thomist Josef Pieper, for whom real philosophy of history must consider prophecy and theology, and whose vision was apocalyptic in the fullest sense. See his *On Hope* (San Francisco: Ignatius, 1986); *Hope and History* (San Francisco: Ignatius, 1994); and *The End of Time: A Meditation on the Philosophy of History* (New York: Pantheon, 1954).

2. Alasdair McIntyre's *After Virtue: A Study in Moral Theory* (South Bend, IN: University of Notre Dame Press, 2007).

3. Pieper, *End of Time*, 22.

in the larger witness to the goodness of the God of Israel and his creation and to its ultimate redemption. Another side of the modern spirit is too ready to hear that we and the world are bound for God; we are less ready to hear, as Daniel would tell us, that such a purpose is nowhere in ourselves, nor in history itself, which is but a succession of monsters before a final snuffing out, distant or not so distant. The end for which we are bound is to be found only in the one coming on the clouds, who comes as a stone from above, and yet not as a stranger. This purposeful location in relation to the creator God attested in scripture helps us to read the specifics of Danielic prophecy as reassurance fixed in God's counting, though we are not to know the day or hour, which is, after all, the nature of hope.[4] At the same time it also forecloses those unhinged dreams of control that might find the stranger aspects of Daniel's vision attractive.

Daniel sets out for us the true stage or scene, as well as the deeper forces and unseen agents, in relation to which we historical creatures are called to hope. For some of the people of God, the martyrdom of the furnace and the pit are found even today. Human history reveals a kind of counterorder as the drive to empire continues and collides with itself (Dan. 7). In such a world the people of God realize in contrition that the world's opposition to God lies within as well as without them (Dan. 9). Those in the West are taught by their brothers and sisters in the Third World to see a wider spiritual dimension to the conflict than they might otherwise perceive (Dan. 10). Were it not for the gospel, the interminable struggle of nations and power blocs would be but sound and fury (Dan. 11). Theology in our time has, in contrast to a century ago, helped us to think seriously, in a realist way, about the last things. And we Christians are well reminded that we sojourn in this history in the company of the original children of Israel.

Thomas Aquinas reminds us, in his account of the virtue of hope, that, of its very nature, we hope *in* someone.[5] It assumes a personal fiduciary bond. That someone is revealed to us as the ascended and returning Son of Man, Jesus Christ, who has been presented after his sacrifice to the Father. Our hope has an irremovably christological center: "What we will be has not yet been revealed. What we do know is this: when he is revealed, we shall be like him" (1 John 3:2). We know that there will be a real break, a hiatus, a discontinuity (end of Dan. 11). We know that the consummation must follow history's disaster (Dan. 11–12), but that the consummator is also the world's creator and redeemer. In this light the Christian account is the most pessimistic, and only then optimistic—the removal of the whole prophetic framework dooms secular accounts to one side or the other.[6]

4. For a concise phenomenology of hope, see Gabriel Marcel's *Mystery of Being II* (South Bend, IN: Regnery, 1951), chap. 9.

5. On this dimension in Aquinas under the rubric of hope, see Stephan Pfuertner's *Luther and Aquinas: A Conversation; Our Salvation, Its Certainty, and Its Peril* (London: Darton, Longman & Todd, 1964).

6. Reinhold Niebuhr, in Kantian fashion, captures this antinomy as well as this fate for secular accounts, though without Pieper's sense of their order or of the definiteness of an end; see *The Nature and Destiny of Man: A Christian Interpretation* (Louisville: Westminster John Knox, 1996).

The virtue of hope accompanies the practice of mission. For that is what the body of Christ, the people of God, are and do in the meantime. History is oppression and will to power headed toward disaster, all bounded by the hope of the resurrection of the dead in Jesus Christ. But it is also, amid the shattering, the coming of the Gentiles, in the victorious train of the Son, back to the Father in the Spirit's eschatological praise. That is what the ascension accomplishes, the goal of the creation itself, the doxology that breaks forth periodically in Daniel, the song of the saints like stars, as historical time is taken up, displayed in judgment, and redeemed in the kingdom of God. But of how the Son of Man will accomplish this, when the seal is broken, there is yet more to hear than Daniel alone can tell.

BIBLIOGRAPHY
FOR DANIEL

Frequently cited works are listed here. Other works are documented in the footnotes.

Calvin, John. 1853. *Commentaries on the Book of the Prophet Daniel*, vol. 2. Translated by Thomas Myers. Edinburgh: Calvin Translation Society.

———. 1993. *Daniel 1: Chapters 1–6*. Translated by T. H. L. Parker. Grand Rapids: Eerdmans.

Chrysostom, John. 1856. In *Patrologia Graeca*, vol. 56. Edited by J. Migne. Turnhout: Brepols.

Collins, John J. 1993. *Daniel*. Hermeneia. Minneapolis: Fortress.

Goldingay, John. 1989. *Daniel*. Word Biblical Commentary 30. Dallas: Word.

Goldwurm, Hersh. 1972. *Sefer Daniel: A New Translation with a Commentary Anthologized from Talmudic, Midrashic, and Rabbinic Sources*. New York: Ziontalis.

Hippolytus. 2000. *Kommentar zu Daniel*. Translated by Marcel Richard. Hippolyt-Werke 1.1. Berlin: Akademie Verlag.

Jerome. 1958. *Jerome's Commentary on Daniel*. Translated by Gleason Archer. Grand Rapids: Baker.

Lacocque, Andre. 1976. *The Book of Daniel*. Atlanta: John Knox.

Melanchthon, Philip. 1543. *In Danielem prophetam commentarius*. Housed at the Cambridge University.

Saadia Gaon. 2006. *The Book of Daniel*. Translated by Joseph Alibaidi. Bern: Lang.

Theodoret of Cyrus. 2006. *Commentary on Daniel*. Translated by Robert Hill. Atlanta: Society of Biblical Literature.

Willet, Andrew. 1610. *Hexapla upon Danielem; that is, a Six-Fold Commentarie upon the Most Divine Prophesie of Daniel*. Cambridge: Cantrell Legge. Accessed via eebo.chadwyck.com.

SUBJECT INDEX

SCRIPTURE INDEX